Moving Mountains

MOVING MOUNTAINS
Communities Confront Mining and Globalisation

Edited by Geoff Evans,
James Goodman and Nina Lansbury

Zed Books
LONDON • NEW YORK

Moving Mountains was published originally by the Mineral Policy Institute, PO Box 21, Bondi Junction, NSW 1355, Australia (www.mpi.org.au) with the Protest and Globalisation research project, University of Technology, Sydney (www.protglob.hss.uts.edu.au) and Otford Press, 49 Station Road, Otford, NSW 2508, Australia in 2001.

Published in the rest of the world by Zed Books Ltd, 7 Cynthia Street, London N1 9JF, UK and Room 400, 175 Fifth Avenue, New York, NY 10010, USA in 2002.

Distributed in the United States by Palgrave, a division of St Martin's Press, LLC, 175 Fifth Avenue, New York 10010, USA.

Cover design by Lee Robinson

A catalogue record for this book is available from the British Library.

Cataloging-in-Publication data has been applied for from the Library of Congress.

ISBN 1 84277 198 1 hb
ISBN 1 84277 199 X pb

Contents

Part Three: Challenges

Part Four: Alternatives

Illustrations, tables and figures

Photos and images: Page/ Details/ Source

Tables and figures

Acknowledgements

The editors would like to thank each of the contributing authors for making time to write about their involvement in issues of corporate mining, and their organisations for supporting this project. Sincere thanks to Lachlan Riches for his legal services. Thanks also to Dave Sweeney, Llywella Smith and Russell Lansbury. Thank you also to the photographers who generously supplied the images used in this book, including Amanda King (Frontyard Films) and Wayne Lawler (www.ecopix.net.au). Thank you to David Pope (Heinrich Hinze) for his cartoon (Scratch! Media, www. scratch.com.au), and to Research Initiative on International Activism (www.international.activism.uts.edu.au).

James Goodman would like to thank the Faculty of Humanities and Social Sciences at the University of Technology Sydney (UTS) for supporting his ongoing research into alternatives to corporate globalisation and for providing valuable financial support for this project.

Nina Lansbury and Geoff Evans would like to thank the supporters and funders of the Mineral Policy Institute.

Royalties from this publication will directly support the campaigning, research and advocacy work of the Mineral Policy Institute, Australia. The Mineral Policy Institute is a non-government organisation that seeks to prevent socially and environmentally destructive mining projects, with a specific focus on Australian mining companies operating in Australia, Asia and the Pacific. For more information about the Institute's work, see the Institute's website at: www.mpi.org.au.

Out of sight, out of mind?

This image of the Ok Tedi River pollution flowing into Sydney Harbour was devised by the Mineral Policy Institute as a campaign tool to raise awareness about the social and environmental devastation caused by the Ok Tedi mine, Papua New Guinea.

Introduction:
Globalisation: Threats and Opportunities
Geoff Evans, James Goodman, Nina Lansbury

Junne Cosmos is a Yonggom woman from the Ok Tedi region in
Papua New Guinea whose traditional land is downstream from the
copper and goldmine owned by the world's largest mining company,
BHP Billiton. Since the mid-1980s, the Ok Tedi mine has dumped
more than 80,000 tonnes of mine wastes into the river each day,
leaving an environmental disaster that threatens the livelihoods and
food security of local people for the next 100 years. Junne states very
clearly the links between local and global concerns and actions needed
to defend environments and communities from the impacts of large-
scale corporate mining.

> 'I'm writing as a concerned Yonggom who comes
> from the mine-affected area. Please bear in mind that we are
> River People. River is the main thing in our lives – its beauty
> has been lost, its symbolic source of life that gives us identity
> as well as all the economic things.
>
> We the local people saw the change in our
> environment first. Even though we did not have the science to
> explain it, we knew. We could see that our mined river was
> changed. We saw the little changes, leaves change colour
> slightly, no pigs eating worms in the soil on the river banks ...
> things the scientists only noticed later or when they had to
> admit there must be because it was so obvious.

> The problem was first seen by us, the river people, then the Fly River Provincial Government, then the National Government, then the rest.

> We saw the change – the problem – and we know what is best for us. Where is our voice in the solution? Or will we be seen again as the ones who don't know? We picked up what was happening to our river and land first. We must be listened to when the solutions are being decided. We must have a say. We the river people need support from all concerned people.'[1]

Mining stands at the centre of the divide between the global North and South. Mining and its products, especially gold and oil, have often been the *raison d'être* for imperialism and its many misadventures. Mining companies have historically played a key role, as partners with both colonial and post-colonial governments, in securing a flow of resources from the global South to North, deliberately exploiting their leverage over weak regimes keen for economic development. Mineral wealth has, however, rarely translated into general local prosperity. Rather, large-scale mining development, like that at Ok Tedi, has in many places in all continents ruined traditional means of livelihood and natural environments, and left once-sustainable local economies and societies dependent on foreign corporations and overseas markets.

Today, economic power is increasingly concentrated not with governments, but with global corporations. Corporate executives wield unprecedented power over societies. They form part of a newly-dominant and assertive global elite that stretches across industrial sectors and encompasses financial institutions, state bureaucracies and inter-governmental agencies.

Multinational mining corporations (MNCs) are among the key agents in the process of globalisation. They embody the emerging logic of global accumulation as they mark out new physical, cultural and economic frontiers for global capitalism. The opposition they face reflects one site in the sharp contest involving communities, governments and corporations over the form and character of globalisation.

Larger than many national economies, mining corporations are in the process of consolidation and self-transformation in order to exploit better and enlarge their opportunities under corporate globalisation. Giant mining transnationals, like Rio Tinto, BHP Billiton, Placer Dome, Newmont, and Anglo American, have the power to shape state policy in both the global North and South. As they compete against each other and other industry sectors for access to resources and capital, they overwhelm the communities and environments in which they operate, driving down environmental, social, labour and fiscal regulations locally, and across the globe. The increased spatial reach and rates of exploitation of large-scale corporate mining accelerate the rate of resource exhaustion. There are huge environmental and social impacts, creating profound crises of social reproduction and ecological sustainability.

The social, environmental and economic consequences of large-scale mining projects can be enormous, and can include the loss of productive and culturally significant land, destruction of environmental systems through the pollution of land, riverine and marine environments, deforestation of sensitive, biologically rich zones, displacement of people, dependence on marginal employment, and destruction of local political structures and value systems leading to increase in alcoholism, domestic violence, child abuse and consumerism.[2]

Mineral projects have a major impact on global climate change by degrading carbon sinks and creating significant greenhouse gases in the mining and processing phases, and locking fossil fuel mining and power-generating regions into long-term dependence on fossil fuels.

The economic impacts are primarily felt in terms of asset-stripping and the irreversible loss of resources, the dislocation of relatively sustainable local economies, and dependence on income streams from foreign-owned and controlled infrastructures and projects. The economic benefits of large-scale corporate mining for many regional and national economies are debatable. Dependence on resource extraction can be a definite disadvantage. Economies and societies are mal-developed and rendered hostage to a minerals export industry – an industry that by definition is extractive, has a limited shelf-life and can create unsustainable expectations. The situation is exemplified in Venezuela – in the words of a political scientist from Venezuela's Simon Bolivar University:

'This is a sick society, and it is sick as a result of an illness called oil. Oil is easy to produce, it can be done by others with imported equipment, and it always sells. As a result, it has asphyxiated the rest of the economy and led the majority of Venezuelans to believe that if they are not rich, it is because someone has stolen what belongs to them.'[3]

Resource exploitation is often associated with the violation of human rights, both by governments and corporations. Mining projects are often associated with the loss of homes, cultures and livelihoods, and forms of pacification ranging from manipulated consent and bribery, to violent suppression of opposition. Resource projects can provide a reliable stream of foreign exchange for corrupt and dictatorial governments, as exemplified by the association between the Nigerian government and Royal Dutch Shell, in the exploitation of oil in Ogoniland.[4]

There are also more general long-term impacts on the political process. In many relatively impoverished regions, including those where indigenous, rural, working-class communities are located in the global North and in many countries of the global South, compliant governments desperately seeking Northern-based private investors, lenders and underwriters accept a development framework characterised by liberalisation, deregulation and privatisation involving tax breaks, concessional access to land, removal of foreign ownership barriers and other incentives. Multilateral agencies such as the International Monetary Fund (IMF) and the World Trade Organisation (WTO) impose market conditionalities in resource extraction and in energy provision forcing Southern governments to seek injections of private capital. The Asian Development Bank (ADB), for instance, specifically requires 'the implementation of privatisation', and loans are held up whenever there is a delay in the privatisation program. In the ADB these adjustment loans have an average of 32 conditionalities per program.[5]

Challenging Globalised Mining

Globalised mining corporations have exploited the relative mobility of capital and the climate of trade and investment liberalisation to put progressive governments, labour and local communities on the defensive. Resistance from locally affected peoples is widespread across all continents. They are increasingly asserting the right of local self-determination and veto over the exercise of corporate power. In some cases, this means forcing mining corporations to meet minimum accountability, environmental and social standards as a condition of consent. In other cases, movements for self-determination may refuse to permit the opening of land for mineral extraction or processing facilities.

An example discussed here is Bougainville, in Papua New Guinea, where a nationalist movement emerged in response to the impacts of the world's largest copper mine on the island and its people. The movement became the first to successfully close a major operating mine, and has been engaged in a struggle for self-government ever since. A further example is the resistance to the proposed Jabiluka uranium mine of the indigenous Mirrar people of the Kakadu region of Australia's Northern Territory.

As corporations become global, social movements defending environmental, labour and human rights have also globalised, becoming international movements. Transnational companies (TNCs) are vulnerable to local confrontation, but also to investor, financier and consumer-focused opposition that targets the corporation in its 'home' territory. Transnational coalitions of non-government organisations (NGOs) have emerged to consciously exploit these vulnerabilities of transnational corporations in many sectors, including mining. They have formed dynamic networks and cross-sectoral alliances, where struggles against exploitation are intertwining labour struggles with environmental campaigns against resource exhaustion and indigenous people's struggle for survival. These alliances match the mobility and reach of the agents of corporate globalisation.

This merging of struggles across sectors to increase solidarity and strength means bridging very different logics of struggle in the common cause of achieving environmental justice – ensuring that environmental and social costs and benefits are carried equitably, rather than by poor and marginalised communities. This book discusses many such struggles. One example is the international coalition that has emerged to target Rio Tinto, until recently the world's largest mining company with a long record of confrontation and accusations over claimed environmental, indigenous and human rights abuses. This unprecedented international campaign was coordinated by the Mineworkers' Confederation, the International Federation of Chemical, Energy, Mine and General Workers' Unions

(ICEM). Launched in South Africa in 1996, the campaign has been hailed as the first global trade union campaign to focus on a transnational corporation. The coalition reached beyond a labour movement campaign aiming to protect workers' collective bargaining rights, to draw in environmental, indigenous and human rights groups also concerned with the abuses perpetrated by Rio Tinto.

The community struggles discussed in this book politicise corporate mining and open up the possibility of an ecological and democratic globalisation with an alternative set of imperatives based on environmental justice, human rights, indigenous sovereignty, and national self-determination. Corporate legitimacy, the informal 'license to operate', has been challenged, and corporations have attempted to defend themselves against the mounting barrage of criticism.

Confidence in mining operations has become unsustainable without informed consent for operations from locally affected people, as well as from national governments, socially responsible investors, labour, and the general public. If corporations fail to secure and maintain these preconditions, their operations become increasingly uncertain, the expectation of future surplus is threatened, and the leverage of NGOs in opposition is greatly enhanced.

It is likely there will always be some mining, in some form, but the current forms of extraction, and the trend of ever-increasing extraction and consumption of mineral products is totally unsustainable, and cries out for change. In challenging the current logic of globalised corporate power, the communities, social movements and NGOs that confront mining transnationals have forced the industry to examine its poor record and reassess its possible future in a world based on an alternative logic of sustainable development.

In the approach to the new millennium, executives of the 10 largest mining transnationals met to launch the Global Mining Initiative and its sub-project Mining, Minerals and Sustainable Development (MMSD). This was an attempt by the industry to 'identify how mining and the minerals industry can best contribute to the global transition to sustainable development.'[6] Sir Robert Wilson, Chairman of Rio Tinto, acknowledged that the mining industry was facing a crisis of legitimacy when he declared, 'Unless the major players in the global mining and minerals industry can present a convincing case that their activities are conducted in line with [sustainable development] principles ... their long term future is in jeopardy.'[7]

Discussing the MMSD project, Sir Robert declared that, 'a pressing concern for the mining and metals industry is the need to overcome its poor public perceptions of our industry's performance in relation to the environment, and our consequent growing vulnerability to increased regulation based not on scientific analysis but popular prejudice.'[8] The chief executives of the world's largest transnational mining companies are trying to improve the 'public perception' of mining to enable them to avoid regulation.

The authors of this book, and the communities and NGOs from which they come, believe there are fundamental problems with corporate mining and that this requires action, not simply a public relations offensive. They are focused on supporting people like Junne Cosmos and the Yonggom of the Ok Tedi region in Papua New Guinea (PNG), and on working with mining-affected communities, including mineworkers, to bring change to the mining industry for the benefit of all peoples and the planet we live in.

The Role of this Book

The editors and authors of *Moving Mountains* are part of a broad-based network of people and organisations, including affected community members, union leaders, academics, campaigners and researchers, who are all in some way committed to challenging the global mining industry, and the transnational corporations that dominate it. They share the common purpose of generating alternatives to corporate power – alternatives that place communities and their environments at the centre of decision-making. Such a purpose may indeed be seen as monumental – the equivalent of moving a mountain.

Through a series of chapters, key issues and campaigns concerning globalised corporate mining are discussed. The authors reflect on their own practice and debate their strategies and directions. This book is presented as a forum for debate on 'why we do what we do and how we go about it'. For these authors, their networks and the people they represent, their collective strength is their most important asset, and to maximise that strength, they must learn from each other and work with each other. Each chapter addresses a particular aspect of mining and globalisation, focusing on specific responses. To illustrate these themes the book is divided into four broad sections, covering contexts, structures, challenges and alternatives.

Part 1: Contexts

The opening section on 'Contexts' explores the logic of corporate power under globalisation, and sketches the current operating framework for mining corporations. There is a focus on the historical and political context of mining, on the role of finance capital, and the responses to controversy and contestation.

In chapter one, David Korten sets the scene with a broad analysis of the emergence and dynamics of corporate globalisation. The chapter places particular emphasis on the linkages between state power and corporate interests, and highlights the ways in which the global 'liberalisation' agenda offers more scope for the abuse of corporate power. Korten outlines how this should be viewed as a new phase in the development of capitalism, and debates how this requires a re-think of strategies of contestation and transformation. In doing so, he charts a series of options and agendas that could become available as opposition to corporate power intensifies.

In chapter two, Peter Colley traces the political and economic history of mineral extraction, and the development of corporate mining. He begins with the emergence of multinational mining companies under the British industrial revolution, tracing their development through to today's globalised mining industry.

The role of the mining sector in the emergence of organised working-class movements is outlined, as well as the close connections between mining corporations with imperial, colonial and neo-colonial governments, and with today's international institutions. He closes with some pointers for social action, emphasising the possibilities for greater economic democracy in the industry and for greater social accountability, including to host governments, communities and workers.

In chapter three, editors Geoff Evans, James Goodman and Nina Lansbury discuss finance, investment and mining. Mining companies are dependent on increasingly volatile finance markets, with investors highly sensitive to the financial and reputational risks arising from escalating social and environmental impacts associated with mining projects.

Mining corporations are acutely aware of these new pressures, and many have embarked on intensive efforts at improving their social and environmental image.

NGOs have seized the opening this offers, pressing their concerns to investors as much as to the general public and to governments. Mining companies have turned to export credit agencies to provide guarantees for their more risky ventures, and NGOs have responded by targeting these, demanding they take environmental and social concerns into account. The chapter discusses these NGO initiatives, debates their effectiveness, and questions whether mining could ever be a sustainable investment.

Part 2: Structures

The second section, 'Structures', shifts to specific cases to outline some of the impacts of corporate mining. These illustrate the ways in which the dominant logic of corporate mining is directly defined against cultures, livelihoods and environments. The cases, drawn from Indonesia, Canada and Australia, clearly illustrate how large-scale mining threatens cultural survival, ecological exhaustion and social dislocation, generating powerful arguments for the construction of alternatives. This section also explores how mining corporations are managing public outrage through public relations strategies.

In chapter four, Danny Kennedy and Abigail Abrash highlight the integration of mining and state power in Freeport McMoRan and Rio Tinto's involvement in the Grasberg mine in West Papua, Indonesia. This chapter introduces some of the key themes explored later in the book, including abuse of indigenous sovereignty and workers' rights, denial of environmental justice and development rights, exploitation of economic dependency, abuse of human rights, and militarisation. The authors question the company's willingness or capacity to reconcile its interests with the interests of the local people, whether defined in terms of environment, democracy, livelihoods, or human rights.

In chapter five, Alison Harwood focuses on the issue of indigenous sovereignty and corporate mining in Northern Australia. For this chapter, she draws on the experience of the Carpentaria Land Council in their negotiations with Rio Tinto about the Century Zinc project in Queensland. She debates the struggles of indigenous people affected by the proposed mine, and their efforts to exercise indigenous sovereignty against an intense campaign conducted by Rio Tinto jointly with the Queensland State government. Corporate and governmental rhetoric about community 'empowerment', geared to managing a consent building process to win approval for the mine and associated facilities, is highlighted and the implications for both the process of negotiation and the outcome are debated.

In chapter six, Catherine Coumans develops a Canadian case study of mining and environmental justice, focusing on contamination of freshwater by mining and the consequences for surrounding communities. This chapter emphasises the challenges mining poses to poor people and to marginal communities in remote regions that are dependent on clean lakes and rivers for their drinking water, their daily subsistence and livelihood, and for social and cultural sustainability.

To illustrate the issue, she uses the example of the proposed Diavik diamond mine in the Canadian north, involving Rio Tinto. This mine is on land subject to unextinguished Aboriginal title, is part of the range for a large caribou herd that is important for adjacent communities as a food source, and threatens an arctic lake at the headwaters of a major watershed. This case illustrates the unwillingness of the Canadian government to enforce regulations to protect national water resources and the rights of Aboriginal peoples. It also shows the complex realities faced by Aboriginal communities dealing with the prospect of a major mining project that threatens their food and water, as well as their cultural identity.

In chapter seven, Bob Burton dissects the public relations strategies increasingly being implemented by major mining corporations to manage public outrage over the devastating environmental and social impacts caused by mining operations. Quoting directly from public relations practitioners, Burton outlines the popular tactics of corporate engagement with NGOs opposing developments, and the dangers posed to the credibility and independence of these organisations if they accept corporate sponsorship. This chapter discusses recent mining incidents, such as the major cyanide spill from an Australian company operating in Romania, and the methods in which mining corporations have strategically managed their response in order to maintain their current practices while improving their public image.

Part 3: Challenges

In the third section, 'Challenges', the book shifts gear to look at some of the challenges to corporate mining posed by social and political movements. This builds on the conceptualisations developed in the previous sections, and forms the central focus for the book. Questions of mining and movements for self-determination are debated, with cases from Bougainville and the Philippines. There is also discussion of the role of organised workers and mining trade unions, focusing on the trade union-led campaign against Rio Tinto. There is discussion of movements for indigenous sovereignty and environmental justice, drawing on the Australian case against the Jabiluka uranium lease. In addition there is debate about the role of international mining advocacy and development NGOs.

In chapter eight, Moses Havini and Vikki John focus on the implications of corporate mining for national self-determination and self-government in Bougainville. They outline the process that led to closure of the Bougainville mine, which at the time was the world's largest open-cut copper mine. This was the first time a major mine had been closed by a movement of local people, and has since marked a highly significant 'line in the sand' for mining corporations. The closure of the Bougainville mine dramatically illustrates the power of local opposition and the 'sovereign risk' associated with corporate mining. The authors debate the issues of self-determination in Bougainville, focussing on relationships between the mining company, the government of Papua New Guinea, and the people of Bougainville.

In chapter nine, Antonio Tujan debates the logic of contesting corporate imperialism in the Philippines. He focuses on the explosion of anti-corporate mining campaigns across the country from the mid-1990s after the legislative amendment to allow 100 per cent foreign ownership of mining operations. Tujan discusses issues of dependency and self-determination, widening the debate to discuss mining corporations as agents of imperialism. Mining corporations in the Philippines have played a key role in the drafting of mining legislation, and have been key beneficiaries of the legislation. In the process, they have directly undermined popular sovereignty in the Philippines. Yet, mining corporations have consistently failed to win over local populations to their 'development' framework, despite active support – including military support – from the Philippine government. Tujan illustrates his arguments with the case study of the Marcopper disaster on the island of Marinduque.

Chapter ten shifts the focus to mineworkers and trade union strategies. Jean McSorley and Rick Fowler address the social impacts of corporate mining, debating the role of mineworkers and their unions in challenging mining corporations. They outline the emergence of a unique trade union campaign that targets Rio Tinto. This has seen mining trade unions construct alliances with non-union NGOs in an international campaign, focused on a single mining corporation.

For the first time, a campaign has confronted a transnational mining corporation with an integrated range of cross-national and cross-sectoral issues, and forced them onto the international agenda through coordinated actions and mobilisations. The authors, who were actively involved in the campaign, evaluate the potentials for this model of transnational social movement unionism in targeting transnational mining corporations like Rio Tinto.

Chapter eleven explores the relationship between NGOs and corporations. Ruth Phillips discusses the logic of confrontation versus engagement between mining transnationals and social movement NGOs. The chapter debates the issues raised for NGOs as corporate elites become increasingly adept at developing responses to the industry's critics. She debates how NGOs can respond to consultative overtures from corporations, and outlines some of the NGO strategies that are emerging. The discussion is informed by the engagement process that some NGOs have embarked on with Rio Tinto, and includes statements from corporate executives, and from NGOs engaging with corporations.

In chapter twelve, Jacqui Katona describes the campaign developed by the Mirrar traditional landowners to halt the development of the Jabiluka uranium mine on their land, situated within Australia's World Heritage listed Kakadu National Park. Katona charts the six years of multi-pronged international pressure on the mining company through blockades, corporate actions and legal challenges, to prevent the mine moving ahead. Through this example, she raises the European economic imperative of mining that directly threatens the legal and traditional rights of the Aboriginal owners to use their land that is intrinsically linked to their living tradition.

Part 4: Alternatives

The book closes with a section focusing on 'Alternatives' to the existing status quo of mining development and corporate globalisation. This deliberately places on the agenda a series of principles and institutional proposals to guide the building of such alternatives.

In chapter thirteen, Geoff Evans, Rory Sullivan and Gabrielle Russell debate the possibilities for international regulation of multinational mining corporations. Corporations like Rio Tinto have proved themselves to be resistant to regulation but incapable of self-regulation that prevents abuses of communities and environments. What scope is there for legal and other controlling principles to be imposed on mining corporations through international institutions and state institutions? This chapter reviews the historical efforts to regulate and control multinational mining companies, in order to provide an understanding of the problems faced in regulating multinational enterprises. Following this, the authors assess the appropriate role for the self-regulation regimes preferred by corporations and many governments, then provide an overview of the strategies and approaches that can be used to ensure that the mining industry operates in a socially and environmentally responsible manner.

In chapter fourteen, Sarah Wright charts pathways towards challenging corporate globalisation, specifically discussing the role of mining corporations. She encourages the role of progressive movements in articulating and debating possible alternative visions for the future that are informed by local community struggles. Wright argues that social and environmental sustainability will not come at the level of a single mine, or an isolated view of the minerals industry, but that an alternative vision of development and community is needed.

The mining and minerals industry is a contested industry, and is in transition. This book, *Moving Mountains*, is a tool for people trying to understand and participate in this process of transition, to ensure that the industry moves towards environmental and social sustainability, avoids exploitation, and prevents global inequalities that allow advancement of the rich at the expense of the poor.

PART ONE: CONTEXTS

1 Predatory corporations
David Korten

'Institutions can exhibit an unbridled desire, a greed that can actually swallow up the earth and its health and the future of its children and that knows no national, ethical, or legal boundaries'[1]

At odd moments, those of us who have enjoyed comfortable and sheltered middle-class lives are jolted by stories of the human capacity for extreme violence against life – even against one's own fellow humans. In our own time the mere mention of the Holocaust, Pol Pot, Idi Amin, and Kosovo, evoke horrifying images and a sense of ultimate evil. Our tendency is to attribute these experiences to the madness of a depraved leader, a Hitler or a Slobodan Milosevic. Yet these were not the isolated acts of a rogue individual – a crazed serial killer senselessly acting out some personal fantasy or vendetta. Nor can they be attributed simply to the momentary social breakdown of mob violence. Many such cases are highly organised, in the case of the Nazi death camps even methodical, and enlist the enthusiastic participation of thousands or even hundreds of thousands of people who in other settings might be models of civility. They lead us to a recognition that violence, pathology, or evil – to use more prophetic language – can be an affliction of institutions, as well as individuals.

Institutions are collections of rules, rewards, and cultural beliefs that shape the behaviours of their participants. Institutions are an essential feature of any clan, tribe, or society that melds individuals into coherent social units with capacities for survival and creative achievement beyond those of their individual members. Institutions are by nature both empowering, in that they extend the capacities of the individual, and at the same time coercive, in that they place constraints on the behaviours of their participants. Healthy institutions, an essential foundation of healthy societies, curb our tendencies toward violence, while nurturing and enhancing our capacities for love and creativity.

Pathological institutions, on the other hand, have the power to evoke a form of collective madness of sufficient power to lead whole societies to destroy the foundations of their own survival. Perhaps the ultimate example is the global capitalist economy, which is consuming the natural, human, social, and institutional capital of the planet – the foundation of all real wealth – to make money for the already rich.

If humanity is to steer a collective course toward a more hopeful future, we must recognise that we are dealing with inherently pathological institutional forms, come to understand the sources of the pathology, and set about eliminating them from society.

Historical Alliance of State and Corporate Power

The modern corporation is a direct descendent of the great merchant companies of 15th and 16th century England and Holland. These were limited liability, joint stock companies to which the crown granted charters that conferred on them vast powers, including the right to monopolies over trade with large foreign territories.

In 1602, the Dutch Crown chartered the United East India Company, giving it a monopoly over Dutch trade in the lands and waters between the Cape of Good Hope (the southern tip of Africa) to the Straits of Magellan (the tip of South America). The charter vested the company with sovereign powers to conclude treaties and alliances, maintain armed forces, conquer territory, and build forts. It subsequently defeated the British fleet, and established sovereignty over the East Indies (now Indonesia) after displacing the Portuguese.[2] Early on it acquired large tracts of land in Eastern Indonesia through a system of lending money to cultivators that led to their eventual dispossession. The growing of cloves on lands not in Dutch hands was prohibited. Unable to produce sufficient food to sustain themselves on the remaining infertile land of their islands, the local people were obliged to buy rice from the company at inflated prices, eventually ruining the local economy and reducing the population to poverty.[3]

The British East India Company was the primary instrument of Britain's colonisation of India, a country it ruled until 1784 much as if it were a private estate. The company continued to administer

India under British supervision until 1858 when the British government assumed direct control.[4] In the early 1800s, the British East India Company established a thriving business exporting tea from China and paying for its purchases with illegal opium. China responded to the resulting social and economic disruption by confiscating the opium warehoused in Canton by the British merchants. This precipitated the Opium War of 1839 to 1842 – which Britain won. As tribute, the British pressed a settlement on China that included the payment of a large indemnity to Britain, granted Britain free access to five Chinese ports for trade, and secured the right of British citizens accused of crimes in China to be tried by British courts.[5] This settlement was a precursor to the modern 'free trade' agreements imposed by strong nations onto weak nations in our present day.

In 1713, the South Sea Company – which subsequently became the centrepiece of one of history's most famous financial scams – was chartered by the British crown for the primary purpose of establishing a monopoly contract with Spain to supply black slaves to Spanish America.[6]

These early chartered corporations were little more than legally chartered crime syndicates with private armies and navies backed by the political and military power of their home governments to engage in extorting tribute, expropriating land and other wealth, monopolising markets, trading slaves, dealing drugs, and profiting from financial scams. From the standpoint of any larger concept of the public interest one must conclude that they exhibit an extreme form of social pathology.

We like to comfort ourselves with the illusion that these are experiences from a distant and less civilised past that, like slavery, we have put behind us in our more civil modern world in which we are respectful of nature and the human rights of indigenous peoples. Yet in some parts of the world, traditional forms of slavery remain very much with us. In others it's called bonded labour, often involving children or prisoners producing goods for sale by the world's largest corporations.

In America, prisoner labour may be both housed in corporate-run prisons and hired by corporate contractors. Work in many sweatshops is only marginally better than outright slavery. While most modern global corporations have learned the skills of projecting a friendly and responsible face to the world, behind the carefully crafted facades we often find a reality not so unlike that of an earlier era. This is especially evident in many of the corporations that specialise in the extraction of petroleum, forest, and mineral resources, ostensibly in response to the insatiable demands of the consumer economy.

The rape of the earth by powerful outsiders to the disregard of nature and the interests of the people whose lands are pillaged has a long and ignoble history.

These community members of the lower Fly River have seen their traditional lands irreversibly damaged by the Ok Tedi mine in Papua New Guinea. This situation highlights the need for sustainable alternatives to corporate globalisation.

Photo by Simon Divecha, Mineral Policy Institute

Enforcing Corporate Priorities

Until World War II, Britain was the world's dominant colonial power, a role subsequently assumed by the United States, which had used World War II to pull itself out of an economic depression and strengthen its industrial base while the European economies were being devastated by war damage. Mark Curtis, author of 'The Ambiguities of Power: British Foreign Policy Since 1945', reports evidence from secret British planning documents from 1945. He outlines plans to strengthen British access to raw materials in Africa and to develop the Middle East; in the words of Ernest Bevin, Britain's post-war Foreign Secretary, as 'a prosperous producing area to assist the British economy and replace India as an important market

4

for British goods'. An explicit aim of the British development assistance policy was to bring 'influence to bear upon other countries' internal decisions' to protect and advance British economic and political interests in the changing circumstances.[7]

This dominant role was subsequently assumed by the United States (US), which had used World War II to pull itself out of an economic depression and strengthen its industrial base while the European economies were being devastated by war damage. Even before the Japanese bombed Pearl Harbour and drew the United States into the war, a US foreign policy elite was laying the groundwork for post-war US initiatives that would capitalise on the consequences of the war to create an integrated global economy dominated by US economic interests.

Haunted by the spectre of the Great Depression, State Department planners believed that to curb capitalism's boom-bust cycles and the resulting political consequences, the US would either have to move to a form of socialism or secure adequate export markets to absorb production in excess of domestic demand. Memorandum number E-B34 issued by the joint planning group to the President and the Department of State on 24 July 1941, outlined the concept of a 'Grand Area'. This was the area of the world that in the planners' view the United States would need to dominate, economically and militarily, to assure materials for its industries with the 'fewest possible stresses ... such as unwieldy export surpluses or severe shortages of consumer goods' that might lead to economic 'disintegration'.

The preferred scope of the Grand Area would consist of the Western hemisphere, the United Kingdom, the remainder of the British Commonwealth and Empire, the Dutch East Indies, China, and Japan. The concept, as outlined in the memo, involved working for economic integration within the largest available core area and then expanding outward from that to weave other areas into the core as circumstances allowed. The more open that economy to trade and foreign investment, the more readily the economic interests of the United States would be able to dominate it. Working from that logic, they placed a substantial emphasis on creating an institutional framework that would advance global economic integration, leading to the creation of the Bretton Woods institutions: the World Bank, the International Monetary Fund (IMF), the General Agreement on Tariffs and Trade (GATT), and ultimately the World Trade Organisation (WTO).

Behind the idealism projected to the public in advancing these policies was a hard-eyed cynicism of the sort revealed in a top secret document written in 1948 by George Kennan, a leading architect of the post-war world: 'We have about 50 per cent of the world's wealth, but only 6.3 per cent of its population. In this situation we cannot fail to be the object of envy and resentment. Our real task in the coming period is to devise a pattern of relationships which will permit us to maintain this position of disparity. ... To do so, we will have to dispense with all sentimentality and day dreaming; and our intention will have to be concentrated everywhere on our immediate national objectives. ... We should cease to talk about vague ... unreal objectives such as human rights, the raising of living standards, and democratisation. The day is not far off when we are going to have to deal in straight power concepts. The less we are then hampered by idealistic slogans, the better.'[8]

In the end, it was necessary to couch this agenda in idealistic slogans to provide cover for intentions, which if revealed, would have been strenuously resisted by the rest of the world and much of the US public.

In the post-war years, the Bretton Woods institutions played their roles well. As country after country emerged from colonialism, the World Bank was able to convince them to borrow foreign exchange to purchase goods from the industrial economies, thus further strengthening their economic dependence on the very countries from which they had presumably just gained their independence. With time, most of their economies became deeply dependent on borrowed money they could not repay.

Then the International Monetary Fund (IMF) stepped in as debt collector, with the backing of the World Bank, to restructure their economies. Restructuring meant diverting more of their own productive resources to export production, privatising public assets and making them available for sale to foreign investors, opening their own markets to unrestricted imports of consumer products and cutting public expenditures for social services so that more money would be freed to repay foreign loans. Conscientious implementation of these policies made them eligible for yet more loans.

Today, the major role has passed to the more recently formed WTO, successor to the General Agreement on Trade and Tariffs (GATT), which is being used to advance further the restructuring of southern economies to serve global corporate interests even as it extends the restructuring process to the high income countries of the North. Here we see a process by which the elites of both North and South are de-linking from any sense of obligation for the wellbeing of those less fortunate – irrespective of country or place – and joining in alliance to enrich themselves without regard to the broader social or natural consequences.

Thus, we now have a world in which the most meaningful boundary is the class boundary between the wealthy elites of the global North and the disenfranchised majority of the global South.

Corporate Power Today

We often overlook the strength of the link between large corporations and government and the extent to which both, even in democratic countries, function as instruments of elite rule and are integrally linked. Perhaps the major difference is that in the days of classical colonial empires, corporations functioned as extensions of government power. Now it seems governments are more likely to act as extensions of corporate power.

Beyond the constant exchange of persons at the top levels of the corporate and governmental sectors, corporate funding increasingly dominates the political process and corporate media shapes the political debates. Meanwhile government freely issues corporate charters with little oversight, maintains little more than a facade of regulating corporate practices to maintain public confidence, and fields police and military forces to protect corporate assets whenever corporate authority is challenged.

Recently we have become aware of the cosy alliance between governmental and corporate elites to circumvent the democratic will of the majority by using international agreements and institutions such as the World Trade Organisation to rewrite any national and local laws that restrain the freedom of the very rich to further build their financial assets at public expense.

Let's stop for a minute to establish the context. Real wealth all ultimately flows from the earth: its inhabitable areas, soils, waters, minerals, the energy it captures and stores, and its climatic systems,

7

forests, and fisheries. Though many of these resources are regenerative, the sustainable output even of regenerative resources is ultimately finite. All of us who inhabit the earth share in common the fact that our very existence depends on the shared availability of these natural resources. Now consider two facts.

Fact #1: Total human demand on these resources already exceeds sustainable limits. Indeed, according to the Living Planet Report of the World Wildlife Federation we collectively depleted these resources by 30 per cent over the 25 year period from 1970 to 1995. The world's pie of real wealth is shrinking at an alarming rate.

Fact #2: Twenty per cent of the world's people account for 86 per cent of total private consumption of these resources, while a less fortunate 20 per cent consumes only 1.3 per cent and suffers basic deficiencies in dietary energy and proteins.[9] This scarcely begins, however, to capture the extent of the mal-distribution in favour of a tiny fraction of one per cent of the world's people. Consider for example that in one year the income (appreciation in the value of his stock holdings) of one person, Bill Gates, was roughly equal to the combined incomes of all the 120 million people of Bangladesh – a ratio of a single year's purchasing power of 120 million to one.

While the global economy has been engineered to create the illusion that it is creating wealth, in fact it is about concentrating a declining pool of real wealth into fewer and fewer hands. As the world's real wealth is increasingly appropriated and ravaged by corporations, these corporations become ever more aggressive in extracting what remains.

As mining corporations engage in the extraction of non-renewable mineral resources to provide often momentary pleasures for the already well off, they create a double tragedy. As well as permanently destroying valuable regenerative resources that might otherwise serve human needs for countless generations to come, they also impoverish those who once lived sustainably from these resources. Usually the devastation takes place in relatively remote areas where it is seen only by the people whose lives are destroyed by it. Those of us who consume the products of this carnage have no idea of the real price our consumption imposes on people and planet, and may even pride ourselves on our environmental responsibility. Given the global scale of the carnage it is no wonder the world's wealthy elite must join power of the state with the power of the corporation to sustain this plunder and injustice.

The Fallacies of Globalisation

It is abundantly clear that abuses of corporate power have a long history. Indeed, the very nature of the limited liability, publicly traded corporation is an invitation to abuse. It is a legal instrument designed to concentrate economic power without accountability. It is inherently both anti-democratic and anti-market.

The modern corporation is a descendent of the chartered corporations – such as the East India Corporation and the Hudson Bay Corporation – that were formed by the British Crown as monopolies to exploit colonial territories. They acted as governments unto themselves, fielded their own armies, and ruthlessly extracted wealth at the expense of the subject peoples. Contrary to corporate propaganda, the corporation was invented not to create wealth, but rather to extract and concentrate it – and that is what all too many of them are still in the business of doing. Indeed, life's closest analogy to the publicly traded, limited liability corporation is cancer. We get cancer when a genetic defect causes a cell to forget it is a part of a larger whole and to seek its own unlimited growth without regard to the consequences.

When corporations are faced with a conflict between profitability and the health of society, they consistently choose profits. Examples include the chemical industry and its release of carcinogenic and endocrine disruptive chemicals that have destroyed millions of lives,[10] the tobacco industry manipulating nicotine content of cigarettes to make them more addictive while falsely testifying that nicotine is not addictive, the nuclear industry burdening future generations with the costs of caring for its radioactive wastes while touting nuclear power as environmentally benign and virtually costless, the genetic engineering industry releasing genetically modified organisms into the environment with the false claim that it is a safe answer to world hunger while it carries out a non-reversible experiment with the life of the planet, and the alliance of the world's largest auto and petroleum companies spending millions to deny the existence of global warming and to undermine efforts to address its causes. In each instance millions have been spent assuring the public that the products involved are both safe and essential to our well-being. Later, after massive harm has been done, we find that those who offered such assurances often knowingly lied for profit.

Yet corporate interests are still identified with national interests, and corporations are top of the list for government assistance. Some data suggests that corporations in the United States now receive more in direct public subsidies than they pay in total taxes. That's only a small part of the story as it doesn't include the costs to society of unsafe products, practices, and workplaces or from outright corporate crime.

In the United States over-billing by defence contractors stands at $26 billion; over-billing by medical insurance contractors is at $23 billion; there is $54 billion a year in health costs from cigarette smoking; there is $136 billion for the consequences of unsafe vehicles and $275 billion for deaths from workplace cancer. Pretty soon it starts adding up to some real money.

In *Tyranny of the Bottom Line*, Chartered Accountant Ralph Estes documented the annual costs imposed on the public by corporations in the United States. His total came to $2.6 trillion measured in 1994 dollars. This is roughly five times the corporate profits reported in the United States for 1994 and the equivalent of 37 per cent of 1994 US Gross Domestic Product.

If we extrapolate this ratio to a global economy with an estimated total output of $29 trillion in 1997, we come up with a likely total cost to humanity upward of $10.73 trillion to maintain the infrastructure of global corporate capitalism – with the benefits going primarily to the wealthiest 1 per cent of the world's population that has any consequential participation in stock ownership.

It is sobering to note that the corporation is one of the most authoritarian of human institutions. In the US system, which is rapidly infecting Europe and the rest of the world, the corporation can virtually hire and fire any worker, open and close any plant, change transfer prices, create and drop product lines almost at will – with no meaningful recourse by the persons or communities affected. Given that our largest corporations command economies larger than those of most states, this represents an extraordinary anomaly in supposedly democratic societies.

With these characteristics in mind, let's review some frequently suggested responses to corporate rule.

- *Appeal to the corporate conscience to act more responsibly.*

This buys into the fiction that the corporation has the qualities and moral sensibilities of a human being. A legal contract has no conscience and no loyalty to people or place. The people who work for corporations are merely employees subject to dismissal if they bring to bear any interests other than the short-term profits of shareholders.

- *Let the dynamics of the global market place take their course and trust that market forces will correct the dysfunctions by rewarding the responsible corporations over the irresponsible.*

This suggestion is based on the false premise that market forces work naturally in the direction of rewarding corporations that internalise their full costs. It is a contradiction in logic, since cost externalisation is clearly an enormous source of profit.

- *Let the market decide as consumers and investors express their economic choices. People who want high labour and environmental standards will make their purchasing and investment choices accordingly – paying higher prices and accepting lower investment returns where necessary.*

This presumes that corporations have a right to externalise their costs onto the community and that if people want it otherwise, they must pay. It also requires consumers and investors to resist corporate wrongdoing, corporation-by-corporation, deed-by-deed, through consumer and investment boycotts. It strips us of our rights as citizens and reduces us to expressing our preferences only in our economic roles as consumers and investors.

- *Regulate corporations through governmental action.*

While regulation is essential in any market economy, relying on governmental regulation to reliably curb the excesses of corporations that command more resources than most states is a weak and temporary solution. States are embedded in an inter-state balance of power and are often constrained in their ability to regulate non-national corporations, especially when those corporation have chosen to assert their power.

- *Realign economic structures in ways that bring economic relationships into a more natural alignment with the public interest.*

11

This requires replacing the present system of unaccountable corporate and financial domination with a system of political and economic democracy – a project comparable to the human project of eliminating monarchy. It involves the elimination of the publicly traded, limited liability corporation as an institutional form. I submit that this is the only option consistent with the goal of creating just, sustainable and compassionate societies that work for all.

De-Corporatising Globalisation.

An ambitious agenda is required, given what is at stake. I believe it is within our reach though, especially given the growing strength of the global democracy movement that first gained public prominence with the massive protests that derailed the World Trade Organisation in Seattle in 1999. The following are some specific agenda items for citizen action to transform economic structures and establish economic and political democracy.

- *Democratise national and local governments.*

Corporate money now corrupts political processes around the world to the point that democracy has become a meaningless charade for all but the very wealthy. The top priority for citizen action in virtually every country in the world is to establish the democratic accountability of national and local governments through reforms that sharply curtail the political influence of corporations and big money. Only then will the way be cleared to create societies that place human and natural interests ahead of corporate interests. In most countries this will require radical campaign-finance reform, with a focus on the public financing of public elections and the provision of free access to the public airwaves for public political debate and campaigns.

- *Eliminate corporate welfare.*

As demonstrated by the costs they impose on the larger society, corporations are extremely inefficient organisations that depend for their survival on massive public subsidies. Eliminate these subsidies and many of them will break up under their own dead weight. The first step is to eliminate direct corporate subsidies and special tax breaks.

Corporations constantly tell us how greater size increases efficiency. It is time they prove it by learning to live without cash payments and tax breaks from government. Similarly, indirect social and environmental subsidies should be eliminated and cost recovery fees should be imposed to offset otherwise externalised costs resulting from dangerous or unhealthy work places, defective and toxic products, depletion of natural capital, and substandard pay.

- *Replace absentee ownership with stakeholder ownership.*

The corporate structures of global capitalism institutionalise the most extreme and pernicious form of absentee ownership. They create massive concentrations of economic power and shield those who hold that power from accountability to society for the consequences of its use. Often individual shareholders and investors have no idea what corporations they own, let alone the negative impact these corporations are having on peoples and the planet. Often their funds are held in managed funds or pension funds, with professional fund managers making the actual investment decisions. Shareholders – the ultimate owners – know only the returns being generated.

Perhaps the most important step toward aligning economic relationships with the public good is to replace this system of short-term absentee ownership with a more stable and locally rooted system of stakeholder ownership. This would mean ownership by those who have a non-financial stake in the corporation – such as its workers, customers, suppliers, and members of the community in which it is located. This can be facilitated by regulatory and fiscal policies that create an increasingly strong bias in favour of this form of ownership. Steps toward stakeholder ownership might begin, for instance, with restructuring worker pension funds to use worker holdings to hold management accountable to the larger range of worker interests in corporate decision making. In addition, as the goal is to encourage the active exercise of ownership rights to hold management and corporate directors accountable to a broad range of stakeholder interests, there will be a need for effective education on economic democracy and ownership participation.

- *Create a strong bias for human-scale enterprises.*

The more concentrated power becomes, the more difficult it is to hold it accountable to the public. Smaller enterprises generally have less power and therefore are less likely to abuse it. One of the defining differences between capitalism and a market economy is size.

Capitalism is about creating massive concentrations of monopoly power immune from market forces and public accountability.

The theory of market economics is quite explicit in stating that market efficiency depends on large numbers of relatively smaller enterprises that have less power to externalise their costs onto the public. Thus, under capitalism, 'the market' is always and everywhere a myth. Ironically, only by dismantling capitalism can 'the market' reign.

If business is to serve more than money, its relationships must be based on more than purely financial ties – including relationships internal to the firm. Sociologists have found it is very difficult to maintain personalised relationships in an organisation of more than 500 employees.

Few economic activities actually require large enterprises. Most of the economic needs of society can readily be met by smaller firms that may join together in networking structures owned by their member firms to carry out larger scale activities. In this context, public policy can and should provide fiscal and regulatory incentives to break up larger enterprises into component stakeholder-owned units.

Appropriate measures include strong anti-trust enforcement, strict prohibitions on mergers and acquisitions, and graduated corporate income and asset taxes that impose significant financial penalties on size.

- *Eliminate special corporate rights and exemptions.*

Corporations have persistently used both courts and legislatures to expand their special rights and exemptions. This began with special limitations on the liability of their owners – an exemption commonly used by corporations to shield themselves from responsibility for the harms caused by their operating subsidiaries. Similarly pernicious is the legal fiction of corporate personhood – which extends to corporations the natural rights of persons.

It seems almost an immutable trade-off: the greater the rights of corporations, the less the rights of real persons. Legal and legislative action is needed to strip away the legal fiction of corporate personhood and clearly establish that corporations are public institutions created by government to serve a public good. They may be granted certain temporary privileges, but they have no rights.

Similarly, legislative action is needed to remove the corporation's limited liability provisions, starting with the removal of limits on the liability of corporations for the actions of their subsidiaries. Corporations and their shareholders should bear the same responsibility and liability for the care and use of the corporate property as does any property owner.

* *Make money creation a public function.*

When new money is created it creates a claim against the real wealth of the community. Logically community members should share in the resulting benefit. This would occur for example if money was issued by a government and used either to pay for public infrastructure and services or was equitably distributed to individuals as a social credit bonus.

Unfortunately, under current practice, most of the money in circulation is created by bank lending. In this instance the benefit of the money creation accrues to the bank that receives the interest on money it has created. When government creates money and spends it, it stays in circulation. Under a debt-based system, money is created as banks lend it. Money is destroyed as loans are repaid. New loans must constantly be issued not only to maintain the money supply, but also to make it possible to repay loans, along with the interest due. With time, the society becomes ever more deeply indebted to its bankers.

If debt does not continue to expand, loan repayment becomes impossible and the economy is subject to a crash. The time has come for citizen groups to demand that their governments look deeply at the possibility of transferring the money creation function from private banks to government, so as to maximise the public benefit from money creation.

* *Favour productive over speculative investment.*

Productive investment requires serious commitment of resources to the creation of new products, services, and productive capacity. Most of what is called investment today is nothing more than speculation on the prices of stocks, bonds, currencies, stock indices and options. Consolidation in the banking industry has transformed the banking system from an industry of financial intermediaries that channel local savings to local investments in housing and enterprise into an engine of global financial speculation. Some of the hedge funds that engage in massive speculative attacks on national currencies leverage their equity capital by as much as 100 times with borrowed money. This credit creation fuels stock bubbles and increases the volatility of share markets.

Financial integrity and stability will be well served by legislation prohibiting banks and financial houses from lending for purposes of financial speculation – such as margin lending or lending to hedge funds, and by placing confiscatory taxes on short-term capital gains, thereby restoring a system of unitary community banks to meet the financial needs of people and communities.

- *Reform international financial markets and economic management.*

The forces of corporate globalisation have melded the World Bank, the International Monetary Fund (IMF), and the World Trade Organisation (WTO) into a corporate dominated global governance that dictates global economic policies outside the framework of the relatively more democratic United Nations. The basic purpose of these policies is to prevent governments from placing regulatory and fiscal limits on global financial speculation and to protect the ability of corporations to pass their costs onto the broader society. The international debts created and encouraged by the World Bank and IMF have placed Third World countries in a condition of international debt bondage.

Corrective actions are needed to eliminate international indebtedness, restore national ownership and control of productive assets, and balance exports and imports. A key step would be to close the World Bank, IMF, and WTO, and restore the right of economic self-determination to people and their governments. Responsibilities for economic management should be transferred to the United Nations.

The capacity and democratic accountability of the United Nations must be strengthened, especially through actions to strengthen its staffing and financial base, to eliminate corporate influence over its decision making, and to reform its structures and procedures, making it more responsive to people rather than to wealth.

Conclusion

Let us be clear: the appropriate goal is not to reform global corporate and financial rule, but it is to end it. A long history establishes beyond reasonable doubt that the publicly traded, limited liability corporation is a pathological institutional form that enables massive abuse of economic power to extract and concentrate the real wealth of society. Financial speculation is similarly predatory.

As a first step, global corporations and financial institutions must be held accountable to the public will, and required to serve the common good. Over the longer term the sources of the pathology must be removed through steps to end speculation and to close down the publicly traded, limited liability corporation as we know it.

2 Political economy of mining

Peter Colley

The extraction of minerals from the Earth has been practised by virtually all societies throughout history. In Australia there is evidence of Aboriginal mining at least 40,000 years ago. What is different about mining since the colonial period is that mining is now often done by one society within the living environment of other societies – rather than 'in its own backyard'. The rate of extraction has experienced exponential growth beyond the wildest dreams of those living only a century ago.

Of critical importance for the issue of long term sustainability, the local impacts – economic, social and environmental – of mining operations are frequently severe. At the global level there are urgent questions about the capacity of the environment to assimilate the waste stream generated, not so much by mining itself as by use of the products of mining.

Perversely for the big corporations of the global mining industry, at the very time they are at the height of their success in terms of their reach, their output, and the efficiency of their production, they account for a shrinking proportion of global economic activity and are at risk of falling into irrelevancy. Where once mining companies and mining employment dominated the landscape of industrial societies (metaphorically and literally), they are now of relatively minor importance for developed country economies and international trade.

Even so, mining activity continues to be one of the largest scale activities conducted by the industrialised world within the developing world. At a time of falling relevance in the developed world, the actions of mining companies have come to represent one of the most obvious points of conflict between large-scale western economic activity and small scale indigenous and self-sufficient communities.

This chapter seeks to present the economic imperatives that have driven the development of the global mining industry to its current situation and why, at the time of its greatest strength, the mining industry also faces its greatest crisis.

The early rationale

Mining has had a significant role in most (if not all) societies because it has been a key means by which people have sought to transform themselves and their environment – for purposes of pleasure, religion, comfort or economic advantage.

The earliest mining activity was little more than the use of mineral products as decoration, as cooking implements and as weapons. In some advanced non-capitalist cultures such as those in parts of Latin America and Asia, certain minerals (usually gems and gold) had substantial importance as items of value, beauty and religious significance.

Particular innovations in the use of minerals had dramatic effects on the scale and nature of economic activity (and arguably still do). The ability to smelt ore into metal, enabling the creation of long-lasting products, enabled some human endeavour to be turned away from the continual replacement of products to other pursuits. This hastened the evolution of economic systems towards capitalist development.

The large empires of the ancient era – Egyptian, Greek, Roman, and Chinese – relied heavily on the wealth by mining and minerals processing. All engaged in exploration and trade that focused in part on access to minerals.

However, the vast bulk of mining activity prior to the Industrial Revolution, and even to the end of the 19th century, relied on local extraction of minerals rather than extensive trade.

20

The essential economic reason for this is the inherent low value of most minerals. Until minerals are refined and processed into a higher value product, they are often not worth the cost of transport to a distant location. Transport costs can often exceed the cost of extraction, making distance to market of more importance than ease of mining. The exception was minerals deemed to be of high value on a value-for-weight basis – notably gemstones and gold. It is only in the 20th century, with rapid development in information technology and bulk transport, that large-scale trade in bulk minerals has transformed mining into a world-scale activity.

The Industrial Revolution

Europe and then the United States were the major sites of the Industrial Revolution that ushered in rapid capitalist development from the mid-18th century. While there was no single innovation, discovery or change of law or culture that triggered the Industrial Revolution, it is undoubtedly true that the development of the steam engine – a continuous controllable source of power based on fossil fuel – was a key factor.

Coal was the main fuel, and some cities and towns of Europe were transformed in the space of a few generations into heavy industrial zones. However, coal was (and is) a low value-for-weight commodity, so industrial development tended to be based in those towns and cities located in or near coalfields – hence the massive industrial developments of the Ruhr valley in Germany and in northern England. Coalmining became a massive employer, and remained so in developed countries until soon after the World War II. In 1961, the UK had more than 720,000 mineworkers out of a workforce of 24.6 million people, or one in 34 workers.[1] Most ordinary people either worked in a mine, in an associated heavy industry, or had relatives who did. Today the UK has less than 10,000 mineworkers.

Oil was the next fuel to have dramatic effects on industrial development. Oil is a far more flexible fuel than coal – higher in energy content per unit of volume, easier to transport and easier to burn. The explorer Marco Polo recorded trade in oil on the Caspian Sea in the 13th century, but it was not until the development of high-volume wells from 1901 in the US that oil became big business. The Spindletop well in Texas in 1901 produced more oil than 40,000 shallow wells then operating in the eastern United States.

Ownership and exploitation of oil assets in the US generated enormous wealth and tremendous economic power. The Rockefeller family's Standard Oil company was one of the first monopolies to be broken up in 'anti-trust' action by the US government. It took a twenty year court battle, and resulted in the formation of twenty smaller companies, three of which (Exxon, Mobil and Chevron) became members of the infamous 'Seven Sisters' identified by a 1952 US inquiry into the global oil cartel.

Europe found itself with few domestic oil resources (until the discovery and development of North Sea oil in the 1980s) but nevertheless developed large oil companies (Shell, British Petroleum and Total) based on trading in their colonial empires and dominance of world financial markets.

The European oil companies also went looking for oil reserves, and identified and developed the Middle East reserves in the period between World War I and II.

The post-war boom

World War II laid waste much of the industry and infrastructure of Europe and Japan. The new economic supremacy of the United States, the establishment of a global trading system based on a gold standard guaranteed in US dollars, together with rebuilding opportunities in Europe and Japan set the scene for massive economic growth. This prompted huge demand for minerals and enabled international trade in them with minimal risk to investors.

A major feature of the growth in international trade in minerals has been Japan. A country with relatively few mineral resources of its own, but with a large population and intensive government – business cooperation in economic planning for most of the post-war period, Japan has been responsible for much mineral development elsewhere in the world. Concerns about resource shortages amongst business and government were felt very deeply:

> Mineral resources are the lifeblood which sustains the life of the people and their industrial activity. Japan depends almost entirely on imports for its mineral resource developments. What is more, deposits of mineral resources are concentrated in a few areas of the world . . . Owing to this peculiar set of circumstances, the availability of mineral resources could pose a short term sporadic

22

threat or a protracted industrial menace to the economic security of Japan. [2]

Japanese policy makers formalised a 'development for import' policy aimed at resource industries in the 1970 MITI White Paper, but it in fact began earlier, with the development of the central Queensland open-cut coalmines in the 1960s by Utah Ltd (now owned by BHP) exclusively for the Japanese steel industry under long-term contracts. The policy was pursued with renewed vigour after the two OPEC oil price crises of the 1970s that particularly hurt the Japanese economy due to a high reliance on oil for power generation. Today Japan is the largest importer of a number of minerals including coal, iron ore and copper.

Most metallic minerals are traded heavily in world markets, in contrast to lower value minerals, such as coal, where the majority of production is still consumed within the nation that produces it. The London Metals Exchange is a key market place, where buyers, sellers and traders not only buy and sell minerals but also (sometime mostly) engage in forward sales of minerals. Future mineral production is frequently bought and sold as a means of risk management for producers and consumers, and as a means of speculation for traders.

The Economic Dynamics of Mining Today

Throughout most human history, and as reflected in conventional economic thinking, minerals have been regarded as a scarce resource. Mine location, and economic advantage in mining, has been based on finding the most accessible resources. The conventional orthodox economic view was expounded by Hotelling in 'The economics of exhaustible resources' in 1931.[3] There was assumed to be an absolute or limited supply of minerals, and mines were therefore supposed to become more expensive and less profitable over time as resources became scarcer. This premise was popularised by the Club of Rome in the famous *Limits to Growth* publication of 1972, wherein forecasts were made of various resources increasing in price and becoming exhausted in a matter of decades or less.[4]

Almost three decades on from the Club of Rome, all minerals are now cheaper in price than ever. Only in the case of oil and gas is there a possibility that resources will be exhausted in the foreseeable future. The fundamental reason for the mistake lies in misreading the tremendous impact of technological change in both exploration and extraction, and in the increasing integration of national economies into world trade.

In the case of oil, known reserves are currently equal to about 40 years of current production.[5] This may not seem long, but the important point to note is that the ratio of reserves to production has been around the same level for decades. This implies that the volume of reserves is limited more by the willingness of companies to explore for oil that they do not yet need, than it is by any absolute limit to the resource.

For most minerals, the resource currently known to exist at affordable/competitive prices ('economic demonstrated reserves') is only a fraction of what probably exists, or which might be cost-effective to extract with new technology. The concept is presented graphically in Table 1.

Table 1: Economic demonstrated reserves relative to known and potential reserves

	Price	
	Economic demonstrated reserves	Known reserves not economically viable at current prices
Geological probability	Inferred resources viable at current prices	Inferred resources viable at higher prices
	Undiscovered resources likely to be viable at current prices	Undiscovered resources viable at higher prices

Commonsense dictates that there are absolute limits to the supply of minerals, but for practical purposes they are not the limiting factor to mining that was once thought. For example, Australia has more than 80 billion tonnes of demonstrated or known coal reserves – enough for over 300 years at current production.[6] Of this, a small proportion is considered cheap enough to mine now. The rest is considered too deep or otherwise problematic. However, the absolute amount of coal in Australia is considered by geologists to be vastly larger than the demonstrated reserves.

The limits to mining are, as discussed elsewhere in this book, the social and environmental impacts and our capacity to cope with them rather than the availability of minerals.

The Increasing Impact of Technological Change

Mining companies will always be on the lookout for new, highly accessible resources. Those areas of the planet which have not been intensively explored by mining companies to date will eventually have exploration teams roaming them – the African and South American continents, and large parts of Asia. Major new mines will be built (governments and communities permitting/acquiescing) in very remote locations if the quality of the resource is enough to overcome the difficulties of building new infrastructure.

Classic examples of this are the major mines built in Indonesia in the last few decades. The Grasberg copper/goldmine, described in chapter four, managed by Freeport McMoRan in West Papua (one of the five largest such mines in the world) is an example of how a massive mine can be built in one of the most remote locations on earth if the mineral resource is attractive enough – with governments willing to fast-track or disregard approvals and regulatory processes.

Added to this is the argument frequently trumpeted by mining companies – that heavy-handed environmental and other bureaucratic regulation is discouraging mining in developed countries and pushing them to relocate. Testing the validity of this argument is inherently difficult – it can only be done in retrospect. There is some evidence of exploration falling off in existing major mining countries such as the USA, Canada, Australia and South Africa, but these countries still retain their pre-eminent position in the global industry. However, over a longer time frame it can be seen that the intensive urbanisation of Europe, and associated regulation, has left mining with little room to move on that continent.

In the last two decades, however, the accelerating rate of technological change is countering the purported flight of mining companies to the developing world. Mining companies are concentrating on getting more out of their existing mines – on redeveloping existing mines to make them lower cost producers. Mines which were once planned to have a 20 year life have been redeveloped and have increased their production life well beyond 20 years. Areas adjacent to existing mines that were once thought uneconomic are now developed in preference to resources in new locations. Making better use of existing infrastructure is part of the story. But a big element is that information technology, combined particularly with satellite-based global positioning systems, is producing major efficiency gains.

For most of the last half of the 20th century, mining companies generally used larger and larger trucks and other equipment to achieve economies of scale (i.e. lowering costs of production per unit by increasing total output). But now information technology is not only accelerating the discovery of new or more efficient minerals processing techniques, it is also enabling redesign of mines to use less equipment and people and increasing the capacity of management to monitor and supervise production.

Large-scale mining has been made possible by the globalised movement of finance.

Photo by Wayne Lawler (www.ecopix.net.au)

Mine managers can now know the exact location and minute-by-minute productivity of each worker, and they will eventually seek to replace as much labour as possible by computer-guided equipment. And where once mine managers filed monthly reports by telex and then faxed to distant head offices, information technology now enables daily and even real-time supply of production data to head office. In the mining industry, Big Brother is already watching you.

Thus Rio Tinto, one of the world's largest mining companies, has recently preferred to expand its existing iron ore mines in Western Australia, and take over the company owning the adjacent mines, North Ltd., rather than develop new mines at Orissa in India. In this type of case, innovations in technology in a core asset – immensely productive and profitable iron ore mines – are enabling a risk-averse approach to be taken to new mines. A new mine in a developing country may offer a good quality mineral that is near to the surface and easy to extract. Local labour may be very cheap relative to that in developed countries. Often these factors are enough to overcome worries about the risk associated with investing in a country that may have considerable political uncertainty, and even to cover the costs of building major new associated infrastructure, such as railways and ports.

However, in recent times technical innovation has seen some companies choose instead to redevelop existing mines. Aydin and Tilton have shown how the US copper mining industry, once steadily shrinking as a proportion of the world market as investors chose to develop new mines elsewhere, has recovered market share since the mid-1980s. The growth in output, and the decline in production costs to a more competitive level, has largely been at existing mines rather than via new mines. [7]

Industry Rationalisation

The combination of massive scale in mining investment, high-tech use of computers and satellite systems and the need for highly competent management to efficiently manage the large investments has meant that smaller producers get squeezed out. The late 1970s and early 1980s resources boom in Australia saw hundreds of small goldmining companies flourish. All you needed was a mining lease, a mechanical excavator/shovel or two, a few trucks, a crusher and a small scale acid bath to separate the gold. Today almost all such companies are gone and the goldmining industry is dominated by a few dozen global producers.

In developing countries there may be more small-scale or artisanal goldminers than ever, but this is conducted on a subsistence level rather than as part of conventional capitalist enterprise. In the case of other lower value-for-weight minerals the degree of rationalisation is even starker. In iron ore, for example, BHP and Rio Tinto in Australia, and CVRD in Brazil, control around two thirds of internationally traded production.[8]

The need to have large projects economically viable or profitable has a major impact on price. For example, in the case of copper and coal, any new world-scale mine is equal to around 3 per cent to 5 per cent or even more of existing globally traded production. So it has a large impact on the supply – demand balance. In practice this means that major mining companies have to gamble on trends in global consumption and on whether their competitors are going to do the same thing.

If more than one or two new mines come into production at the same time, global oversupply occurs and prices fall rapidly. This has in fact been the trend of the last 20 years, making much mining unprofitable except for those who are most efficient. This has accelerated the squeezing out of smaller companies (and by small we can mean companies that may have some billions in assets and thousands of workers).

The pricing problem has been made worse by the existence of buyers' cartels in some key minerals. For most of the last century, manufacturing capital has been larger and wealthier than mining capital, with the result that the inherent balance of power has rested with the buyers.

Added to this has been the practices of Japanese heavy industry which, in cooperation with government, has bargained as a group with mining companies for supply of key minerals – coal, iron ore, natural gas.[9] The aim has been to set ceiling prices for these minerals so that wealth can be maximised elsewhere in the production chain. When one nation is such a large importer of minerals (often the largest in particular minerals) and its industrial consumers operate as a united purchasing bloc, the global price is adversely affected.

The final result has been a persistent decline in long-term prices for most minerals, and the emerging dominance of the global industry by just a few major companies in each commodity. These companies are frequently regarded as giants in the global economy, but later in this chapter we will see that the reverse is true.

The Clash: Large-scale Collides with Small-scale

Major modern mining projects are physically massive. Some large brown coalmines in Germany are even able to be viewed from space with the naked eye. They are usually characterised by massive pits that stretch into the distance both horizontally and vertically. Trucks that seem quite small from a distance, tower several storeys high as they approach. A large 'dragline' used for removing soil from the top of coal seams can be higher than a ten-storey building and consume enough power to supply a town of several thousand people. It is usually operated by one or two people.

Though physically large, such projects are, in economic terms, usually only a small part of the activity of a developed nation. Even in Australia, a major mining nation, mining forms less than 4 per cent of Gross Domestic Product, the annual wealth produced by a nation (although it is 30 per cent of export earnings). They are not major employers.

In certain regions, such as central Queensland or northern Western Australia, mining may be a prominent activity. But the overall scale of economic activity in developed nations means that any particular project is of limited economic impact.

The situation in developing countries could not be in starker contrast. Though it is the task of other chapters in this book to detail the social and environmental impacts of certain projects, it is worth examining here the clash of economic systems produced by major mining projects in developing countries.

National Economic Impacts

Major mining projects frequently have an impact on the national economies of developing countries that simply could not happen in developed nations because of their much greater wealth. Developing countries are more likely to have the majority of their population engaged in subsistence or near-subsistence living, with only a minority of the workforce operating in the formal or cash economy. So national governments have only a small proportion of the population from which to raise taxes and provide government services. In this context large mining and industrial projects become very significant taxpayers.

In Australia, the largest resources company is BHP. It ranks as one of the nation's ten largest companies with a market capitalisation (price of all shares in the company) of around A$34 billion. In 2000 it made an operating profit of A$4.7 billion (before tax and financing adjustments) which may be thought of as the wealth it contributed to national income.[10] The Gross Domestic Product for Australia in the year ending June 2000 was A$621 billion. Hence BHP's contribution was roughly 0.76 per cent.[11]

Contrast this with the impact of BHP's Ok Tedi mine in Papua New Guinea. The country's entire GDP in 1998 was estimated at 7.7 billion PNG Kina or A$5.98 billion.[12] This single large mine contributes 10 per cent of that.[13] When it comes to export earnings the contrasts grow. PNG relies on mining for more than 70 per cent of its export earnings, with the Ok Tedi mine – just one operation – supplying about 20 per cent. In Indonesia it is a similar story for the Grasberg copper/goldmine, which for decades has been the largest single contributor by far to national government revenues. In Australia only the largest of BHP's many operations might reach towards 1 per cent of export earnings.

The national economic impact of large mining projects on developing countries is therefore massive. Governments in poor countries tend to become heavily reliant on particular projects as the solution to their budgetary problems. Even without obvious corruption of government officials demonstrably rampant in PNG and Indonesia, the influence of such projects on public policy will be dramatic.

Local Impacts

At the local level the problems are magnified a thousand-fold. The province of Kalimantan on the island of Borneo in Indonesia was once a remote, densely forested region with little involvement in the cash economy. But over the last two decades major resource projects have brought massive injections of cash. There has been a huge influx of workers and entrepreneurs from other parts of Indonesia. Local indigenous people have found themselves evicted from their land with minimal or no compensation and, due to their low education levels, denied employment in the new projects.

The desire of big companies for political certainty almost inevitably leads to encouragement and support for militarisation. Until the fall of the Soeharto regime, the central government's requirement to protect the interests of the big resources companies contributed to

30

heavy political repression. The political uncertainty that has occurred since Soeharto's fall has led to a winding back of new investment and to a devaluing of existing investments.

Booming cash economies will, unless carefully planned and regulated, produce social upheaval and dysfunction. Gambling, alcoholism, prostitution and crime all rise rapidly in regions experiencing a mining boom.

Finally, and only indirectly related to the economic impact, is the clash of culture of the large-scale with the small. The large-scale of mining activities is a shock for citizens of developed countries when they see it for the first time.

For indigenous people, used to all activity being undertaken on a family and community basis with only little infrastructure, the shock of the large-scale is a major problem contributing to social upheaval.

Protesters against globalisation in Sydney, Australia.

Photo by James Arvanitakis, AID/WATCH

The New Dilemmas for Mining MNCs

Large mining companies are today one of the most obvious features of the impact of globalisation on developing nations. However, this is not the result of any massive shift by mining companies from the developed world. Most mining activity continues to be in developed nations or in places in developing countries (e.g. South Africa) where it has occurred for many decades.

The scale at which the large projects operate, costing hundreds or even thousands of millions of dollars, with relatively few people employed – reflects competitive pressures to reduce mining costs per unit of output. There is unquestionably vigorous competition amongst large mining companies with many losing out and being swallowed by the victors. It is this competition, a feature of capitalist development in most industries where there is no government ownership or private sector monopoly, that leads to most minerals being cheaper and more plentiful than a century ago.

Large mining companies tend to transplant the technology and designs that have been successful for them elsewhere when developing a new project. So a design for a large-scale mining operation is simply transplanted from the USA or Australia to Indonesia, with perhaps some modification to make more use of the cheaper labour available. A large mine is something of a shock for a regional community in the USA or Australia – for a remote community in a developing country it can be cataclysmic.

Perversely for the mining companies, their ruthless competitiveness and efficiency has not paid off in terms of making them of continuing merit to their shareholders and the financial markets. In one sense it can be argued that the major multinational mining companies are turning themselves into small companies even as the scale of their operations grow.

Some mining companies are now bigger than they ever have been. The world's two biggest mining companies in terms of market capitalisation are AngloAmerican and Rio Tinto. The former was South African but has recently shifted its head office to London. Rio Tinto also has its head office in London (although legally it is two companies – one in the UK and one in Australia). Both are giants in terms of their operations. Rio Tinto operates more than 60 sites in over 40 countries, with an emphasis on Australia, the USA, southern Africa and South America.

AngloAmerican is more concentrated in southern Africa, but is now rapidly buying assets in other countries. During the era of apartheid sanctions against South Africa, Anglo was forced to confine itself to the country. It ended up buying a lot of non-mining assets that it is now shedding to concentrate on mining. Anglo has A\$27.88 billion in shareholders funds and is valued by international financial markets at A\$34 billion. Rio Tinto, which is more popular with investors, has shareholders' funds of A$12.23 billion but in mid-2000 it was valued by financial markets at A$43 billion.

But scale is always relative. Mining corporations are large, but they pale into significance compared to the giants of the information technology industries. In October 2000 – well after the 'tech-wreck' crash of shares in technology companies of April 2000, Microsoft Corporation was valued at more than A$700 billion – probably more than the value of all publicly-listed mining companies worldwide. In Australia, News Corporation with a market value of A$66 billion, dwarfs BHP with A$34 billion.[14]

The broader picture is that with fewer mining companies left standing the overall value of mining companies has declined as a proportion of the value of the total stock market. In Australia, where they have been largest in the post-war period, mining shares accounted for 50 per cent of the stock market at the height of the resources boom in 1980. Now they account for less than 15 per cent. Globally, mining companies account for only a couple of percentage points of the share market. As part of the world of big business mining companies are, in fact, fading fast.

Two inter-linked factors are at work here. Technological change and innovation inevitably means that new industries will grow and employ people in areas or activities which were not even thought of a generation ago. On top of this, older industries, in an effort to generate greater profits, have become extremely precise and/or ruthless in their management. This helps sustain profits, but ultimately – in conjunction with competition – it means that rates of return will become very predictable and not move far from the threshold rate of profit needed to attract risk-averse investment.

Basically, this is a little higher than the rate governments pay on government bonds – the money that governments borrow from the public. This means that the mining industry becomes uninteresting for speculators – there is a lesser prospect of spectacular movements in prices, profits and share prices. Whereas most shares in the USA trade at 20 times or more their annual earnings, shares in mining companies typically trade at less than 12 times their annual earnings. This is a measure of the relative lack of interest by investors in the mining industry.

These two factors – the growth of new industries, and the

33

transformation of mining from an anarchic, high risk process to a routine, predictable operation, has meant that mining companies are declining as a part of the global economy. The response of the MNCs has been the only one possible within the capitalist dynamic in which they are locked. They seek to streamline and further rationalise their operations. The only option is to generate more profits by reducing costs, in a context where revenues are not likely to increase much, due to intense price competition and slowing growth in demand for minerals.

They pursue further technical innovation and ever larger scale, whilst cutting jobs and payments to suppliers and governments. They merge with and take over each other in order to achieve greater efficiencies. This produces some momentary interest from investors, but ultimately it perpetuates the trend already described.

Where to for Mining Giants?

The final dilemma for the multinational corporations of the mining industry is that, at the very time they are at the peak of their efficiency, they are being spurned by the stock market. In their pursuit of ever-cheaper resources they have cut jobs and spin-off benefits in mining regions of developed countries to the point where they are losing the support of communities in those areas. In developing countries they have become the focus of hostility against globalisation as they represent the epitome of large-scale, ruthlessly efficient, high technology industry that is thoroughly out of step with the small-scale, low-tech life styles of indigenous and traditional communities.

Were it not for the sometimes substantial environmental impacts of mining and the flashpoints of confrontation with communities, the mining industry would become a 'boring' part of the stock market, an area of modest financial returns in a highly predictable industry, an industry that is large in the scale of its operations but small in its employment, and one that is 'out of sight, out of mind' for most people. However, the aforementioned environmental impacts and confrontations mean that mining in many instances faces a legitimacy crisis; it runs the risk of being deemed an unacceptable industry. This crisis can influence the decisions of those who invest in mining; where mining projects face continual opposition the investors may turn to less controversial investment options.

Thus, despite hundred of years of effort in becoming a high

technology, highly efficient industry, mining faces an uneasy and often difficult relationship with the communities in which it operates. The more things have changed the more they have remained the same.

While some environmentalists envision a future where there is very little mining – where most materials are sourced from recycling rather than new mineral extraction – it is likely that large-scale mining will continue to be a feature of developed economies. The absolute number of mining projects will decrease, but the scale of those that remain will be bigger than ever.

The mining TNCs will be required to put huge efforts into environmental management and community relations if they are to survive even in those fewer locations.

Because of the need for political stability, a highly skilled (albeit small) workforce, and, to minimise conflict by being located away from large populations, mining is more likely to take place in the remoter parts of developed nations than in developing nations.

Nevertheless, mineral deposits in developing nations that appear to be highly prospective will continue to attract some mining companies. While they will be the projects that arouse the most controversy, they will not be typical of the bulk of the mining ndustry.

Where To for Labour and NGOs?

It is not the purpose of this chapter to describe, forecast or prescribe the responses of organised labour and community groups to these trends, as this is addressed by other chapters. However, it is worth pointing out a few obvious parameters to response actions.

For unions, in both the developed and developing world, mining is generally a declining source of employment and membership. Large challenges remain within mining; in particular resisting the efforts of the MNCs to increase working hours and to reduce security of employment. An even greater challenge is to unionise the new emerging industries and to build links among workforces in mining and the new industries.

For the broader community, and the non-government organisations, that seek to represent them, the challenge is to pressure companies to improve their environmental and social performance to the level where mining is acceptable to the community.

Political economy of mining

Where the impacts of mining are unacceptable (and this is often not simply a matter of science but of economic and cultural choice) the challenge is to propose an alternative path of development that meets the needs of local and national communities. Mining is often highly problematic, but often so too are the alternatives.

3   Politicising Finance

Geoff Evans, James Goodman, Nina Lansbury

Mining is a high-risk industry, often requiring massive injections of capital prior to realising any returns. Consequently, large mining companies are heavily dependent on backing from large financial institutions acting as investors, lenders and project insurers. The mining industry, focused as it is on resource extraction in ever more remote and often environmentally and culturally sensitive regions, may be seen as a sunset industry of dwindling attractiveness for investors. Finance raising for new resources projects is becoming increasingly difficult, especially as fund managers face increased pressure for short-term performance.

According to Hugh Morgan, the CEO of the Australian-based mining transnational WMC, these pressures are effectively 'starving' the mining industry of funds.[1] This issue of financial dependence and vulnerability poses particular problems for the mining sector. The industry's search for funds is becoming more urgent, raising both threats and opportunities for communities and NGOs that argue for greater corporate accountability to prevent harmful environmental and social impacts.

Institutions that provide finance for mining range from private banks, investment analysts, stockbrokers, pension or superannuation funds or insurance agencies, to publicly owned multilateral development banks (MDBs) such as the World Bank and the Asia Development Bank, and government-backed export credit agencies (ECAs). These institutions are key players in corporate globalisation, operating across the world in partnership with governments and transnational corporations, and facilitating many large-scale 'development' projects. With an eye on profits, they often pay scant regard for the social and environmental impacts of the projects they fund. NGO campaigns targeting the projects supported by these financial institutions are not just challenging the projects and the corporations that promote them, but are also campaigns for accountability of global financial institutions.

This chapter discusses the expanding range of NGO campaigns that target the financing of mining. NGO strategies fall into three broad categories: campaigns that rely on the market, campaigns that focus on self-regulation by financial institutions, and campaigns that rely on local and national regulation. Each of these strategies is part of a process of politicising finance. The chapter closes with an examination of the opportunities that these various campaigns open up – and the questions these raise for the financing of mining and minerals projects in the future.

Export Credit Agencies – Public Risk, Private Profit

Corporations generally hedge against risk through private insurers or underwriters. But in many cases private financial institutions are unwilling to back projects unless there are significant 'cast iron' guarantees available from a state agency. Historically, it has been the publicly owned multilateral financial institutions, such as World Bank Group, the Asian Development Bank, and the European Bank for Reconstruction and Development, that have played the key role in providing these guarantees, through subsidies, security and legislative enforcement, and investment guarantees.

Increasingly, this role is performed by Northern governments, which provide investment guarantees through agencies explicitly set up for the purpose, such as the US Overseas Private Investment Corporation (OPIC) or through generic Export Credit and Investment Insurance Agencies (ECAs). These nationally owned, Northern-based ECAs provide guarantees to private banks, agreeing to refund costs plus 'a reasonable rate of return' if projects falter or face political risks. Agreements are then signed with 'host' governments, through the ECA, so that in the event of a project falling through, liabilities incurred by the Northern agency are simply converted to debt owed by the 'recipient' government.

Through this process, ECAs have become the largest long-term official creditors of Southern countries. Between 1988 and 1996 ECA lending rose fourfold to US$105 billion, amounting to 56 per cent of overall official debt. This amounts to twice the lending of the World Bank and all other multilateral development banks combined for that period.[2] About half of this – US$50-60 billion per year – was long term investment funding. This, according to the World Bank, is destined for 'large infrastructure projects', making ECAs 'the single largest public financiers of large-scale infrastructure projects in the developing world, exceeding by far the total annual investments of multilateral development banks and bilateral development aid agencies'.[3] Table 2 illustrates the large percentage of mining funding provided by ECAs.

Table 2: Multilateral and bilateral funding of mineral projects 1995–99[4]

Institution	($USmillion)
World Bank	5,950
European Bank for Reconstruction & Development	946
Asian Development Bank	2,025
Inter-American Development Bank	1,073
Export Credit Agencies (oil & gas only, 1994–99)	40,500

Most OECD nations have at least one ECA, and this usually an official or quasi-official branch of their government. Northern states are increasingly – and to a remarkable extent given the dominant worship of markets over state interventions – taking on the role of collective (national) capitalist. They directly offer to underwrite projects as a means of levering-in private finance and enabling projects to proceed. These public-private package deals illustrate the 'corporate welfare' role that Northern states are acquiring under globalised neo-liberalism.[5] Northern governments still present themselves as promoting their 'national interest' by facilitating locally based corporations gaining access to international business opportunities in a competition for lucrative ventures. This is seen as a key aspect of statecraft, as far as possible to be preserved. ECA activity is explicitly excluded from the World Trade Organisation (WTO), despite its direct impacts on trade.[6]

An interpretation of Australia's Export Credit Agency, EFIC.

Cartoon by Fiona Katauskas

ECAs are also generally exempt from important national legislation that would impose critical environmental, social, transparency and accountability standards. In Australia, for instance, the government's Export Finance and Insurance Corporation (EFIC) was specifically exempted from the *1999 Environment Protection and Biodiversity Conservation Act.*[7]

ECAs use the revenue raising powers and legal authority of Northern states to guarantee risky projects, yet even Northern politicians and NGOs often cannot get access to information about ECA decision making. Likewise, the local landowners whose environments, economies and societies are irrevocably affected by large-scale projects financed and insured by ECAs are not privy to such information.

The USA's OPIC and the World Bank's Multilateral Investment Guarantee Agency (MIGA) have adopted limited environmental screening processes, and other ECAs have started to accept the need for increased 'transparency'. The structural pressure is downwards though, towards the lowest common denominator.

ECAs that have chosen to adopt a set of standards for screening projects must compete with less scrupulous agencies that have not chosen to use screening. This 'race to the bottom' in social and environmental standards is illustrated by the example of the Lihir mine in Papua New Guinea, a project that was rejected on environmental grounds by OPIC, but then supported by EFIC and MIGA.[8] With commercial disincentives such as these, the vast majority of private investors, lenders, insurers and ECAs have been unwilling to adopt rigorous standards and systems of accountability.

ECAs collaborate to set a standard fee but otherwise have no common means of assessing the merit of projects. Even the member states of the European Union have been unable to agree on a common policy, despite being comitted to 'harmonisation' since the 1957 Treaty of Rome. As the European Commission noted in 1994, 'states are extremely reluctant to renounce even a small part of their independence in matters of export credit insurance'.[9]

Ironically, many corporations assisted by ECAs are rarely in any sense expressions of Northern 'national interests'. Many of the transnational corporations that make use of ECAs are deliberately – and often nakedly – involved in exploiting global divides in the 'race

41

to the bottom' that directly subordinates Northern as well as Southern peoples. It has been pointed out, for instance, that the main corporate beneficiaries of the US government's OPIC were shedding jobs in the US at the same time as they were embarking on OPIC – backed infrastructure projects in the South.

Once a contract has been signed with an ECA, Southern governments are required to accept potential liabilities under ECA – backed projects, and in the process are disciplined into protecting the interests of Northern corporations. ECAs thus socialise risk, first shifting the burden from private corporations to Northern governments, and then to Southern governments. ECAs are not only a 'debt-creating vehicle for developing countries',[10] but they are also a very effective means of securing against regulation or expropriation by 'host' Southern governments. Contracts are inviolable, so their disciplinary effects are maintained regardless of the government in power.

A compelling contemporary example is the insistence by Northern ECAs from Switzerland, Germany, US and Japan, that contracts with Indonesia's Soeharto Government be upheld in the post – Soeharto period. ECA – backed projects are associated with 'massive corruption, malfeasance, improper contracting procedures, environmental devastation and human rights violations', yet the ECAs insist the contracts must remain in place, and have warned that any attempt to renege on contracts may 'harm new foreign investment and delay Indonesia's economic recovery'.[11]

As the UK-based research institute, Corner House, argues, 'Northern Governments are using Third World money to subsidise their exports [and investments], the chief beneficiaries being the shareholders of some of the richest companies in the world'.[12]

Not surprisingly, the mining sector is particularly dependent on ECAs. According to the World Resources Institute, international financial institutions allocated around US$51 billion to projects in the minerals sectors between 1994 and 1999, in addition to providing significant leverage for other sources of project capital, adding to total project investments, as shown in table 2 on page 39. Of this, ECAs provided more than US$40 billion or eighty per cent in loans and guarantees to upstream oil and gas development, as shown by table 1.[13] Some investment guarantee agencies focus almost exclusively on providing support for the mining sector. Australia's EFIC, for instance, committed 97 per cent of its program for Papua New Guinea to the sector in 1992, amounting to a total of A$902mil dollars of support.[14]

Ultimately, corporations can rest secure in the knowledge that whilst not all private investors, lenders, insurers or ECAs will fund or underwrite their proposals, there are many that will. ECAs are thus the ideal source of support. They are unencumbered by unpredictable decision making, sufficiently discreetly obscured, out of the public eye, and uncomplicated by anything other than the financial 'bottom line'. It shouldn't be surprising then that so many companies have 'turned to national ECAs to featherbed their Third World projects', and that NGOs have specifically targeted ECAs for reform.[15]

Context of Liberalisation

The rapid growth of transnational mining corporations over the last 20 years has occurred in a climate of investment liberalisation, deregulation and privatisation. Liberalisation and the opening up of the global South to transnational corporations has been heavily promoted by the mining sector. Corporations have lobbied for increased access, more security and less taxation, exploiting the intensifying competition between liberalising countries for foreign mining capital.[16]

The globalisation of investment finance greatly enhances the structural power of corporations – increasing their leverage over dependent economies and their governments. There are many examples of this process from the mining sector. One example is the Philippine Mining Act of 1995, which was deliberately designed to attract foreign corporations, and offered tax concessions, access to indigenous peoples' land, and removal of barriers to 100 per cent foreign ownership.

This process has been replicated across the global South. A quarter of all 'developing' and 'post-communist' countries are now 'mineral economies', where at least 10 per cent of national income or 40 per cent of export earnings are derived from mining. From the mid-1980s many of these began deregulating, and by 1989, 75 states had privatised state-owned mineral assets, and many more have now followed.[17]

Images associated with projects funded by the Australian Government's EFIC, including the Indonesian military, the Ok Tedi mine in PNG, nuclear power stations and Laotian dams.

Montage created by the Mineral Policy Institute

As a result, mining corporations have gained 'unprecedented access to a larger proportion of the earth's surface than ever before ... shaped by a world marketplace where countries must compete for private sector investment'.[18]

Mining projects, especially in the global South, often involve the imposition of commodity exchange on peripheralised peoples on the fringes or outer reaches of state power. Invariably, the corporations involved can claim no local base, and while they may operate with the approval of national governments, they often fail to gain freely given, informed consent of local peoples. Reflecting this, they often attract popular opposition, facing claims for compensation and ultimately the risk of closure or local or national expropriation, as the example of Bougainville, detailed in this book, illustrates.

Due to the risks of controversy, many, if not most, mining projects in the global South would not go ahead without political and financial risk insurance by government – backed or private financial institutions. Increasingly, ECA and MDB investment guarantees are used to overcome private sector concerns about political and financial risks in the extractive and energy sectors. The terms and conditions under which access to 'development finance' is gained become critical to the exercise of power in the global arena. They are therefore heavily contested by corporations, governments, communities and NGOs.

Multilateral institutions such as the World Bank and the Asian Development Bank have a development mandate and must pay lip service to developmental goals and environmental standards. They must also be seen to operate within a relatively accountable multilateral decision-making framework. Recent courtships between some multilateral financial institutions and critical NGOs only underline the extent to which these institutions are in some sense bound to a broader 'public' mandate.

Private investors and ECAs are free of these environmental, social and accountability constraints. This increases financial and political risks associated with projects, the very risks ECAs are supposed to protect against.[19] While multilateral institutions create opportunities for private and publicly owned financial institutions, private investors and ECAs are in many ways defined against them. Private financial institutions and ECAs compete with each other for business, and have been quick to back projects rejected by multilateral development banks. Liberalisation and competition thus undermine the limited multilateral social and environmental standards, and other standards that have been adopted by some private investors and some ECAs.

NGO Responses to ECA Activities

Not surprisingly, a series of southern and northern based campaigns have emerged that target harmful private finance and ECA projects. northern based NGOs have been working to target financial institutions as agents of social dislocation and environmental destruction. The mining sector, as a major recipient of finance sector support, is particularly vulnerable to these pressures, and has been a key focus.

In recent years, governments as well as environmental and social justice NGOs have called on public and private financial institutions to adopt and improve environmental and social policies.[20] The G8 Summit, an association of industrialised states, acknowledged in their 1997 summit that financial flows from Northern to Southern contexts had implications for sustainability. Significantly, they also acknowledged the resulting need for more rigorous standards: 'Private sector financial flows from industrial nations have a significant impact on sustainable development worldwide. Governments should help promote sustainable practices by taking environmental factors into account when providing support for investment in infrastructure and equipment'.[21]

While Northern campaigns are primarily focused on the introduction of social and environmental standards to allow the screening of proposed projects, Southern-based groups more often seek the cessation of externally driven development agendas, while also asserting indigenous sovereignty and anti-colonialism.

A reference point for many Northern campaigners was the effort to force the US based ECA, OPIC, to withdraw its support for Freeport's Grasberg mine in West Papua, Indonesia. The campaign, led in the US by Friends of the Earth, the International Rivers Network, and Project Underground, exploited an on-paper comitment, introduced in 1985, that OPIC assess the environmental impacts of its projects. In 1996, OPIC responded with an 'environmental audit' of Freeport, and, as a result of this, cancelled political risk insurance for the mine. This was followed by the announcement of environmental standards for OPIC, described as 'amongst the strongest guidelines of any international finance institution'.[22]

In 1998, several of the NGOs involved in the Freeport campaign shifted focus to target the ECA sector as a whole. NGOs convened a strategy meeting of 18 environment and development organisations, and produced a statement calling for 'the reform of export credit and investment guarantee agencies'. This was signed by 163 NGOs and sent to the governments of the Organisation for Economic Cooperation and Development (OECD). The statement supported ECAs as vehicles for development, arguing that 'publicly supported private capital flows have the potential to foster environmentally and socially responsible development'.[23]

The relatively weak position no doubt reflected tactical sensitivities, but it also, perhaps, reflected Northern assumptions. At the follow-up meeting in Jakarta in August 2000, there were many more Southern based NGOs, and the meeting produced a much more critical declaration. The institutional reference points for standards were widened beyond the World Bank to include the International Labour Organisation and the United Nations. The demands for consultation were bolstered with explicit reference to 'indigenous and local peoples right to land and livelihood'. There was direct criticism of mega-projects supported by ECAs, and of the arms trade backed by export credits.

The declaration also broached the issue of Southern debt, demanding that 'ECA debt for the poorest countries' be cancelled. Most important there was no endorsement of ECAs as potential vehicles for development: instead it was argued they embody 'a form of corrupt, untransparent, environmentally and socially destructive globalisation'. The declaration was signed by 350 NGOs from 46 countries before it was presented to the June OECD Ministerial.

The changing logic of the finance sector focused campaigns reflects a central issue in the politicisation of development finance – namely the need to bridge the gulf between Northern and Southern perspectives. The key shift has been to a position where it is no longer assumed that unbridled foreign investment, including that provided through the World Bank and ECAs is a potentially legitimate vehicle for development. This has enabled a more sustained critique, rooted in the issues faced by affected peoples.

Environmental Justice and Financial Investment

Concepts of environmental justice highlight the uneven environmental and social impacts of human activity. Negative impacts fall most heavily on poor and marginalised communities whilst the rich and powerful reap the rewards. NGO campaigners are now demanding that investors be made accountable for the negative impacts of their activities rather than simply banking the profits. This is necessary for environmental justice but it also may be in the interest of investors, lenders or insurers to reduce risk and liability in the event of disasters.

Put simply, if mining projects were to promote environmental justice, then mining disasters would be less likely. Mine waste would not be dumped into rivers, destroying entire river courses and associated livelihoods, as at BHP Billiton's Ok Tedi mine in PNG and Freeport's Grasberg mine in West Papua. Cyanide use and inadequate tailings dams would not be constructed, leading to collapses and the poisoning of living environments, for instance as occurred at Cambior's Umai mine in Guyana in 1995 and Esmeralda Exploration's Baia Mare mine in Romania in 2000.

NGOs have taken the lead in promoting principles of environmental and social justice, directly campaigning against investors that fail to act on them. One example is the Jabiluka campaign in Australia which demanded that private banks and shareholders withdraw funds unless the proposed Jabiluka uranium mine was abandoned. The proposed mine was located in the World Heritage listed Kakadu National Park in northern Australia, and was opposed by the Mirrar people, the indigenous owners, by environmentalists and a wide range of other groups, including the Mineral Policy Institute (see chapter 12).

Campaigners mounted protests and boycotts outside the retail operations of high-street bank, Westpac, a major investor and lender to the project. The campaign mobilised shareholders of the project developer, North Ltd, to call for an Extraordinary General Meeting to discuss the proposed mine, and launched actions inside and outside of the AGMs of both North Ltd and the mine's current owner, Rio Tinto.

These campaigns directly challenge the legitimacy of investment in projects and companies that have particularly negative environmental and social impacts. They directly pose the question of why such projects and companies should exist in the first place, and in doing so, imply the need for tighter regulation of investment flows to rule out risky projects. As the Western Mining Activists Network of the US and Canada, argue, a key objective of these 'follow the money' strategies is also 'to get greater direct or indirect access to investors to make them think twice about keeping money flowing to "high risk" projects'.[24]

The forest downstream of the Ok Tedi mine in Papua New Guinea suffers from 'dieback', a phenomenon caused by waterlogging of tree roots after mine-related changes to the river.

Photo by Simon Divecha, Mineral Policy Institute

Responding to NGO pressures, and to the high-risk context, investors are increasingly claiming both a responsibility and a right to know the potential impacts of industries they are investing in. Many financiers have created 'socially responsible' investment funds (SRI), in which investors, lenders and insurers actively use positive and negative screens and standards to shape investment. Ethical investment funds, engaged in this form of conscientious investment, have emerged across Northern countries – especially in the US, where it is estimated that $US2.16 trillion is invested 'ethically', accounting for 13 per cent of private investment.[25] Increasingly the sector is entering the mainstream as larger financial institutions start to compete for the growing market of ethically aware investors, and realise that rates of extracting surplus can be as high, if not higher, in 'ethical' activities as in 'unethical' ones.

There have been some important victories in shifting large financial institutions to embrace SRI principles and practices. One example is the Ethics for USS campaign by the UK-based NGO, People and Planet, to get the university academic and senior administrative staff's pension fund, Universities Superannuation Scheme (USS), to commit to active socially responsible investment of its £ 20 billion (US$40 billion) in funds. This commitment requires the fund to set standards in seven areas of corporate behaviour: environment, overseas operations, workplace, product/service, community, animal welfare and political activity.

It also requires the fund to use its voice as a shareholder to raise environmental and ethical issues with management, liaising with other investors, voting against or abstaining on resolutions, supporting special shareholder resolutions, and preparing a detailed annual report listing its investments, detailing specific actions taken and progress in engagement with individual companies.[26] Increased risks and sensitivity to environmental and social issues is also reflected in a greater reliance on governments, which are increasingly taking on a key role in guaranteeing mining projects.

NGO Campaign Strategies for Finance Sector Reform

Campaigners on financial institutions face sharp political dilemmas. There are at least three strategies being pursued and all centre on developing modes of regulation, whether self-regulation in the market, regulation through international financial institutions, or forms of local or state regulation.

Market-based Approaches

In recent years, with the neo-liberal and globalist turn in political ideology, many NGOs have turned away from the state, focusing instead on corporations. Corporations have certainly become more powerful and are now often seen as the primary agents of social change. Instead of looking to the state to reign in corporate power, many NGOs look to the market, arguing that social conscience and the risks of globalised production can influence market actors. Market-based campaigns around mining have developed consumer strategies – for instance, a product labelling system for diamonds and a campaign to undermine the demand for gold – but for the most part they have focused on investment markets.

Many Northern NGOs are embracing the idea that investors can be persuaded to participate in boycotts of unethical corporations and shift their support to more ethical enterprises through what have been called 'buycotts'. Here, investment is seen as an instrument of social change, that, as the editors of the US book *Sustainable Banking* put it, can 'change finance', rather than simply 'finance change'.[27]

However there has been criticism of ethical or 'socially responsible investment' (SRI) for its failure to produce measurable changes and for legitimising corporate self-regulation. There are procedural problems: a clear image of an ideal or sustainable model is often absent; there is often a lack of independent information on corporate practices and on the views of peoples affected by company operations; and there is often a reluctance on the part of so-called SRI funds to move from expressing concern to actually disinvesting from recalcitrant corporations and from harmful projects.

There are many ways of addressing these imbalances, for ethical investors to proactively challenge corporations, combining positive with negative screening, participating in shareholder activism and imposing divestment time-lines if companies fail to produce change. Continued pressure on the corporations and their financiers from NGO campaigners is crucial.

Such pressure can only intensify. Indeed shareholder activism has almost become a genre in NGO campaigning, especially for mining advocacy groups. The London-based campaign against Rio Tinto – PARTIZANS – pioneered this approach in the late 1970s and early 1980s. NGO activists often buy small numbers of shares in order to get a voice at company annual general meetings (AGMs), or create partnerships with institutional investors (especially with large church-based funds) to encourage existing shareholders to press their concerns and to submit and vote on resolutions at general meetings. Often NGOs organise for affected peoples to get a voice at the AGMs, organise publicity events, mobilise demonstrators, and form conscientious groupings for shareholders.

The focus on the market, though, is inherently self-limiting, with changes subject to unstable market conditions and to corporate whim and manipulation. Increasingly, corporations respond to shareholder activism with the offer of private 'dialogue', and SRI fund managers and many NGOs have been drawn into unaccountable corporate-controlled discussions, with no public outcome.

Related to this is the more general problem of linkages with Southern peoples – ethical investment may improve corporate practices, but who has the right to say what is and what is not an ethical corporation? It may be argued that SRI fund managers and Northern-based international advocacy NGOs are often closer to Northern-based corporations than to affected peoples and have no right to set this standard. To avoid this problem, clear dialogue and accountability mechanisms need to be in place, linking SRI fund managers, NGOs and affected communities.

Standards for Financial Institutions

Instead of relying on the market to impose standards, many NGOs argue that international financial institutions should take on this role. Again, this approach is vulnerable to manipulation. The problems are already clearly evident, especially in relation to standards introduced by the World Bank, often in consultation with NGOs, which at best have mired the Bank in controversy and at worst have simply served to legitimise existing policies.[28]

There are similar problems as private financial institutions and ECAs introduce 'codes of conduct' and establish 'consultative' arrangements with prominent Northern NGOs. The Australian ECA, EFIC, in 2000, responded to criticisms by introducing environmental and social screening and posted an Aid/Watch and Mineral Policy Institute screening submission on its website. The process of challenge and response may have made some gains but there needs to be ongoing pressure to ensure that these do not become part of a cynical public relations exercise as ECAs demonstrate their reasonableness and openness to criticism without fundamentally changing investment practices.

Even if standards are accepted and implemented there are problems. Private financial institutions and ECAs may adopt standards relating to social and environmental sustainability and human rights and the process may become more accountable, transparent and consultative. But this will do little to change the structural logic of most large finance sector activities – which is to support accumulation by Northern transnationals in subordinated Southern contexts. The approach may simply recruit Northern-based NGOs as partners for financial institutions, dividing them from affected peoples.

Like ethical investment, the argument for standards assumes that Northern-based international financial institutions and international NGOs have the will and capacity to monitor corporate practices and to withdraw support for corporations that are flouting standards. It also assumes that the standards are acceptable to affected peoples – that the provisions for local influence over corporate decision making meet local expectations, and do not facilitate manipulation and distortion of local opinions.

Local and National Regulation

A strategy of wholesale rejection of international financial institutions, including multilateral banks and ECAs, with the demand they be dismantled, may grant greater mileage. Financial institutions are market-creating as well as debt-creating institutions, imposing a particular development model that favours the rich over the poor, the North over the South. It may reasonably be argued, then, that they are unreformable.

In Southern contexts this approach may be framed as an attack on neo-colonialism, affirming the rights of Southern peoples to autonomy and self-determination. This may be highly problematic, given the pervasive influence of other Northern-centred bilateral and multilateral agencies. Rejecting standardsetting via either markets or international institutions forces a default to existing national and local forms of regulation. In large part these are already locked into developmentalism and dependency, and often lack capacity to independently monitor and impose sanctions, although the institutional structures are spatially and ideologically closer to the affected peoples, and thus may be forced to become more responsive. Yet there are problems where post-colonial states have already been required to accept constraints on their freedom of action.

In the North, meanwhile, an abolitionist approach may be framed as an attack on 'corporate welfare' and 'capitalist accumulation'. Yet, in the absence of a viable alternative model of public intervention in financial flows, the position can implicitly suggest that non-subsidised market relations are legitimate.

The UK-based Corner House argues, 'as a rule, private sector projects and exports should be covered through the market and the [Export Credit Guarantee Department, the British ECA] should not assume risks that the market is itself not willing to bear'.[29] Not surprisingly, the mainstream financial press has also taken up this position. In July 2000, a *Financial Times* editorial argued that ECAs had 'led to waste and distorted markets ... leaving the market to price [insurance] cover would encourage greater commercial rigour'. The editorial ended by arguing that ultimately ECAs should be dismantled: if projects were viable they should be 'left to the market', if they were not viable they should be 'rejected or referred to development agencies'.[30]

Clearly the alternative, in both contexts, is for more effective local powers to monitor and control the impacts of financial flows into and out of communities, and greater local, state and international regulation. States can, and should regulate corporations, including financial transactions. There is some evidence that this is beginning to occur, especially as governments become aware of the risks associated with unregulated corporate activity and financial flows. In the mining sector, for instance, the European Parliament has passed a resolution urging the monitoring of European Union-based companies that have operations in non-OECD countries. In Australia, the mining company BHP was sued for causing environmental destruction at its Ok Tedi mine in Papua New Guinea. In 2000, legislation was being discussed (by minority parties) that would oblige Australian-based companies to abide by Australian law in their 'offshore' operations. These, and other regulatory initiatives, are discussed in greater detail in chapter 13.

Conclusion

Mining is in many ways a 'sunset' industry. Sir Robert Wilson, Chairman of Rio Tinto, made this point clear when he confirmed that for the thirty years since 1970, 'few companies have earned their cost of capital ... worse still those that had, have fallen behind the levels achieved in several other sectors. The fact remains that investors today, unlike their predecessors, can quite easily choose to avoid the mining sector altogether'.[31] At the same time, the pressure for the regulation of corporate mining – whether through the market, through financial institutions, or through the state – is on the increase. What does this mean for the future of mining?

The numerous ways the mining industry abuses peoples and environments have been well documented in this book and elsewhere.

Why, then, shouldn't investment in mining simply be halted? This is the position of many activist groups who demand an end to investment in any industry associated with mining and fossil fuels.

For example, in July 2001, Friends of the Earth International called for international financial institutions (MDBs and ECAs) to phase out investments in fossil fuels and mining within five years, except for small community-based mines that do not pose serious threats to the environment or human health, do not involve any forced resettlement, and are managed by and for the benefit of local people.[32]

Even at the very mainstream end of the spectrum there are demands for significant change. One Australia-based SRI fund, for instance, identifies basic principles for selection of stock in the Australian Stock Exchange mining index as:

- Minimising exposure in resources which are considered 'industries of the past', e.g. gold, thermal coal and uranium;
- Minimising exposure to companies that are heavily involved in mining in developing countries and have not clearly demonstrated their commitment towards more sustainable development; and
- Demonstrated commitment to the environment, workforce (including health and safety) and community.[33]

The vast bulk of investment remains outside this SRI framework, but increasingly is characterised as 'socially irresponsible investment', and as a result is increasingly politicised as illegitimate and irresponsible investment, requiring some sort of regulation (see chapter 13).

Social justice organisations in Southern countries have worked on models for mining that might benefit local people while still protecting the environment. Friends of the Earth's Colombian Branch, Censat Agua Viva, considers that mineral reserves should only be exploited to a level that can be sustained and regenerated by ecosystems, and should be controlled by community and worker-owned organisations, geared to maximising the collective social benefit.

Mining activity should contribute to the collective desired future of a region, and promote the rational use of mineral resources as well as sustainable, equitable and diverse economies: it must be orientated towards the satisfaction of basic needs of society, contributing to the solution of dilemmas of human wellbeing, food security, communication, adequate shelter, public services and the conservation of natural ecosystems. For Censat Agua Viva, the inclusion of ethical decision-making processes in mining is essential to the construction of just and sustainable livelihoods for both present and future generations.[34]

Clearly, a truly sustainable minerals industry would have to shed any focus on the continual extraction of resources – and this implies rejection of any model that relies on an ever-increasing demand for minerals. A sustainable and socially responsible minerals industry would also accept and pay for environmental and social impacts. Given that the real costs of mining are potentially infinite and that minerals are extracted permanently, companies would have to shift toward managing the resources once they are out of the ground, focusing on salvage, re-use and resale of minerals. A future-focussed minerals company would thus quite possibly not practice mining at all, but instead become a custodian of mineral resources, practicing 'closed loop' life cycle management through the continual use and re-use of mineral resources, while ethical energy corporations would focus on energy conservation and renewables.

This debate about what is and what is not socially and environmentally sustainable – and how mining might be affected by this – is the central one. The mineral industry is already seeking to create and promote its interpretation. In a deliberate attempt at capturing the agenda, the industry has funded the 'Global Mining Initiative', a project geared to promoting mining as a sustainable activity for the 2002 United Nations conference on environment and development. The project is aimed at creating a common definition and standard of sustainability across the industry, and has sought participation and endorsement from non-government organisations in doing this.

The Mineral Policy Institute (MPI) and many other mining advocacy NGOs, have not participated in the project, preferring instead to work with mining affected communities independent of an industry-driven process. MPI has put forward a set of preconditions for any involvement including a meaningful role for NGOs in shaping the project. It has also presented a set of minimum requirements that the mining industry would need to accept before entering into any serious conversation about sustainability. These include:

- the cessation of mine waste dumping into rivers or oceans;
- disinvestment from uranium mining and the nuclear fuel cycle;
- phasing out investment in fossil fuels and instead focussing on renewable energy systems;
- an end to mining and exploration in national parks and other protected areas;
- active promotion of human rights and end involvement with corrupt and repressive regimes;
- an end to lobbying for weaker environmental regulations, labour rights and indigenous rights, whether directly or indirectly through industry bodies;
- active provision for workers' rights, for collective bargaining through independent trade unions; and
- a demonstrated commitment to refocusing on mineral resource and energy conservation, rather than the promotion of increased resource consumption. [35]

The challenge is to build common perspectives that express different conditions in Northern and Southern contexts, and, at the same time, democratise the process of determining the 'who, where, when and how' of minerals and energy development.

The answer to this challenge lies in the political process of building local, state and international powers to contest corporate power and prevent harmful project financing. There is no pristine model, campaign strategy or ultimate answer that will supersede differences of perspective on how to do this. Rather, there are a range of complementary approaches and a series of convergences around the common agendas of politicising finance. The key issue is to strengthen that process, countering the current corporate model of unaccountable, confidential boardroom decisions with a democratic and participatory alternative.

PART TWO: STRUCTURES

4 Repressive mining in West Papua

Abigail Abrash and Danny Kennedy

Grasberg in the Global Context

Economic globalisation has been described as imperialism on amphetamines. While the process of European conquest and colonialism in Africa, Asia, the Western Hemisphere and the Pacific took centuries to take control of people and places, today's purveyors of neo-liberalism are moving even more rapidly, acting to incorporate within a few decades all known resources into the global economy through processes of commodification, privatisation and liberalisation.

Since humans began to name their epochs in terms of the minerals they could dig up and the metals they could smelt, the flag of empire often has followed the geologist. Romans of the Bronze Age built an empire in part in the pursuit of copper, critical to their favourite alloy. And in our own era – whose signature commodity is oil – we have seen the United States, the remaining global superpower, wage war to ensure access to petroleum half a world away in the Persian Gulf and deploy an imperial foreign policy in many other places to secure continuing petroleum supplies.

Indeed, mineral development comes, more often than not, at the expense of nature and of native peoples. It is often the spark that ignites war and other violent conflict and that irreparably alters the lives, cultures, lands and economies of indigenous landowners in often harrowing, sometimes brutal ways. These linkages between economic globalisation, social conflict, environmental degradation and mining are well represented by the experience of two indigenous communities in the troubled Indonesian territory of Papua (Irian Jaya/West Papua) and Freeport McMoRan Copper & Gold's mining operations there.

If a mine can be personified, then Grasberg is the Incredible Hulk on cocaine, driven mad by the demands of its owners on the other side of the planet, and set to destroy all in its path. The world's largest operating copper and goldmine has many of the ingredients that make resource development under globalisation problematic: private ownership by absentee landlords who have little connection or shared interest with local people; a rate of production so rapid its consequences cannot be measured let alone mitigated, and extreme physical and political force to allow the wheels of this form of 'progress' to turn over smoothly. The Amungme and Kamoro peoples – the original indigenous landowners of the areas that now comprise Freeport's mining, infrastructure, and exploration operations areas – have been at the receiving end of these conditions for more than 30 years.

When Freeport arrived in the late 1960s, the Amungme and Kamoro were living subsistence lifestyles in a spiritually significant landscape. They now live amidst a sea of industrial technology that has transformed their homelands into a heavily populated, militarised metropolis, mining pits, hazardous waste dumps, and flooded coastal plains where tropical rainforest once stood. The pace and scale of change are hard to imagine. A deluge of economic migrants to their homelands, and daily deposits into their rivers of more than 200,000 tonnes of mine tailings, have destroyed the life they knew. Meanwhile, Indonesian soldiers and police – provisioned by Freeport and operating with a mandate to protect the company – have cracked down ruthlessly on those who have protested the invasion. No good neighbour arrangements were struck; instead the company arrived with its own agenda and prejudices, reinforced by the military power of a corrupt regime in Jakarta, and imposed a way of existence on the Amungme and Kamoro without consultation or their consent.

Freeport signed its first contract of work – to mine the Erstberg copper deposit – two years before the United Nations had recognised Indonesian sovereignty over Papua. The contract was the first signed by a multinational corporation with Indonesia's New Order government, headed by Army General, and later President, Soeharto. As would happen in other newly independent countries during the Cold War and beyond, the regime had come to power with the backing and assistance of the US government, including the Central Intelligence Agency, because of its foreign-investment-friendly economic policies.

Indeed, Freeport's history in Indonesia exemplifies the dynamics of multinational corporate investment in the extractive industries and the relationship of these corporate investors with governments. Freeport and other US commercial interests in Indonesia's natural resources, low-wage labour and lax regulatory regime have dominated US policy towards Indonesia. This influence has blocked effective US policy approaches to address the Indonesian government's repressive practices and policies. In addition, the US Embassy in Jakarta has provided considerable diplomatic support to these interests in the face of attempts by Indonesian communities and non-governmental organisations, and more recently the democratically elected government of Abdurrahman Wahid, to hold companies accountable for their social and environmental impact and allegedly unfair business deals with the Soeharto regime.[1]

In 1991, Freeport CEO James Robert ('Jim Bob') Moffett signed a new Contract of Work with Soeharto to exploit the huge deposit of gold that Freeport had discovered at Grasberg in 1988. There is circumstantial evidence suggesting that the deal was fraught with the corruption and collusion for which the Soeharto regime has become infamous.[2] As the Soeharto regime faltered, the company decided to pursue a get-rich-quick approach, obtaining permits to escalate mining throughput at Grasberg. Freeport also sought large injections of foreign capital, provided primarily by Rio Tinto, to finance this massive increase in the rate of mining.

Against this backdrop – and Indonesia's moves to address the concerns of local communities who have been exploited – opportunities now exist for the Kamoro and Amungme, Freeport, the Indonesian government and other actors to resolve the problems associated with Freeport's mining activities. Set in the context of

Papuans' intensifying, yet peaceful struggle for self-determination against a colonising government that is backed by the might of the United States, Freeport's hole in the ground is central to the fate of the entire nation.

There is some hope that the human rights and environmental abuses perpetrated by Freeport will be exposed and in some ways ameliorated. But enormous challenges exist for Papuans to be heard and to have a voice in the debate about what now needs to be done. We cannot speak for the Amungme and Kamoro, but we can reflect on the successes and challenges of their struggle to defend their lands and basic rights, and the lessons that the international community should learn from their experience.

History of the Conflict

The Amungme and Kamoro tell us that their conflict with Freeport began in 1967, with the company's confiscation of indigenous communities' territory, without consultation or the consent of local landowners. Seven years after Freeport's arrival, and at the insistence of the Amungme community, a three-way meeting involving the Amungme, Freeport and the provincial government was held to discuss local concerns. This meeting resulted in a document known as the 1974 January Agreement, in which Freeport pledged to construct facilities, including a school and health clinic in exchange for the approval by indigenous landowners of mining activities.

In the ensuing 20 years, the non-transparent land acquisition process – and forced resettlement of local communities – continued. In 1995, community members understood for the first time that, according to government records, they had ceded all ancestral lands in the Timika area (nearly one million hectares) to the government for transmigration settlements, along with the town of Timika and Freeport's new town, Kuala Kencana.[3]

Over the course of their struggle, local landowners have appealed to the Indonesian government, military and civil society institutions, the United Nations, United States courts and policymakers, and directly to Freeport and Rio Tinto management and shareholders in an effort to be heard and to have their concerns effectively addressed.

In a series of formal letters to the government and the military from 1995, in public statements and in face-to-face meetings, community representatives have demanded:

- compensation by Freeport for all lands that have been confiscated;
- independent environmental and human rights assessments to determine the extent of damages;
- accountability for military personnel who have perpetrated human rights abuses;
- explanations by Freeport and the Indonesian government of plans for the company's mining plans and activities under its Contract of Work;
- community-led development programs;
- cessation by the government of the transmigration program and of 'spontaneous' migration;
- responsibility by Freeport for reclamation of land degraded by mining activities;
- cessation by Freeport of tailings deposition into local river systems;
- compensation to the communities by Freeport for pollution-related suffering;
- cessation by the government of military involvement in the management of natural resources;
- compensation by the government for past losses suffered as a result of land seizures and exploitation of Amungme lands;
- the return by the government and Freeport of traditional Amungme lands confiscated without the community's permission; and
- Amungme permission and consent for all activity on Amungme land.

The company has responded by injecting enormous sums of money into local communities. LEMASA (*Lembaga Musyawarah Adat Suku Amungme* or the Amungme Tribal Council) and the area's three Christian churches have denounced these actions for having a divisive impact on indigenous communities and for fostering a dependency mentality amongst them. In a June 1996 resolution, LEMASA 'unconditionally and absolutely' rejected Freeport's 'One Percent Trust Fund Offer,' which designates one per cent of the company's annual revenues for regional development programs. LEMASA declared that 'with the help of God we shall never succumb to the offer of bribes, intimidation or [be] dishonestly induced into accepting PT Freeport Indonesia's 'Settlement Agreement.'[4]

More recently, and with few alternatives remaining to them, the Amungme and Kamoro have had to adapt their resistance strategies. After a protracted period of attempted cooption by Freeport, Amungme community leader Tom Beanal reluctantly – and with the backing of LEMASA – joined PT Freeport's Board of Commissioners in June 1999. Citing the devastation to local communities caused by Freeport's provision of monies through the 'One Percent Offer' – including the deaths of 18 indigenous people because of inter-ethnic conflict sparked by Freeport's divisive tactics – Beanal has written with some bitterness about accepting the Commissioner position, and the role of Vice President of the regional development organisation established with Freeport's One Per cent funding. He describes his participation as the only option left to him in defending the rights of his people.

Beanal states: 'What Freeport has done to me is to present me with a single limited choice, prepared by the company, so that I was not able to choose freely, but was always obliged to choose what was desired by Freeport. People see me as working with Freeport now. Perhaps it's true! Nevertheless in the depths of my heart, I feel that I must do what is best for my people.'[5]

Moving a Mountain A Day

It is not easy to create one of the largest excavations on earth, and much of the literature about Grasberg marvels at the engineering feat involved in developing the mine. In some way this fixation is no mere boast: the company is moving 700,000 metric tonnes per day of material. This is the rough equivalent to moving the Egyptian Great Pyramid of Cheops once a week.[6] What makes this mine even more remarkable, and damaging, is that Freeport's operations are at elevations of more than 4,100 metres in the central highlands of the province of Papua. Try to imagine a mountain, with a backdrop of glaciers, jutting out of the largest contiguous expanse of rainforest outside the Amazon. The mountain has been decapitated: the top is gone, and the remains are strewn all over the surrounding region.

The Amungme's cosmology depicts this mountain as the sacred head of their mother and its rivers are her milk. To the Amungme, Freeport is digging out her heart. In a disturbing echo of this analogy Freeport CEO Jim Bob Moffett told shareholders at the company's 1997 annual general meeting in New Orleans that the company's operations were like taking 'a volcano that's been decapitated by nature, and we're mining the oesophagus.' Indeed, as the Grasberg open pit is exhausted it will become the world's largest underground mine.[7]

Already Freeport has ground more than 120 metres from the top of the mountain and all that will be left will be a 450 metre crater surrounded by machine-made tunnels, mountains of crumbling, acid-leaching rock waste and a riverine dumping ground stretching to the coast more than 80 miles away.

Overburden is a mining term describing everything on top of the ore that the mining operation seeks – trees, topsoil, the earth's crust. Overburden exists in a ratio of nearly three to one at Grasberg which means that during the life of the mine, the company will remove a quantity of rock and other debris equivalent to twice the amount of earth extracted to build the Panama Canal, or about three billion metric tonnes. This is being piled in two adjacent alpine valleys: to the west 114 hectares of an alpine meadow known as Carstenszweide will be covered more than 800 feet deep, while on the other side of the mine the Wanagon Valley will be filled 450 metres. [8]

In order to counter considerable criticism of environmental management choices, Freeport has, in recent years, employed paid environmental consultants. The resulting reports[9] have been widely criticised by scientists, environmental organisations and company shareholders as being incomplete and/or misleading.[10] In addition, it seems clear that Freeport has not fully implemented the concrete recommendations made in the reports.

In a 1999 report written for Freeport, the environmental consultants Montgomery Watson stated that the company had 'incorporated modern, state-of-the-practice geotechnical stability techniques in siting and designing the Wanagon and Carstenz [Overburden Stockpiles].'[11] Just months later, the Wanagon stockpile underwent a massive rockslide that entered Lake Wanagon, generating a pulse of water that washed downstream like a tidal wave into the populated valley below. Previous overflows had occurred at the site, yet Freeport management ignored and suppressed consultants' recommendations to regulate dumping at Wanagon. The result: four workers were killed by the May 2000 wave.

An even more chilling example of expedient environmental management is the tailings disposal system chosen by Freeport. Tailings are the slurry of finely ground ore from which minerals have been removed. In this case, they are a combination of mill wastes including unrecovered copper, fine clays and sediment, chemical precipitates and slimes. They are potentially the biggest source of heavy metal pollution resulting from Freeport's mining activity and are the most difficult by-product to contain. Recent rates of production have resulted in emptying the equivalent of a ten tonne dump truck filled with untreated tailings every five seconds.

Much of that 200,000 tonnes or more of tailings per day is being dumped into the Aghawaghon River, which merges into the Otomona and Ajkwa rivers. To place this quantity of discharge into a regional context, the controversial Ok Tedi copper mine in Papua New Guinea disposes of approximately 80,000 tonnes of tailings per day into the Fly River system. Recently the World Bank, and even the Australia-based parent company, BHP, have concluded that this form of waste disposal – small in scale compared with Freeport's volumes – should not be practiced because of the environmental damage it causes.[12]

Riverine tailings disposal is not practiced in the United States, Freeport's home country, and is banned in all other developed countries. The practice has attracted condemnation from the international community and was cited as the primary reason for the cancellation of Freeport's political risk insurance by the US government's Overseas Private Investment Corporation (OPIC) in 1995. OPIC states that the termination is based, in part, on 'unreasonable or major environmental, health and safety hazards' and severe degradation of surrounding rainforests caused by mining operations at Grasberg.[13] That the US Ambassador to Indonesia forgot this and claimed that Freeport is doing an excellent job on the environment at Grasberg[14] is evidence that ignorance, hypocrisy and double standards in this case are not limited to the corporate decision makers involved.

Downstream the rainforest is dead, although Freeport now claims that this is all part of the plan and has designated a one hundred square kilometre sacrifice zone as the tailings deposition area. The area, more than 80 kilometres distant from the mine site, was once a source of livelihood for local indigenous communities. The area of 'die back' in the forest caused by suffocation and poisoning of the trees by the mine wastes could increase by at least 50 per cent if the better-understood Ok Tedi experience is any model. It is precisely this risk – and the loss of livelihood and environmental health – that has caused the parties involved to recommend shutting down the Ok Tedi mine.[15]

Another example of note is the Panguna Copper mine in Bougainville, which seems to share the same cursed vein of porphyry as Ok Tedi and Grasberg. There the mine deposited 130,000 tonnes of tailings per day into the Jaba River and inundated the downstream communities and environment.[16] The result there – when the concerns of disgruntled locals, outraged by the impacts of the mine, went un-addressed for years – was the civil war that beset the island for much of the 1990s and cost more than ten thousand lives. When it comes to its partnership with Freeport, Rio Tinto, the parent company on Bougainville, seems to have learnt little about the germinal influence of bad mining practices on local conflicts.

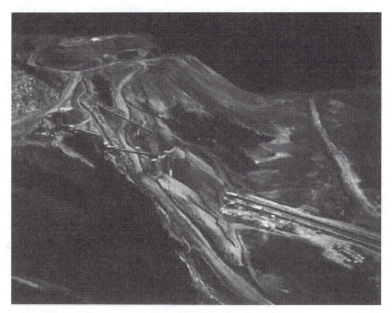

Freeport's Grasberg copper and goldmine, West Papua.

Photo from ICEM

Human Rights Violations and International Scrutiny

The human rights conditions associated with Freeport's mining operations are indicative of the problems experienced by local communities facing large-scale resource extraction around the globe. This is particularly true of regions in which multinational exploitation of resources has provoked resistance by indigenous peoples subsequently sparking 'counter-insurgency' operations by national militaries supported by the US government.

During some 30 years of mine operations, documented human rights abuses have included:

- Torture, rape,[17] indiscriminate and extra judicial killings, disappearances, arbitrary detention, employment and racial discrimination, and severe restrictions on freedom of movement;
- Violation of subsistence rights resulting from seizure and destruction of thousands of acres of rainforest, including community hunting grounds and forest gardens, and contamination of water supplies and fishing grounds;
- Violation of cultural rights, including destruction of a mountain and other sites held sacred by the Amungme; and
- Forced resettlement of communities and massive destruction of housing, churches and other shelters.

In their public statements, the Amungme, in particular, state clearly that they view themselves as victims and as oppressed people. Community members consistently speak about the loss of human dignity and mistreatment – physical, psychological, spiritual and economic – they have experienced since Freeport, its agents and by-products (subcontractors, military protectors, transmigrants, spontaneous migrants and others) arrived. As one Amungme community leader expressed it, ' … we feel that [Freeport] and the Government of Indonesia have blatantly disregarded our existence as the owners of the land which was confiscated. They have humiliated our existence, our dignity, our self-esteem, and pride and we, as human beings, have been belittled and trodden over. We are wondering ourselves if, in fact, we are human beings or merely creatures which are in the process of evolution to become human beings.'[18]

Another Amungme community leader asked, 'What do they think the Amungme are? Human? Half-human? Or not human at all?

If we were seen as human . . . they would not take the most valued property of the Amungme, just as we have never wanted to take the property of others . . . I sometimes wonder, whose actions are more primitive?' [19]

Despite Indonesian government and company interference with scrutiny of human rights conditions in the Freeport area, the 1990s brought increased domestic and international attention to the Amungme and Kamoro's human rights and environmental concerns. In particular, there have been inquiries into specific human rights violations that occurred in and around Freeport's project area in 1994 and 1995 by the Catholic Church of Irian Jaya (1995), Komnas HAM (1995), the International Committee of the Red Cross or ICRC (1995), and by Australian and United States diplomats (1995 and later).[20]

The Catholic Church report, based on eyewitness testimonies, provides the most detailed and disturbing account of the torture and other human rights abuses experienced by Amungme and other local indigenous people: 'Torture caused bleeding head wounds, swollen faces and hands, bruises, loss of consciousness and death because of a broken neck. The torture was conducted in Freeport containers, the Army Commander's Mess, the police station and the Freeport security post.'[21]

In September 1995, Indonesia's National Commission on Human Rights (Komnas HAM) concluded that clear and identifiable human rights violations had occurred in and around Freeport's project area, including indiscriminate killings, torture and inhuman or degrading treatment, unlawful arrest and arbitrary detention, disappearance, excessive surveillance, and destruction of property. Komnas HAM noted that these violations 'are directly connected to [the Indonesian army] . . . acting as protection for the mining business of PT Freeport Indonesia.'

Komnas HAM called on the Indonesian government and military to investigate these occurrences and prosecute those responsible. The Commission also recommended government compensation to the victims and their families. To date, Indonesian authorities have carried out an investigation and prosecutions with regard to only one of the confirmed incidents. No victims have received compensation.

The government's failure to implement the Komnas HAM

recommendations and the Commission's own lack of attention to the company's role in the human rights violations has continued to frustrate community members.

In a detailed response to the Komnas HAM findings, the Amungme state, 'For us, the Amungme people, the root cause of the human rights violations is Freeport . . .'

They continue: 'Considering that the government decided to designate Freeport as a 'vital project', why was the matter not first discussed with the people who are the owners of the natural resources before the company began its operations? Or is it that because the company was designated as a vital project, it was deemed necessary to sacrifice the interests of the people? If the company is indeed a vital project, making it necessary for the government to sacrifice its own people, we regard this as economic colonisation by capitalists in contravention of our national economic system. . . . The fact that Freeport has been allowed to operate here in Irian Jaya and dig up and exploit our mineral resources, to destroy the very means of our existence, to drive us out of our ancestral lands, to impoverish us and kill us on our own territory, is all the result of a policy which has been determined at the centre in Jakarta. It is the Central Government that must take responsibility for reaching a solution to this problem.'[22]

In February 2000, more than 45 Amungme community leaders again voiced their dissatisfaction with the government's lack of attention to the human rights situation and with Freeport's intransigence in cooperating with an independent assessment of these problems. In a written statement, these community members, describing themselves as 'The Victims in Society,' emphasise their ongoing problems with Freeport and state their desire for an independent assessment of the company's impact on human rights. In their words: 'For all this time many problems have occurred in our land, the Amungsa area, which have never been completely or thoroughly resolved. Then our land has been occupied by PT Freeport Indonesia from 1967 to the present. Since this giant American-owned mining company has been operating on the land of our ancestors we have experienced much suffering.'[23]

Recent Developments

The struggle of the Amungme and Kamoro has become intimately entwined with Papuans' territory-wide struggle for independence. Not surprisingly, many Amungme community members support the goals of or have become active in the Free Papua Movement *(Organisasi Papua Merdeka* or OPM), the amorphous, multi-faction Papuan political movement that has employed tactics of armed resistance and international diplomacy in resisting the takeover of the territory by Indonesia.

Since Soeharto's forced resignation from the presidency of Indonesia in May 1998, the Amungme have also had greater influence as part of the renewed independence efforts by Papuan civil society. Amungme and Kamoro concerns, common to many indigenous communities throughout Papua, are reflected in the statements of Papua's independence movement. As Tom Beanal and other Papuan community leaders have stated: 'Could it be that the Indonesian government is drawn to Irian Jaya not by its people but by its natural resources? The legislative and executive bodies have proven incapable of responding to the genuine aspirations of the people within the context of the Republic of Indonesia.'[24]

The Indonesian government of President Abdurrahman Wahid, which came to power in late 1999, has taken some steps to hold Freeport accountable for environmental impacts and to examine the social and human rights concerns associated with the mine.[25]

WALHI, Indonesia's largest environmental organisation, has sued Freeport in the courts for the company's failure to provide accurate information about the environmental impacts of the mine – a first in the country and yet another example of change there. Some national political parties in Indonesia are beginning to address the issue of indigenous land rights.

Members of Indonesia's democratically elected legislature, challenging the validity of Freeport's contract on the grounds that it was signed in the context of the Soeharto regime's high-level corruption and collusion, have asserted that the contract must be renegotiated. Whether or not this occurs, the fact that the possibility has been raised is undoubtedly a mark of the success of the Amungme and Kamoro's struggle.

There are mixed signals though, with implications of a new law decentralising decision making over natural resources to the provincial level remaining ambiguous. Of greater immediate and perhaps ultimate significance, the Papuan independence movement is gaining momentum. It is fed by outrage over the dispossession, displacement and other human rights abuses, the environmental degradation, and lack of political participation associated with military-backed natural resource exploitation, especially at Freeport's Grasberg mine.

Thousands of Indonesian troops have moved into the province and a military-backed militia has joined with Indonesian security forces to attack Papuan independence supporters. Papuan leaders have been arrested and international observers denied access to courts. Domestic and international observers have expressed concerns that another brutal Indonesian assault on Papua's indigenous population may be forthcoming, and that the situation could deteriorate into conditions similar to those in East Timor in 1999.

As always, Freeport management is playing an active role in warding off perceived threats to its continued operations. The company has been hedging its bets by cultivating connections with both the Indonesian government (especially the military), and with Papua's indigenous civil society and independence movement.

The company reportedly gave financial support for the Second Papuan People's Congress in 2000, which was used as a public demonstration of support for independence of the province from Indonesia. At the same time, Freeport CEO Moffett said the company was pursuing an agreement with local community leaders for 'significant additional compensation'[26] beyond what is required under Indonesian law.

In 2000, Freeport publicised a Memorandum of Understanding (MOU) signed by the company with representatives of the Amungme and Kamoro people, including long-time opponent Tom Beanal. According to Moffett 'Freeport has for many years demonstrated its commitment to ensure the social and economic well being of the local people around our operation by investing significant human and financial resources in our social programs. This MOU, the result of years of patient dialogue, is further evidence of our commitment, and now means we will continue this effort hand in hand with the local people.'[27]

The MOU offers nothing in terms of addressing local concerns regarding public health, land tenure, and environmental protection. While its announcement boosted Freeport's stock rating by financial analysts, there is no indication that the MOU represents a retreat from the local communities' commitment to holding Freeport accountable for its social and environmental impact.

Beanal remains critical of the continuing dynamic of exploitation that Amungme and Kamoro experience. He recently told a journalist, 'The Indonesian Government eats at the table with Freeport, they throw the leftover food on the floor and we Papuans have to fight for it.'[28]

Mining Indigenous Lands: Sustainable Community Development or Mal-development?

The struggle of the Amungme and Kamoro peoples against the US mining corporation Freeport McMoRan Copper & Gold is one of the best-documented examples of how local communities have experienced, resisted and confronted the seizure of their traditional lands by national government backed multinational mining enterprises.

The experience of the Kamoro and Amungme typifies that of so many local people who find themselves at the mercy of unregulated global capital in the extractive industries. Indonesia's legal system offers no effective protection for community land rights or for traditional livelihoods and cultures. Highly centralised and militarised governance structures have prevented communities from participating in decision making regarding use and management of natural resources and environmental conservation.

In the repressive political environment that has dominated Indonesia for more than thirty years, basic rights to freedom of expression and subsistence, among others, have been violated in the name of a monolithic model of extraction-based, trickle-down 'development.'

This system has siphoned the vast majority of short-term resource profits to foreign stockholders and the national elite, leaving local people dispossessed, displaced and marginalised.

The experience of the Kamoro and Amungme is also one of 'ersatz development', indeed 'mal-development', in which dominant powers – Freeport, the central government and the military – have used coercion, intimidation, force, divide and conquer strategies and other undemocratic, non-transparent and non-participatory means to impose the cash-wage nexus, in which land and other natural resources become exchangeable commodities.

Their story asks us to consider what sustainable development really is, and whether it is possible to achieve, particularly in indigenous communities, via large-scale mineral extraction designed, imposed and for the benefit of multinationals and governments. It also demonstrates the harm to human life and threat to community existence that results when economic interests are allowed to take precedence over the protection of basic human rights.

Finally, the Freeport case is a microcosm of how the management strategies of multinationals are changing as local resistance becomes more visible. It shows, too, how shareholders, human rights and environmental organisations, public and private insurance and financial lending institutions, and government bodies are taking on new roles in influencing the behaviour of multinationals.

The story of the Amungme, Kamoro and Freeport continues, now in its fourth decade. The future is uncertain. But what is clear is that by taking a determined stand in defence of their rights, the Kamoro and the Amungme have focused the eyes of the world on the severe problems that local communities experience in the face of multinational mining operations.

Their struggle is changing the rules of the game for the mining industry, making it increasingly unacceptable that corporations and governments devastate communities and the natural environment in the name of corporate profit-taking and trickle-down 'development'. Their story, too, underscores the urgent need for more successful mechanisms for safeguarding the rights of indigenous communities in the face of mining assaults in Indonesia and worldwide.

5   Indigenous sovereignty and Century Zinc
Alison Harwood

Introduction

Indigenous peoples are intervening in, and to some extent transforming, processes of economic globalisation. This chapter focuses on the responses of Australian Aboriginal groups in the southern Gulf of Carpentaria in Queensland, Australia, to the global mining giant, Conzinc Riotinto Australia (CRA), now known as Rio Tinto. This case illustrates the complex nature of power in the context of processes of economic globalisation. It is argued that despite the huge disparities of 'wealth' between local Aboriginal communities and multinational corporations such as CRA, Aboriginal communities are by no means powerless within these processes.

As a 'resource locality', the southern Gulf of Carpentaria has been affected by multifaceted changes related to the ending of the Cold War, economic globalisation (and associated changes in global resource markets and political dynamics), and adaptation of cultural identities. Economic globalisation creates new 'geopolitics' of resources in which place-based social, political and environmental relations become highly significant in the dynamics of natural resource management (NRM) decisions. This produces a range of new ideas about territoriality, identity and power.[1]

The significance of geopolitics within processes of economic globalisation, specifically as they relate to NRM, is illustrated through the concept of developmentalism. Developmentalism has been described as a philosophy which is characterised by an unquestioning acceptance of economic growth and development as core societal goals, and which imposes great costs on those who are marginalised from its benefits, notably often traditional owners and indigenous peoples.[2] Western NRM systems largely serve the dominant, developmentalist paradigm. In the case of mining development, NRM systems facilitate the transformation of mineral lease applications and project proposals into Projects.

The processes by which this is achieved are formal and technocratic practices that do not adequately accommodate the values, understandings, concerns and aspirations which prevail in Aboriginal domains such as the southern Gulf of Carpentaria.[3] Thus a conflict arises between two different philosophies: global developmentalism and Aboriginal community-based aspirations.

The two philosophies construct landscapes and resources in specific and often conflicting ways. This ethno-geographic conflict sees, on the one hand, a resource locality such as the Century Zinc Mine as a deposit within a sparsely populated region where there exist no preferable use patterns. On the other hand, these areas hold great cultural significance for Aboriginal people and embody connections between people, country and culture.

Both development processes and political struggles exist and take place within a social and cultural context of power. Specifically, this concerns the power to make decisions over how resources are to be managed. Those who have the most power are able to marginalise alternative visions and aspirations regarding resource management. When these resources happen to belong to indigenous peoples' country and to be part of sacred places, those who have power influence not just resource management futures, but the futures of people and how they will relate to and interact with their country, their culture, and with one another.

Aboriginal People and the Southern Gulf of Carpentaria: Aboriginal Landscapes

Aboriginal country is shaped by the activity of Creation Beings and contemporary Aboriginal identity remains connected to the creation Time, or Dreamings. Indigenous culture, or Aboriginal common law, is embodied within and adapted from teachings derived from the Dreamings.[4]

76

A vital cultural aspect in the region is the identification by Aboriginal people with specific species in the landscape, called totems, and understandings about how each person will relate with and make use of their totemic species, specifically as food resources, and with other totems. Because the landscape is occupied by a myriad of totemic species and totemic identities, it is possible to describe country as a totemic landscape and to understand culture as effectively encoding a system of natural resource management. Thus, people are effectively embedded within landscapes in ways that construct and reflect social, cultural and economic considerations and values.[5]

The Bynoe River on the eastern side of the project is an important place for the Gkuthaarn and Kukatj people, and is implicated in the construction of the Century Zinc mine's slurry pipe.

Photo by Alison Harwood

Colonisation and ongoing attempts at dispossession have resulted in significant social, economic and cultural impacts on Aboriginal people in the Southern Gulf of Carpentaria. Nonetheless, relationships with country and enduring cultural practices continue to shape the values and aspirations of Aboriginal communities in the region. Since European contact the maintenance and protection of culture has required the adaptation and modification of traditional forms, including the reinterpretation of Dreaming stories. Cultural adaptation has been accompanied by negotiations and re-negotiations of meanings, values and priorities related with country. Country should be seen as a dynamic landscape, inhabited and shaped simultaneously by 'the tracks of the Dreamings'[6], and by contested notions of connections between country, culture and people.

Enduring cultural values and understandings continue to inform Aboriginal community development goals and aspirations. As such, these aspirations are frequently seen to be in conflict with the assumptions of the dominant developmentalist paradigm regarding the economic and technical imperatives for natural resource development and economic globalisation.[7] One arena of conflict lies in the ways of seeing and constructing places and landscapes. Enduring indigenous ways of seeing and doing resource management continue to be characterised by culturally-based and place-specific philosophies. These philosophies centre on the idea of country as a 'nourishing terrain' where all aspects of the landscape are connected through caring for one.[8] As such, Aboriginal people's concerns and aspirations for country, culture and people are inseparable.

Aboriginal people's assertions of rights to land are frequently described as obstacles to development which is in the 'national interest', and seen as attempts to 'lock away' valuable resources.[9] Thus, practices of resource development have frequently resulted in the 'progressive dispossession of Aboriginal people and incorporation of country into productive economic uses'.[10]

Alternatively, traditional Aboriginal ontologies characterise country as a living entity, the sacredness of certain places resulting from the ancestral activity which took place there during the creation time, or Dreaming. People's identity and place in the universe is derived from their relationship with particular aspects of the landscape, known as totems.

Thus, the nature of Aboriginal responses to the Century Mine proposal are characterised by spiritual, cultural and economic understandings of place, and opposition to the project frequently arises from a knowledge of and concern for a system of connectedness between people, culture and place.

Colonial Landscapes

The Century Mine proposal, and local Aboriginal people's responses to it, should be viewed within an historical context of colonial invasion. Century Zinc mine and the processes surrounding it represent a continuum with the events of the colonial past and contemporary Aboriginal/non-Aboriginal relations. Despite a history of brutal and violent dispossession at the hands of European pastoralists, of forced removals and relocations to authoritarian missions (known as 'reserves' in Queensland), and of systematic attempts to prevent the maintenance of traditional cultural practices, the various Aboriginal traditional owner groups in the Gulf of Carpentaria region continue to know the region as country and to struggle for recognition of their rights.

During the 1800's, Aboriginal groups in the region responded to invasion with armed resistance against European pastoralists. Conflicts were characterised by atrocities carried out by pastoralists and representatives of the Queensland Mounted Native Police Force against Aboriginal people. One historical account observes that perpetrators were seen: 'smashing children against trees and rocks ... , and after shootings, cutting up bodies, burning bodies, and hanging up parts of corpses in trees where other Aborigines [sic] would later find them'. [11]

Despite resistance, large numbers of Aboriginal people were murdered, forced to flee from their country, and later forcibly relocated to European-controlled settlements. Reduced ability to access traditional food resources also resulted in many Aboriginal people eventually settling on pastoral stations and in camps on the periphery of European settlements known as 'fringe-dwellings'.

Aboriginal communities in the region have also suffered the effects of forced removals from families and country. Thefts of Aboriginal people are believed to have commenced officially in 1912 and to have continued until 1936. Justification for the 'removals', mainly of young children, relate to the threat posed by Aboriginal people to non-Aboriginal people, the need for children to receive European schooling, and the need for Aboriginal people to be provided with 'protection' and medical care. [12]

In 1933, a Christian Brethren mission was established at Dumaji on the Bayley Point Reserve. The contemporary community at Doomadgee has its foundations in principles of evangelism and administrative authoritarianism, and has for the most part been governed by the Chief Protector of Aborigines. Administrators of the institution were driven by a paternalistic desire to be the 'complete caretakers' of the people from babyhood to old age. Despite the authoritarianism of the administration and the Doomadgee community's founding missionary principles, Aboriginal people have continued to resist the complete subjugation of traditional cultural values and practices, often incorporating Christian theology with traditional cosmology and knowledge. Today the town of Doomadgee is a large population centre, governed by the Doomadgee Aboriginal Community Council as a separate local government authority. [13]

Contemporary Landscapes

The various tribal groups in the region are incorporated as Traditional Tribal Corporations, and are represented by the Carpentaria Land Council Aboriginal Corporation (CLC) as the central, regional representative body. Aboriginal leaders in the southern Gulf of Carpentaria established the Carpentaria Land Council in 1984. This was viewed by many Aboriginal people in the region as an attempt to 'return to indigenous self-government based on traditional affiliations'.[14] The CLC have been vigorous in the struggle for recognition as an Aboriginal representative body, the rights of Aboriginal people to land, and for community development and natural resource management that reflects the needs, values and aspirations of local Aboriginal people. With passage of the *Native Title Act 1993* the role of the CLC in facilitating the return of land to traditional owners intensified.

The CLC was recognised in 1994 as a Native Title representative body and has since been the central representative body in the region. Continued uncertainties regarding the existence of native title on pastoral leases, and provision within the Act of the 'Right to Negotiate' regarding proposed developments, has ensured that the CLC has been a significant participant in negotiations about the Century Zinc mine and other proposed resource developments in the Southern Gulf of Carpentaria. Since the early 1990s, the Century Mine proposal has inspired various responses from Aboriginal people and groups in the region. Debates surrounding the proposal have provided for dialogue, negotiations and contestations about country, community aspirations and cultural values and identity. The Century Zinc Mine thus illustrates challenges which economic globalisation poses for Aboriginal people and their country, in the Southern Gulf of Carpentaria.

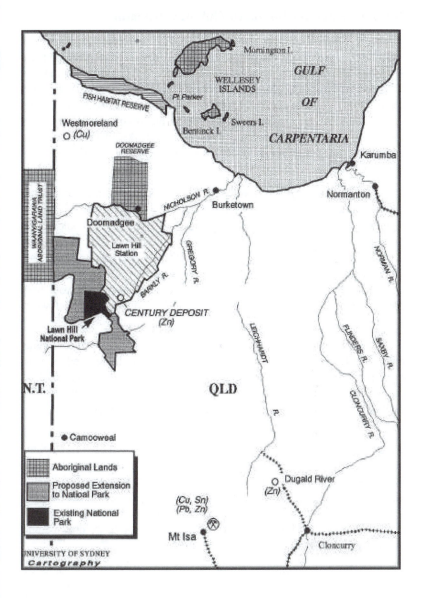

This map shows the location of the Century Zinc deposit in Northwest Queensland, Australia.

Map by Cartography Department, University of Sydney

Resources and the Southern Gulf of Carpentaria

Since the colonial invasion, the way in which non-Aboriginal people and institutions relate with and value the natural resources of the southern Gulf of Carpentaria has shaped understandings of the region. During the 1840s, the savannah grasslands enabled pastoral activity. Today, the region attracts many tourist visitors, the major attractions being fishing and hunting activity. Additionally, the region has been acknowledged for its largely unexploited mineral wealth and is described by mining company and government institutions as the 'Carpentaria Mt Isa Minerals Province'.

The first proposed development in the context of the Carpentaria Mt Isa Minerals Province was the Century Zinc project that involves a significant lead, zinc and silver deposit at Lawn Hill, 250 kilometres north-north-west of Mt Isa. In 1995, two mining leases covering a 23,585 hectare area were granted to CRA for the mine, under the Queensland *Mineral Resources Act 1989*. In addition, CRA, in the guise of Gulf Metals and Minerals, also purchased a number of surrounding pastoral leases.[15] As a result, CRA became the largest single landowner in the region.[16]

The proposal involved the operation of an open-cut mine extending below the water table. In addition to the mine itself, it was proposed that a 300 km slurry pipeline traverse waterways to the coast of the southern Gulf of Carpentaria and a coastal loading and transportation facility be constructed at the town of Karumba, on the Normanton River.

The Century Mine site is situated on Waanyi people's land and adjacent to Gangalida country. The proposed slurry transport pipeline crosses country to which the Gkuthaarn and Kukatj people hold traditional affiliations. The 'sea country' belonging to the Lardil, Kaiadilt and Yangal people is implicated in the operation of coastal and off-shore loading and transport facilities.[17] Thus, the local Aboriginal people likely to be affected by the Century Zinc project are drawn from culturally and geographically diverse groups.

The current cultural landscape in part reflects the impacts of colonisation, such as forced removals, massacres and the establishment of reserves. It is not surprising, therefore, that the Century Mine proposal has generated conflict amongst Aboriginal people in the region.[18] Nonetheless, Aboriginal people have also constructed common responses to CRA and the Century Mine. For example, Aboriginal people's connections to country and culture continue to be asserted in part through their relationship with the 'running water' of the river systems around Gregory, Doomadgee, Burketown and Normanton, and with the sea around the Wellesley Islands. The cultural and economic importance of fishing activities in these areas 'generates a critical relationship between their potential health and local marine pollution'.[19] Since identification of the Century deposit in 1990, Aboriginal people in the region have expressed concern regarding the potential for negative impacts on the cultural and environmental integrity of country, and the need to address community-based development goals and aspirations.

A complex set of negotiations took place between Aboriginal groups, State and Commonwealth governments, and CRA regarding the Century Mine proposal. The context for these negotiations was a rapidly changing political and legal arena. Key developments included the Common Law recognition of Native Title, the High Court decision regarding the relationship between native title and pastoral leases in Queensland, and the subsequent passage of State and Commonwealth Native Title Legislation.

There were six key elements to negotiations which occurred as part of the formal decision-making process: the consultation period (late 1990–1991); the production of an Impact Assessment (1991–1996); the gazettal of Lawn Hill National Park (1992); hearings before the Mining Warden's Court (1993, 1995 and 1996); the Waanyi Native Title Claim (commenced June 1994); and the Mediation stage (commenced March 1995). These processes consistently reflected the failure of natural resource management systems, despite the 'cross-cultural' relations implicit within them, to accommodate alternative ways of understanding landscapes and local community-based (rather than global commodity-based) ideas about development.

CRA Exploration (CRAE) approached Aboriginal communities in late 1990 in an attempt to gain approval to continue with drilling operations that began in May 1990.[20] In meetings throughout the region in 1991, Waanyi, Garrawa, Gangalida, Kaiadilt, Yangal and Lardil people consistently expressed concern regarding the impact of the proposed mine and pipeline on the fishing grounds of the estuarine and marine environments, and on sacred sites. Whilst Aboriginal people felt that their concerns regarding sacred sites should be influential in *determining* the pipeline route, CRAE felt that once a preferred route was determined, it was sufficient to engage Aboriginal people in site identification processes and to manoeuvre the pipeline around any sites of significance. Considerable anxiety was also expressed by these groups that the Doomadgee communities alone had been consulted when in reality it is 'people all over who belong to that area'.[21]

Between December 1990 and October 1994, Century Zinc Limited (CZL) were involved in 55 meetings and consultations with Gulf Aboriginal groups.[22] Early consultations in this period were characterised by the absence of experienced personnel qualified in cross-cultural consultation and negotiation. Initial approaches to Aboriginal groups at Doomadgee were made by a CRAE geologist. Few opportunities existed for Aboriginal people to intervene in the course of events. During a consultation meeting with Gulf Aboriginal people in August 1991, a CRAE representative made it known that 'we don't have to [negotiate access for Aboriginal traditional owners to Lawn Hill station]. It would be a good neighbourly activity if we did'.[23]

One of the most lasting, and possibly destructive, legacies of CRA's actions in the initial stages of negotiations was the creation of a level of distrust towards the proponent and within and between Aboriginal communities in the region. This was fostered by a privileging of certain groups of people in negotiations, specifically those affiliated with the mine site area and those whom CRA believed would be most easily accommodated within their own priorities.[24] Furthermore, some observers have argued that CRA effectively tried to make a highly complex indigenous political landscape one-dimensional by assuming that all Aboriginal people in the region would have the same opinion about the mine and understanding about country.[25]

Following the consultation period, initial Impact Assessment (IA) was undertaken. This work failed to address issues and concerns related to Aboriginal people and landscapes in the region despite the fact that considerable effort went into the production of Impact Assessment Guidelines by the Queensland Social Impact Assessment Unit (SIAU). Despite concerns raised, the Queensland Government determined that the IA Guidelines had been addressed, thus effectively signing-off on the process whilst substantial IA work remained incomplete.

Despite the value of Impact Assessment as a decision-making tool, it occurred in the context of an expedited development approval process characterised by the privileging of corporate interests over those of local Aboriginal people.

At the same time, a Native Title claim for land ownership was lodged with the National Native Title Tribunal (NNTT) by Waanyi traditional owners in June 1994 over an area known as *Wugujaji*. The area contains a site of considerable cultural significance to Waanyi people which is known to have been used for traditional purposes. This period and subsequent years were characterised by increasing public interest in the ability of the Native Title Act to protect the rights of Aboriginal people and pressure from pastoralist groups, mining industry interests and sections of the State and Commonwealth Governments to legislate to protect the interest of industry.

As the Mine proposal developed, Waanyi people grew increasingly concerned about the impacts of the mine on the area, specifically the pollution of the river systems which run through the Park. In October 1994, 200 Waanyi people occupied Lawn Hill National Park, adjacent to the Century Mine site, for three weeks. [26] One protestor explained that 'this used to be our home and we're happy to come back home'. [27] During the occupation people engaged in traditional hunting and fishing activities and the passing-on of traditional knowledge to younger generations.

The Waanyi people agreed to leave the Park in return for the establishment of an Advisory Committee of Waanyi People to facilitate the management of the Park. [28] The assertion that Lawn Hill was and would remain country which belonged to the Waanyi people was a powerful and symbolic act of opposition to what they saw as the Queensland government's and CZL's attempts to deny Aboriginal people's continuing rights and responsibilities to country. Furthermore, it illustrated the potential for the Carpentaria Land Council to organise campaigns of protest and opposition. The CLC were able to draw attention to what they felt were the inadequacies in the Draft Impact Assessment Study Report (DIASR). As a result, the Queensland government became aware of the need to address Aboriginal social impact assessment issues. [29]

In February 1996, a group of 26 Waanyi people flew to Canberra, the capital of Australia, to hear the decision by the High Court in its ruling in the Waanyi claimants' favour that the National Native Title Tribunal (NNTT) should accept the Waanyi claim for registration. In being a visible presence at the court, Aboriginal people indicated the importance of their continued connections to traditional country and their preparedness to engage in formal, legislative processes in the interests of pursuing their rights. Furthermore, the presence of Waanyi traditional owners at the High Court in Canberra also illustrates the interface that occurs between local place – and culture-specific development aspirations and broader processes of economic globalisation.

In 1997, traditional owner groups in the region and CZL reached a settlement regarding the future of the Century Zinc Mine and its implications for local Aboriginal people. This agreement was known popularly as the '$90 million offer' and involved the provision of funding, employment and training for Aboriginal communities. Despite continued wariness about the cultural, environmental and social impacts of the Century Mine, questions about the integrity of 'offers' by CZL, and a sense of weariness amongst traditional owners who had for the best part of the 1990s been struggling against overwhelming pressures to have their say in the future of their country and their communities, the settlement represented a significant shift from the days when CRA were prepared to engage only a limited number of traditional owner interests in site clearance activity.

Throughout the conduct of formal decision-making processes, Aboriginal people attempted to participate in a way that safeguarded their rights and interests. Nonetheless from the outset the processes and the key protagonists failed to meaningfully accommodate Aboriginal people. The limitations of formal processes meant that if the rights of Aboriginal people were to achieve any recognition, and if the integrity of their culture and country was to stand a chance in the face of overwhelming corporate and political pressures, they needed to act outside of these structures and to participate in informal acts of protest.

By refusing to participate in processes that marginalised and disempowered them, Aboriginal people in the region engaged in autonomous actions which challenged the notion of corporate ownership of natural resources and the processes designed to safeguard this. These actions put Aboriginal people's concerns and development aspirations on a decision-making agenda that increasingly received more attention both in Australia and internationally, and counteracted attempts by CRA and the Queensland Government to make Aboriginal interests invisible. It is significant that protest actions occurred within places that continue to be sacred to Aboriginal people (such as Lawn Hill National Park) and that are characterised as Aboriginal domains (such as the town of Normanton).

The way in which local Aboriginal people participate and intervene in resource management decision making and broader processes of economic globalisation, involves the exercise of power. If one considers power as the myriad of actions within a dialectic, where access to resources, control of identities, and influence over country is being constantly contested and negotiated, then 'power' does not necessarily require one entity to have power and another to be without power – the one holding power over the other.

In tracing the patterns and structures of power within processes surrounding the Century Mine proposal processes, the concept of power can be defined as 'distinct from conventional western models of social interaction which entrench notions of domination, superiority and conflict'.[30]

This concept of power involves a focus on relationships and processes by which decisions affecting future outcomes in the region (and within and between the social groups involved) are constantly constructed, contested, challenged and re-negotiated. As a process, this concept of empowerment 'builds directly on the existing strengths of Aboriginal groups – continuing interests in land, cultural traditions, knowledge and values'.[31] In referring to empowerment through protest, resistance and opposition, the intention then is not simply to refer to outcomes, but to highlight the relationships and their implications.

Such actions and processes afford Aboriginal people an informed and experienced sense of possibility within future negotiations. Empowerment means having a significant degree of autonomy in realising ones own goals and aspirations. Thus: 'empowerment is understood here to be about improving people's ability to secure their own survival and development, and to increase their ability to participate in and exercise influence over crucial decisions affecting their survival.'[32]

Conclusion

Historically, recognition of Aboriginal people's interests in Australian natural resource management systems has been significantly limited. Ironically, where it has occurred it is often conditional on Aboriginal people conceding to agreements that result in the destruction of sacred country in exchange for a form of 'charitable cooperation' with mining companies. The notion of rights and compensation has been largely absent.

Community action that steps outside 'formal' decision-making frameworks disrupts corporate and state narratives of dominance and legitimacy that surround processes of economic globalisation. Local oppositional and protest actions in response to CRA's Century Mine proposal illustrate a broader process that fundamentally involves the negotiation of power.

At Century, Aboriginal people acted simultaneously to assert their rights to participate meaningfully in formal processes, *and* to challenge the integrity of these processes, *and* to put Aboriginal concerns and aspirations onto the broader agenda for the region.

The role of 'place' has been central to these actions. Aboriginal people have acted strategically at significant places in an attempt to assert their continuing connections to country and development goals based upon intimate cultural understandings about places and communities. In contrast, multinational mining companies view landscapes in terms of what can be extracted from it in the interests of generating corporate wealth through global economic markets.

Thus, what are for Aboriginal people sacred places shaped by ancestors, inhabited by totemic species, and encoded with knowledge that is central to the maintenance of life and culture, represent for multinational mining companies resource-rich landscapes valued only in terms of their potential commodification.

The recognition of the persistence of Native Title has changed the legislative and political landscape in Australia, establishing a means by which Aboriginal interests are legitimated within formal processes and strengthening support (both locally and from the wider non-indigenous population) for informal protests. It remains to be seen whether the Commonwealth *Native Title Act* is a means of promoting indigenous interests, or whether, like environment and heritage legislation, Impact Assessment and limited land title concessions, it simply provides another means of marginalising indigenous people, or co-opting them into decision-making structures that ultimately dispossess them.

In the context of the Century Mine proposal, Native Title has facilitated a shift in the balance of power and the dynamics of regional development in remote Aboriginal domains such as the Gulf country. Nonetheless, it has not displaced corporate ideologies from their influential position in development narratives. Formal development processes at Century continued to primarily reflect corporate ideologies and the assumption that mineral resource development is *the* preferred land use pattern in the region. Thus, processes of economic globalisation as they occur locally, continue to place indigenous people at risk of further dispossession.

Despite a long history of opposition by local indigenous peoples, processes of economic globalisation and the institutions complicit within them largely fail to acknowledge and accommodate the significance of locally-held values. As such, resources are effectively disembodied from the places, communities and the cultures which have managed, or cared for them since creation. A fundamental conflict thus arises between the paradigm of economic globalisation and the values held by local Aboriginal people in relation to natural resource landscapes.

While this chapter has focused on protest and participation around the Century Mine proposal, the material and discursive significance of place and power are useful in attempting to reach an understanding of indigenous people's responses to processes of resource development and economic globalisation in other settings.

Throughout the world, indigenous people's oppositional strategies and protest actions are an attempt to insert their concerns, interests and rights within broader political agendas, to assert their rights to participate and intervene in decision-making processes, and to counteract the propensity of processes of economic globalisation to make local people and places invisible.

6 Mining, water, survival and the Diavik diamond mine

Catherine Coumans

Introduction: Pure Water is More Precious than Diamonds[1]

Large-scale mining poses significant environmental challenges. It threatens the world's remaining natural forests,[2] it contaminates soil, degrades air quality, and has a serious impact on the world's water resources. Water has been called 'mining's most common casualty'.[3]

This chapter focuses on contamination of freshwater by mining and on the consequences of water pollution for poor communities. Large-scale mining is increasingly taking place in developing countries, made accessible through trade liberalisation, and in remote regions of both developing and developed countries, made accessible through modern technology. This chapter emphasises the challenges mining poses to poor people and to marginal and indigenous communities in remote regions that are dependent on clean lakes and rivers for their drinking water, their daily subsistence and livelihood, and for social and cultural sustainability.

Pure water is increasingly recognised as a precious and limited resource likely to be at the centre of serious conflicts in the 21st century.

'By 2015 nearly half the world's population – more than three billion people – will live in countries that are water stressed. ... as countries press against the limits of available water between now and 2015 the possibility of conflict will increase'.[4] According to the Council of Canadians, 'The demand for water is doubling every 20 years – that's twice the rate at which the world's population is growing. By 2025, two-thirds of the world's population will not have enough water'.[5]

Hard rock mines always exploit at least two precious resources: ore and water. Most hard rock mines use vast amounts of water in drilling and in processing ore. Copper mining, for example, 'uses approximately 200 gallons of water per ton of ore milled'.[6] De-watering mines that reach below the water table can impact huge areas by draining underground aquifers of pristine reserves of water that have built up over centuries and even millennia. In addition to consuming fresh water, mining also threatens water resources by diverting rivers and streams and by polluting water.

Primary causes of water contamination are acid mine drainage, heavy metal leaching, processing chemicals such as cyanide, and sedimentation. In the United States alone more than 19,500 kilometres of rivers and 72,000 hectares of lakes have been polluted by mining. No global estimates exist.[7] The impact of mine pollution on water is often severe, with fish populations wiped out, wildlife habitats destroyed, watershed vegetation die back, and drinking water sources contaminated. The impacts can last a long time, making water, 'unusable for literally thousands of years'.[8] Moreover, the costs to society of treating polluted water are enormous. Water treatment alone for Acid Mine Drainage has cost Australia, AU$930 million a year.[9]

Globalisation and trade liberalisation are making it more difficult for both developed and developing nations to protect their water resources from mining. Developed nations cannot easily ban a foreign investor based solely on a bad environmental track record, and competition for mining revenues with countries that have lower environmental standards places downward pressure on the enforcement of national regulations protecting water. Developing countries often have weak environmental legislation. Where adequate environmental legislation does exist, developing countries often lack the financial, technical and human resource capacity to evaluate mine proposals, monitor compliance, and enforce existing laws.

Furthermore, developing countries are not encouraged to enforce strict environmental laws as, in order to generate revenues needed to finance development and pay back loans, they experience pressure from international financial institutions to provide a favourable investment climate for foreign mining companies.

There is an urgent need for stringent international standards for mining to provide a 'level playing field' that protects global water resources.[10] Regulatory authorities in developing countries need to be provided with financial resources to develop high standards for mining, and to hire and train environmental monitors to enforce their laws. In the absence of such provisions, efforts focus on building the capacity of local communities to resist mining projects that are likely to degrade their water resources. This means providing communities with accurate and thorough information on the possible impacts of mining and on the highest technical and legislative international standards for mining practice, and by supporting processes that will provide indigenous people with a greater role in the governance of their land and water resources.

The case study used to illustrate the arguments I make is based in the Canadian north and involves a diamond mine proposed by the British Australian mining giant Rio Tinto. This mine is on land that is the subject of unextinguished Aboriginal title and part of the range for a large caribou herd that is important for adjacent communities as a food source.

This mine will be located within a pristine arctic lake that is at the headwaters of a major watershed. This case illustrates the unwillingness of the Canadian government to enforce Canadian regulations protecting national water resources and the rights of Aboriginal peoples. It also shows the complex challenges faced by Aboriginal communities dealing with the prospect of a major mining project that threatens their food and water, as well as their cultural identity.

The Race to the Bottom: Legislative Failures to Protect Water in Canada

One fifth of the world's freshwater supply is located in Canada.[11] Rather than encourage regulators to see Canada as a guardian of water, this fact appears to make Canadian authorities cavalier about the need to protect and preserve water resources. Canadian authorities too often do not enforce the regulations that exist and the mining industry puts constant pressure on regulators to lower standards.

Canada's Fisheries Act contains prohibitions against the, 'harmful alteration, disruption or destruction of fish habitat'[12] and the release of 'deleterious substances' into waters frequented by fish.[13] In 1977, the Metal Mining Liquid Effluent Regulations (MMLERs) were enacted under the Fisheries Act, setting maximum limits for a number of toxic substances and for 'total suspended solids' that may be deposited into waters frequented by fish. Total suspended solids may not exceed a monthly average of 25 milligrams/litre. A review of the MMLERs, currently underway, will likely further reduce this allowable limit. The limit on total suspended solids effectively rules out the deposition of mine waste ('tailings') into Canada's rivers, lakes and seas.

While these regulations are meant to protect Canadian waters, reportedly about 25 per cent of the mines currently operating in Canada are out of compliance with the MMLERs, and in the 24-year history of the regulations, few mines have been prosecuted under the MMLERs.[14] Between 1992 and 1998 Placer Dome dutifully reported that river discharge from its Dome mine in Northern Ontario was lethal to the indicator fish species.[15] No sanctions were ever imposed. Furthermore, in spite of the MMLERs, lakes are now being used as tailings disposal sites in Canada.

For the past 20 years, the MMLERs have been successful in one area, and that is in stopping ocean dumping of tailings in Canada. Submarine Tailings Disposal (STD) is the disposal of mine tailings into the sea through a submerged pipe. Major mining companies and their consultants are actively promoting this tailings disposal method in various parts of the world, particularly in the Pacific and South-east Asia, as both economical and environmentally sound.[16]

Submarine Tailings Disposal contravenes provisions in both the US Clean Water Act and the Canadian Fisheries Act and is not being practised in Canada or in the US. Nonetheless, US and Canadian companies, such as Placer Dome, advocate STD in developing countries where they mine, such as in the Philippines and in Papua New Guinea, where Placer Dome also dumps mine tailings directly into a major river system at its Porgera mine.

Pressure by the industry to overturn Canada's regulatory provisions against STD in Canada has been intense of late. Industry-sponsored workshops and conferences, often in partnership with Canadian government departments, regularly feature sessions on this topic with speakers – frequently from environmental consulting firms that work for mining companies and specialize in STD – who argue that the sea can safely absorb mine tailings and that the technology and scientific knowledge exist to dump mine waste into the ocean responsibly.

The industry and their consultants invariably point to what they consider to be success stories with this technology, in countries such as Papua New Guinea, and they argue that Canada is losing mines to countries willing to allow ocean dumping. Natural Resources Canada, a government ministry, is currently spending a large amount of taxpayer dollars on a three year study of the impacts of historic mine tailings in the Atlantic Ocean off Canada's coast.

In public presentations, Natural Resources Canada officials indicate that this study may change how the Canadian government will evaluate ocean disposal of tailings in the future.

Rio Tinto's Diavik Diamond Mine

' ... the system that approved Diavik has also resulted in the environmental disasters at the Giant, Faro, Colomac, BYG, and other mines'. [17]

(Louise Hardy, Member of Parliament for the Yukon)

In the early 1990s mineral claims were staked in a large area of Canada's central Northwest Territories (NWT), covering a region the size of France, including some that were just 30 kilometers south of Canada's first diamond mine, the BHP-owned Ekati mine, in the Lac de Gras area.

In 1992, Rio Tinto, through its subsidiary Kennecott Canada Inc., acquired a 60 per cent interest in the unincorporated joint venture claim in exchange for providing the necessary financing and expertise to develop what will now become Canada's second diamond mine.

In 1996, Diavik Diamond Mines Inc. (Diavik) was formed, as a wholly owned subsidiary of Rio Tinto, to oversee the management of the proposed Diavik diamond mine. The Diavik project is a joint venture between Diavik Diamond Mines Inc. (60 per cent) and Aber Diamond Mines (40 per cent), itself now 14.3 per cent owned by the jeweller Tiffany & Co.

The location of the proposed mine is about 300 km north of Yellowknife and about 100 km north of the tree line in a tundra area designated as a southern arctic ecozone. The mine is on lands used traditionally by five Aboriginal peoples: the Dogrib Treaty 11 Tribal Council, Yellowknives Dene First Nation, Lutsel K'e First Nation, North Slave Metis Alliance and the Kitikmeot Inuit Association. It is also in the heart of the range of the Bathurst caribou herd, the largest caribou herd in the NWT.

The mine will be located inside Lac de Gras, a large lake at the headwaters of the Coppermine River system, which feeds into the Arctic Ocean. Massive dykes will be built in Lac de Gras, with the water behind the dykes pumped out and layers of glacial till and lake sediments removed to expose four kimberlite 'pipes', the ore containing diamonds, that will be mined through an open pit process.

At least two of the pipes may eventually be further exploited through underground mining. A 20 square kilometer island in Lac de Gras will serve as a base for waste rock dumps, power generation facilities, accommodation and administrative buildings, a diamond recovery plant, an airstrip and a water treatment facility.[18] The projected life of the mine is 16 – 22 years.

Diavik triggered a formal environmental assessment when it filed project descriptions and applications in March of 1998 and an environmental assessment report in September. Following a process of some technical review and public consultation, Canada's Department of Indian Affairs and Northern Development, Fisheries and Oceans, and Natural Resources, filed a Comprehensive Study Report (CSR) under the Canadian Environmental Assessment Act, in June 1999.

This report sets out Diavik's claims, presents some of the concerns that were voiced, and concludes that, 'with the mitigation measures proposed by Diavik, no significant adverse environmental effects on the biophysical and socio-economic environments have been identified'.[19]

The report notes that environmental and socio-economic impacts about which uncertainty remains, including ultimate effects on caribou and the water of the Coppermine watershed, can be adequately dealt with at later licensing and permitting phases. There were 30 days in which comments on the CSR could be filed by interested parties.[20]

Critical environmental and social concerns about the Diavik proposal fuelled informed and committed participation by some Aboriginal organisations and NGOs such as the Canadian Arctic Resources Committee (CARC), throughout the project's review process. These groups ultimately requested that the project be referred to a full environmental review panel, as set out under section 23 of the Canadian Environmental Assessment Act, for the following reasons: failure to take cumulative environmental and social effects of mineral exploration in the region into consideration;

- undue reliance on the project proponent's assurances that environmental impacts to water and caribou will be minimal or mitigative without sufficient independent scientific evidence to back up these predictions;

- undue reliance on the ability of future permitting and licensing processes to accurately identify and resolve key outstanding environmental issues;

- failure to consider seriously less-risky alternatives, such as underground mining; and

- an abject failure to respect the views and concerns expressed by affected First Nations whose rights and official representation were undermined in the review process.

In spite of these concerns, and after months of intense lobbying by Diavik's proponents and local businesses, Environment Minister David Anderson released the project from further environmental assessment on 1 November 1999, when he provided conditional approval of the Comprehensive Study Report. Minister Anderson's position provided in the government press release was brief, stating simply that with the implementation of mitigation measures the project, 'is not likely to cause significant adverse environmental effects'.[22]

Statements by the Minister of Indian Affairs and Northern Development, Robert Nault, perhaps provide greater insight into the economic priorities of the government, 'the Diavik project is important, not only for the Northwest Territories, but for all of Canada. Northerners stand to realize very significant direct benefits from job creation and business opportunities.'[23]

Mining in the North: Degradation of Water and Human Health Impacts

'*Much of the history of mining in our traditional territory is a national disgrace. In the 1940s and 50s there was a uranium mine at Rayrock that turned part of our territory into a hazardous waste site. Clean up, assuming there can be one, has been left to the Canadian taxpayer.*'

John Zoe of the Dogrib First Nation.[24]

The social and environmental concerns about the Diavik project raised by stakeholder groups need to be understood within the broader context of cultural and socio-economic life in the Canadian North and the existing legacy of mining there. The Canadian North is one of the remote parts of the world that now is being explored aggressively for exploitable ore bodies as advances in technology, infrastructure and communications make these areas logistically and economically more attractive.

Like other remote regions in the world, the Canadian North is sparsely populated with a relatively large indigenous population. Subsistence harvesting plays a major economic and cultural role in the lives of these communities, whose members have traditionally low participation in the wage economy. Many of these Aboriginal communities rely on rivers and lakes for their drinking water and food sources. The Diavik mine, through its potential impacts on a major river system and on caribou herds, has the potential to threaten both the livelihood and the health of local Aboriginal communities. It will not be the first time this has happened in the region.

While diamonds are a new industry for the North, past mining booms, as well as more recent mines, have left behind serious environmental problems that now threaten indigenous lands, foods and community health. Although impacts on wildlife and on human health have not yet been adequately studied, there is broad recognition of the environmental problems related to these mines and the likely costs to clean them up.

Louise Hardy, Member of Parliament for the Yukon, noted, 'Since there is no policy or law that requires zero public liability from mining operations in northern Canada, the system that approved Diavik has also resulted in the environmental disasters at the Giant,

Faro, Colomac, BYG, and other mines. All of these required abandonment plans and they were still disasters.'[25]

The most infamous case is that of the Giant Mine in Yellowknife which closed in 1999 when its owners went bankrupt. The mine contains 270,000 tonnes of highly carcinogenic arsenic trioxide laced dust, a by-product of 50 years of gold roasting. The arsenic is stored underground, is soluble and threatens the entire Mackenzie River Watershed. This mine is also known to have pumped out airborne arsenic through its roasting operations for years. The Yellowknives Dene First Nation asserts that two children died when they drank arsenic contaminated melt water from snow during the early 1950s when people were warned against continuing this traditional practice. Estimates for clean-up of the arsenic range from tens of millions to over 1.5 billion dollars. To date, no acceptable method has been proposed for cleaning up this waste.[27]

While government officials admit that many of the abandoned mines in the North are in need of environmental rehabilitation, there have been almost no studies done on the impacts of toxic seepage and metal contamination on the animals native people eat, the water they drink, or on the health of native communities living near these mines. Two Yukon First Nation communities have recently taken matters into their own hands with alarming results. Sarah Johnnie, of the Little Salmon Carmacks First Nation, located near BYG Resources' abandoned Mount Nansen mine, says, 'We are worried about the health of the fish and wildlife in the area, so we sampled the water ourselves.'[28]

Unacceptable levels of cyanide, arsenic, copper, lead, aluminium and iron were found in Dome Creek, a few kilometres down stream from the mine site in an area that is used by native people for fishing and hunting. Similar sampling by members of the Ross River Kaska Dene First Nation at the Ketza River mine, which is also abandoned, found toxic levels of lead and copper in uncontained water and toxic levels of arsenic, lead, and iron flowing into the Ketza River. The Ketza River area is used by native people to harvest berries and medicine and to hunt sheep, moose, and caribou, as well as for fishing, 'this was a rich place to go in times of scarcity, why do mines always go into areas which are full of food?' asks Vera Sterriah of the Ross River Kaska Dene First Nation.[29]

In spite of clear evidence that existing mines threaten the ability of Aboriginal peoples to sustain themselves in a healthy manner from the land, and in spite of the overwhelming public costs associated with the clean-up of abandoned mines, the main argument proponents make in favour of Diavik rests on social and economic development. According to Mayor Dave Lovell of Yellowknife, 'if Diavik doesn't go through, I think we'll know what a recession's all about'.[30]

In an open letter the NWT and Yellowknife Chambers of Commerce and various worried corporate supporters argued, 'Mr. Prime Minister, this is an appeal from the people of the Northwest Territories. Prompt approval for Diavik to proceed to the next stage will encourage companies sponsoring additional diamond projects as well as other mining and oil and gas developments, to enter the environmental review process. We look to your support for environmentally responsible projects like Diavik that will contribute significantly to our social and economic future.'[31] It is important to recognise that while the open letter claims to speak for all people of the Northwest Territories, Mayor Lovell and the signatories of the open letter, both corporate and individual, are overwhelmingly non-native and urban-based.

There is no doubt that the expeditious permitting of Diavik will encourage proponents for at least three other possible diamond mines in the same area to proceed with applications. But the Comprehensive Study Report does not address the issue of cumulative effects should these other mines come on line and does not provide a regional framework against which the effects of Diavik can be gauged.

In June 1998 an important legal precedent was set in Canada when failure to consider and assess cumulative effects prior to project approval led to a Federal Court judgement against a proposed coalmine.[32] The question whether Diavik itself should be described as 'environmentally responsible' also needs further examination.

Water: Lac de Gras, a Unique Ecosystem

Lac de Gras has exceptional characteristics, 'the water of Lac de Gras is likely some of the purest natural water on the planet. Its hardness and levels of contained metals, suspended solids, and nutrients are in the range of the lowest concentrations recorded for lake water'.[33] The lake has been given a rare ecological classification – 'ultra-oligotrophic' and little scientific knowledge exists about this kind of lake. Renowned Canadian water expert David Schindler notes that, 'if total phosphorus concentrations are as low as measured by Diavik, the lake represents a unique system'.[34] The lake appears to be a 'regionally, and perhaps internationally, rare resource'.[35] And yet, little is known about its biodiversity in a regional context.

Purely for scientific reasons and to preserve a unique ecosystem it could be argued that this lake should be protected from the impacts of mining within the lake itself. But the lake is also situated at the headwaters of a major river system that culminates in the Arctic Ocean and includes critical fishery resources and drinking water for native communities, such as the residents of Kugluktuk. The Coppermine River has also been designated as a Heritage River although there is no legal protection with this status.

The unusual nature of this mine, which proposes open pits directly connected to unlimited volumes of groundwater in an arctic environment means that many of the engineering challenges are unique and untested. The potential threats to Lac de Gras that have been established by Diavik and by independent scientists are substantial and most have not been adequately addressed according to independent assessments. These include ongoing uncertainty about the impacts on aquatic resources of blasting, and about 'mine drainage quality, volumes of water, storage capacity of tailings facility, security of containment from groundwater access, water treatment process, discharge water quality, leaching rates of cadmium from water retaining dams, and ultimate ecological effects of water quality changes in Lac de Gras.'[36]

According to Diavik's own predictions, sulfide oxidation in the waste rock piles could last two hundred years or more, 'collection and treatment of waste rock and tailings impoundment drainage, cited as technically and economically unfeasible by reviewers in the comprehensive study process, will almost certainly be necessary for two centuries or more.'[37]

Diavik predicts that heavy metal releases during dyke construction will exceed thresholds for the protection of aquatic life.[38] Diavik also predicts that higher nutrient mine water discharge will change 20 per cent of the surface waters of Lac de Gras to a eutrophic system, at least during the lifetime of the mine.[39] The use of an

101

impermeable liner under its tailings and waste rock dumps was rejected by Diavik as 'uneconomical', relying instead on permafrost to provide a barrier for waste effluent.[40] Numerous recent studies point out that with climate change permafrost in the Canadian North is no longer permanent.

Diavik's 'Special Authorisation'

So how did a unique lake that falls within the jurisdiction of the Canadian federal government and under the provisions of the Fisheries Act, as described above, become subjected to these impacts?

In brief, although Diavik does not deny that fish habitat will be destroyed, the company managed to get a special 'authorisation' to alter and destroy fish habitat (under Section 35(2) of the Fisheries Act) upon the understanding that the company will have 'compensated' for the loss by the time the mine is closed and the dykes removed, assuring, ultimately, no net loss to fish habitat. The authorisation Diavik received recognises that the project will destroy not only fish habitat in Lac de Gras, but also in six additional lakes and some streams on East Island in Lac de Gras where the mine will be located. [42]

It assumes that the mining company has the competence to compensate for these habitat losses and lost fish production during the years of mining, through a series of environmental engineering feats that will actually improve upon existing fish habitats. This is entirely speculative, a certain leap of faith, all the more so as Diavik does not have to provide the design specifications for these major environmental enhancements until two years after the issuance of its authorisation to alter and destroy fish habitat, which it received on 2 August 2000.

Diavik's authorisation to alter and destroy fish habitat in a rare environment such as Lac de Gras is particularly questionable as the guidelines set for Department of Fisheries and Oceans (DFO) officials clearly state that 'compensation specified is viewed as the least preferred approach'. DFO recognises that '[I]t is often difficult to predict the success of compensation measures ... there is greater likelihood of achieving No Net Loss by maintaining, to the extent possible, the existing integrity, structure, and function of the attributes of fish habitat which sustain a fish's life processes'. [43]

Finally, even recent experience and existing impacts from mining on Lac de Gras seem not to have deterred DFO from granting Diavik's authorisation. Canada's first diamond mine, BHP's Ekati mine north of Lac de Gras, went through a more rigorous type of environmental review than did Diavik, and BHP assured regulators that surrounding waters would not be adversely affected.

Nonetheless, on 9 June 2000, just two years into Ekati's operations, BHP was cited for eight charges under the Fisheries Act (three for disturbing fish habitat and five for putting a deleterious substance in water frequented by fish) dating back to the mines construction between 1994–1997. Silt and sediment were deposited into three lakes near the Ekati mine site. These lakes drain into Lac de Gras. In addition, in 1998 sewage effluent and other organic material was dumped into Kodiak Lake causing oxygen levels to plummet. Once alerted, BHP responded by pumping air into the lake.[43] Other unpredicted aquatic effects at Ekati included increased nutrients downstream of the project, higher metal concentrations downstream, and the presence of increased acid content in waste rock seepage areas that may be linked with Acid Mine Drainage.

Indigenous Peoples Threatened

'... we find that our rights to live as we choose, just as our forefathers did, are threatened by a host of forces beyond our current ability to manage or control. There is no threat that is currently more pressing than the anticipated impacts of the Diavik project ... it has the potential to destroy our lands and resources, our way of life and our people.'

North Slave Metis Alliance, 1999[44]

At a conference of women affected by mining held in the Yukon, a young Aboriginal woman told of laboratory test results that confirmed her people's fears that an abandoned mine is poisoning water on their land. In a strained and halting voice, she expressed her fear that this pollution may be the thing that will ultimately destroy her community. She said the toxic contamination is threatening their ability to live from the land and that as a people they cannot move from their ancestral land or they will lose their rights and their identity as a people.[45]

Five Aboriginal peoples are affected by the Diavik project; the Dogrib Treaty 11 Tribal Council, Yellowknives Dene First Nation,

Lutsel K'e First Nation, North Slave Metis Alliance and the Kitikmeot Inuit Association. The capacity of these peoples, who will be most directly affected by the Diavik project, to review and evaluate Diavik's claims is limited and their ability to influence decision making on the project has been proven to be negligible.

The Aboriginal peoples are disempowered in a number of ways. They are at a disadvantage because land claims and self-governance issues for most of these groups have not been settled. Concerned stakeholders advised the government that multiple land claims to the area of the mine should be settled before mining be considered. The Dogrib Treaty 11, on whose traditional and unceded land the mine will be located, declined a seat on the Steering Committee reviewing the mine because they wanted to focus their efforts on making progress on their land claim. The capacity in the Dogrib community to do both is clearly limited.

The Dogrib did commission an independent environmental review of Diavik's proposal, which raised serious concerns that were not adequately addressed in the government's Comprehensive Study Report (CSR).[46]   The CSR recognizes that, 'the Government of Canada has a fiduciary obligation to minimise the infringement of Aboriginal Rights caused by resource development initiatives on Aboriginal Lands.'[47]

This governmental obligation is set out in the Delgamuukw decision of the Supreme Court of Canada. However, Aboriginal groups, like other concerned stakeholder groups, such as NGOs, had advisory status only, ' ... the environmental agreement requires agreement from the territorial government, federal government and the company. It does not require the consent of the five Aboriginal groups affected by the project.'[48] The Dogrib's advice to the Minister of Environment to send the project to a full environmental panel review was not heeded. John Zoe of the Dogrib wrote of their independent report, 'It seems to have disappeared in the bureaucracy. Our concerns are nowhere in evidence in the industry's current lobbying campaign.'[49]

The Dogrib, along with the other Aboriginal groups have expressed special concern for the fate of the Bathurst caribou herd. The mine is in the middle of the summer range of the herd:

'The Bathurst caribou herd is the lifeblood of our people. We still depend heavily on wildlife harvesting for basic subsistence. (...) What is the special rush in this case, that such a threat must be tolerated? The diamonds aren't going anywhere. We have been harvesting on this land and the Bathurst caribou have been traversing it since before human memory. How can the demands of Diavik for an immediate approval be balanced against this history and these needs today?'[50]

The Kitikmeot Inuit Association did initially sit on the Steering Committee but withdrew because of concerns over the effectiveness of the review process. Studies paid for by Diavik to gather Traditional Environmental Knowledge (TEK) in preparation for the CSR, such as the West Kitikmeot/Slave Study, were not completed when the CSR was submitted to the government. The North Slave Metis Alliance (NSMA) prepared a lengthy document that outlined their environmental, social, economic and cultural concerns, based on their traditions and knowledge, and identified seven areas in which Diavik's environmental assessment did not conform with the Environmental Assessment Guidelines. Yet just one month before the NSMA document was published, the CSR was submitted.[51] This document attests to the rage felt by native communities over the way they were treated in the review process:

'Diavik extended its hand and lent its ears to Aboriginal communities, but it refused to engage us on a level that would make a difference for the project, for us, for everyone ... Neither Diavik nor government has given NSMA any assurance that the Diavik project is anything more than a "big experiment" and that we, Aboriginal people of the region, are the guinea pigs.'[52]

The North Slave Metis Alliance accuses the Department of Indian Affairs and Northern Development of incorporating the NSMA's concerns in an earlier draft of the CSR but then removing these sections again in the final draft without further consultation. 'Our "active participation", while obviously warranted, back-fired, producing the same results as never having "participated" at all'.[53]

The Mackenzie Valley Environmental Impact Review Board (MVEIRB), newly set up by a federal Act specifically to provide local and Aboriginal representation in assessing projects such as Diavik and to advise the Minister, was barely in place in time to comment on the CSR. Nonetheless, the Board identified five major areas of concern related to the review process itself and the CSR findings and advised that failure to address these issues should result in a full environmental panel review. Perhaps most damning was the Board's assessment that the comprehensive study process did not meet the 'goal of meaningful involvement of First Nations.'[54]

The Board also expressed concern over Impact and Benefit Agreements (IBAs). Until indigenous communities have settled their land claims, they are not in a strong position to negotiate an IBA. Furthermore, land claim settlements may void the provisions of an IBA, and an IBA may compromise the governance powers of a community.[55] According to the MVEIRB, Diavik negotiated private IBA-type agreements with some of the Aboriginal peoples, but not all, these were negotiated outside of the environmental assessment process and before there was a full assessment of socio-economic and environmental impacts that should inform IBAs. These 'participation agreements' have not been made public.

Rio Tinto: Behind the Scenes

Throughout the review and permitting process, Canadian government agencies doggedly kept the process on track. All public respondents to the environmental review process commented on the fact that in the face of serious environmental uncertainties and Aboriginal concerns, the Canadian government continued to express faith in the assurances given by Diavik.

The MVEIRB board recorded the astounding fact that, 'Diavik completed the early drafts of the CSR leaving the impression that the proponent was driving the process ... '![56] Undermining the very purpose of the environmental review, outstanding concerns and unresolved issues that came to light during the review process were put off to be 'resolved' at the permitting and licensing phases for individual aspects of the operations.

It was only when it appeared that environmental concerns might in fact delay the approval of critical land lease and water license applications by the Department of Indian Affairs and Northern Development that Rio Tinto's powerful behind the scenes lobbying role was revealed through an access to information request. Rio Tinto's director, Gordon Sage, directly lobbied Roy MacLaren, the Canadian High Commissioner in London, for 'urgent action' on Diavik's behalf.

In particular, Sage requested, in a 27 March 2000 letter, that the land license be granted before the Mackenzie Valley Resource Management Act, established to provide greater input from local people, would take effect on 31 March. According to Sage, 'if the land leases are not issued prior to 31 March 2000, a new review process will have to be conducted with respect to the project. Significant delay of at least one year would inevitably result.' Diavik got its land license on 29 March. [57]

Conclusions

Rio Tinto has responded to growing global criticism of its environmental and social impacts by drafting very general corporate social and environmental policies. As in the case of other major mining companies taking the same course, these carefully worded policies appear to provide guidelines that could potentially mitigate bad practice. With respect to Aboriginal peoples, Rio Tinto's community policy states, 'in parts of the world the Group recognises that claims to land based on ancestral or indigenous title exist. In these areas, the fullest possible understanding will be sought including ways in which such rights can be accommodated.' [58]

The problems with these social and environmental policies lie in lack of implementation. When Rio Tinto's Diavik project faced possible delays through the establishment of a Resource Management Act expressly designed to provide local people with a better process through which to express their rights and concerns, Rio Tinto put pressure on the Canadian government to grant the necessary permits before the implementation of the Act.

This example provides considerable insight into the ways in which Rio Tinto has dealt with critical environmental and social concerns related to the Diavik project. On the whole, Rio Tinto has preferred to stay in the background, exerting pressure when necessary, and letting Canadian government agencies subvert their own regulations and responsibilities on behalf of the project.

This chapter illustrates an abject failure on the part of the Canadian government to protect precious water resources, as well as a failure to uphold the rights of Aboriginal peoples to affect decisions that will impact on their lives. By granting Diavik a special 'authorisation' to destroy fish habitat, based upon entirely speculative assurances that this rare habitat can be compensated by the end of mining, the government undermined the intent of the Fisheries Act. By granting critical land lease and water license applications before the Mackenzie Valley Resource Management Act took effect, the government ensured that the concerns raised over previous years by Aboriginal peoples of the area would not have a chance to impact on the project.

Clearly, the first people to be affected by the failure of governments to protect clean water resources are poor, geographically remote and Aboriginal peoples who rely on these water resources directly for physical survival and for cultural continuity. Yet ultimately, the increasing loss and contamination of clean water sources through short-sighted policies aimed at immediate economic gains, will affect us all.

7 When corporations want to cuddle
Bob Burton

In a sombre speech in late 1999, the Chairman of Rio Tinto, Sir Robert Wilson, confessed to the Securities Institute of Australia that the global mining industry faced major problems. 'What on earth went wrong?' Wilson asked rhetorically about the economic fall of the mining industry. Over the last 30 years, he said, 'few companies have earned their cost of capital during most of that period'.[1]

The prognosis, he told the audience, was not good. 'There is a perception held, often tacitly, by a growing number of people that the global mining ... industry is incompatible with sustainable development', he said. As far as Wilson was concerned, doing nothing was not an option. 'Unchecked it will drive legislation and distort markets in ways that will ultimately harm our business and developing economies alike – and produce unlooked for environmental and social consequences', Wilson said.

A few months earlier the Minerals Council of Australia (MCA) – of which Rio Tinto is one of the largest members – invited one of the corporate world's most sought after public relations (PR) consultants, US-based Peter Sandman, to address its 1998 annual environmental workshop in Melbourne.[2] That Sandman was called on at all was testimony to the mounting concern within the industry that increasing grass roots mobilisation around the world is frustrating industry ambitions.

Sandman was evangelical about his medicine for unpopular industries and companies: deal directly with your harshest critics, make concessions, and maybe even let them 'win'. This may seem like unusual advice, but some of the largest companies in the world pay big bucks – between \$US650 and \$US1250 per hour – for Sandman's analysis. His clients have included Rio Tinto, Western Mining Corporation, BHP, Placer Pacific, Pasminco, BHP Petroleum, Energy Resources of Australia, North Ltd, Exxon and Shell International.[3]

Sandman's niche in the PR world is advising his corporate clients against counter-attacking critical NGOs. 'Counterattack is tempting and emotionally satisfying, but it rarely helps. Gestures of respect and offers to cooperate are much more productive', he suggests.

Through humility and concessions, he argues, companies can 'open communication channels,' forcing stubborn activists to moderate their position. 'Lure them into collaboration (by making the only alternative public unreasonableness and possible marginalisation). This is always worth trying, even if the group seems unlikely to prove willing. It can't hurt', he suggests. The hardest but most effective approach, he suggests, is to 'legitimate the activist group' by offering to co-operate with the activists.

The purpose of the cooperation he says is 'outsourcing trust' – rebuilding tarnished corporate credibility by involving activist groups in corporate decision making. 'This is indeed a way of getting external groups to face hard choices, and of out-sourcing controversial decisions that would have little credibility if made within the company', Sandman says.

Having studied the mining industry's attempts to regain its political ascendancy, Sandman gave a Mineral Council of Australia (MCA) environmental workshop some frank advice.[4] He pointed to a string of mining controversies from the Bougainville rebellion, BHP's Ok Tedi debacle in Papua New Guinea, the Marcopper disaster in the Philippines and the attempt to build the Jabiluka mine adjoining the Kakadu National Park against the wishes of the traditional Aboriginal owners.

'There is a growing sense that you screw up a lot, and as a net result it becomes harder to get permission to mine', Sandman said. The solution, he advised, lay in finding an appropriate 'persona' for the industry.

The best option he suggested would be to present the industry as a 'team player,' but Sandman told the miners that it couldn't get from its current persona of 'bad actor' to 'team player'. 'As a characteristic of human nature, I don't think people can go from thinking you are bad guys to thinking you are good guys, without pausing somewhere in the middle', he said.

Sandman suggested a 'middle' role that the industry could adopt on its path to salvation. The image, he suggested 'that I think works by far the best ... is the "caged beast."' 'What is the persona of this "caged beast"? 'Useful, perhaps even indispensable, but dangerous. This is the image I would recommend to you. If you want to come back from "bad actor" to "team player", the easiest path back is to make a case that you would continue to be bad actor if you could, but you can't, because the cage works.'

Why should the industry portray itself so negatively? Because, Sandman said, it was a 'saleable image' that at least would convey the idea that the industry was no longer harmful: 'You are behaving much better, not because you want to, not because you have become the Mother Theresa of the mining companies, but because NGOs have been successful, regulators have been successful, your neighbours have been successful, the entire society has been successful in persuading you at least that you will make more dollars if you reform.'

The first step is to persuade critical NGOs that the industry is committed to change, and unless NGOs affirm their first steps towards change, companies are unlikely to persist. 'Activists and others must notice that companies have changed and reward them for changing,' Sandman argues.

One way of overcoming scepticism amongst NGOs, he suggested, is the repeated public confession of past sins. 'Acknowledge your prior misbehaviour,' he advises. Honesty has certain practical limitations, however. 'I don't chiefly mean things you have done that nobody knows you have done and when we find out you will go to jail,' he adds. 'If there are any of these, I urge you to seek legal counsel before you seek communication counsel. I'm talking about negative things on the public record.'

Sandman's analysis, which is superficially attractive, is based on studying largely conflicts over chemical plants in densely populated areas of the US. It assumes, moreover, that community activism is undertaken without fear of reprisal in a democratic country

where activists can access support networks, information and the media. All of these are assumed to be vital checks on the temptation for corporations to indulge in greenwashing. These assumptions are tenuous enough in the US but can only be considered fanciful in many parts of the world dominated by military dictatorships.

Many companies are increasingly adopting at least some of Sandman's ideas in their efforts to woo activist groups. Central to the success of Sandman's approach is ensuring a focus on issues determined to be the 'common ground' by a broad-based constituency, and developing voluntary measures that allow the industry to create its 'caged beast' persona.

A Shell service station sign adorned with a hanging man as part of a protest against Shell's involvement with the execution of nine Ogoni people who opposed Shell's oil extraction activities on their land.

Photo by Project Underground

Welcome to the Table, said the Spider to the Fly

Following the disaster at Union Carbide's Bhopal plant in India, the credibility of the chemical industry in the US was in tatters. Peter Sandman suggested the industry propose the expansion of Community Advisory Panels (CAPs), modelled on the experience of the US chemical industry. It is a model he suggests the mining industry adopt.

Although companies sometimes fear letting outsiders get involved in making decisions that affect their business, Sandman says their concern is misguided. 'The usual problem with these committees isn't orchestrating the chaos. It is sustaining interest and attendance. Erstwhile troublemakers let onto the panel start learning about the industry's problems and limitations, acquire a sense of responsibility to give good advice, and pretty soon they are sounding a lot like industry apologists. This is not hypocrisy or cooptation: it is outrage reduction.'

Ben Woodhouse was Vice-President with Dow Chemical at the time, and is now a PR consultant in Australia. Among his clients is the Minerals Council of Australia. A critical step in developing a community panel, he said, is selecting the 'core members for your team.' 'Find three to four people from the community who want to work with you to make you successful. Use that core of members to draft the terms of agreement and to recruit the members,' he says.[5]

'How should companies deal with "tricky" people on the panel?' asked a participant of a workshop by Woodhouse. 'The selection of your core members is important,' Woodhouse said. 'You pick three or four people that on a bell shaped curve tend to be right here in the middle. Then you ask them to help you find people that not only fit with the middle of that bell curve but represent both ends. What happens is that that middle part kind of keeps the two end parts from getting too radical on you. About the time they start going off in some direction that seems too weird or unbelievable, you'll find the rest of the panel will bring them back in. It's not quite as bad as trying to herd cats', he told the audience.

Peter Sandman also candidly explains that participation in such committees has the benefit for companies of generating a social pressure on even the most outspoken critics to conform. 'The experience of breaking bread with company representatives, chatting with them before and after meetings encourages many CAP members to feel that harsh criticism would be somehow rude. CAP members who don't respond this way are likely to feel some social pressure from their fellow members to conform or quit.' Thus, says Sandman, 'the embattled company has a great deal to gain from visible collaboration with activists'.

While industry may be enthusiastic about such committees, at least some participants are starting to re-think. When the Placer Dome managed Porgera mine, in the highlands of Papua New Guinea, commenced disposing of mine tailings and overburden into the Strickland River system in 1992, local people began to complain about environmental impacts.

Increasing national and international media coverage of the issue in 1995 pushed the company to act. Placer funded the Australian Commonwealth Scientific and Industrial Research Organisation (CSIRO) to undertake a major study of the impacts of riverine disposal at the mine. CSIRO made numerous recommendations including that tailings solids and waste rock be stored on-site.

Placer then established a multi-stakeholder committee, Porgera Environmental Advisory Komiti (PEAK), to oversee the implementation of the CSIRO recommendations. After various changes to the committee composition, Yati Bun, the Executive Director of Foundation for People and Community Development in Papua New Guinea, was appointed as Chair.

As the years ticked by little changed in Placer's management of the mine wastes. Finally, prompted by the unauthorised use of his name in what he described as 'propaganda materials', Bun resigned.[6] 'Placer has now had four years to carry out these studies and implement their recommendations, yet nothing has changed from the situation in 1996 when the CSIRO report was started,' he wrote. While the committee gave the impression that progress was being made on the issues, little in fact was changing on the ground.

How Now, Green Frog?

After influential discussions in 1995 with the US corporate giant, Weyerhauser, Rio Tinto's Australian predecessor, CRA, reviewed its public relations program. The first step was to commission the US-based 'management and communications consultancy', HRN, to survey opinion leaders on perceptions of the company. With poor results in a number of key areas, CRA (and subsequently Rio Tinto) decided to undertake a program of partnerships to communicate that it was a responsible corporate citizen.[7]

Rio Tinto Australia's External Affairs Manager, Dr Tim Duncan, argues that corporations have to develop much closer relationships with community groups. Corporations, he says, 'need to find platforms into the community, or the part of the community that through self-selection has got some sort of interest in our business or our industry'.[8] One method of establishing a platform is through corporate sponsorship of these community groups.

Corporate sponsorships are often an explicit 'divide and conquer' strategy of PR firms. A rare window into how this strategy works emerged from a PR company in New Zealand working for the government-owned logging company, Timberlands. Leaked papers referred to strategies for 'bridge building' with 'Environmental Lobby Groups.' One strategy paper stated: 'Identify key opposition groups and the individuals within them who are likely to be more supportive/less opposed to Timberlands'.[9]

It set out to court World Wildlife Fund for Nature (WWF), New Zealand. The place to start, one paper suggested was to 'develop points of agreement or commonality with these groups, ideally leading to joint agreements/statements, etc.' The plan was to 'establish or develop existing relations with individual group members on common or non-contentious areas e.g. scientific research on forest wildlife.' To cement the courtship, it suggested offering 'appropriate support' for some of their projects.[10]

WWF, especially in Australia, has become the preferred group for the mining industry and individual companies to seek out. WWF itself says it prefers a 'mutually beneficial approach' of working with industry with its internal guidelines stating that it 'emphasises co-operation rather than confrontation as the key to achieving WWF's mission'[11]. WWF Australia's Chief Executive Officer (CEO), David Butcher, says it will accept corporate funding providing it is, 'consistent with WWF's ethical and environmental principles ... The ones that are squeaky clean we are not all that interested in.'[12]

For example, two weeks after Sir Robert Wilson's sober speech to the Securities Institute in Melbourne, WWF Australia and Rio Tinto announced a $1.2 million 'partnership' over four years called 'Frogs Alive!'. The project is to develop a program monitoring and researching Australia's frog population.[13]

While WWF argues the main aim in corporate partnerships is to change corporate practice, Butcher concedes there is little prospect of persuading Rio Tinto from participating in campaigns against WWF priorities. Why develop partnerships with companies if there is no prospect of achieving the conservation goals of most importance to WWF? 'There are more ways of getting those positions in place than just working with mining companies. There's a whole suite of other forums involved from governments at one end to individuals at the other', he said.

Corporate sponsorship carries a price to organisational independence too. Butcher agrees it is common for corporate donors to ask to review draft reports that may criticise them. 'Oh sure, if they don't agree with the report they can have their connection removed', he said. However, he agreed that reports could be changed 'if they can show that it is not factual what we have written ... But when it is factual material then if it has some negative effects upon the donor then you are morally-bound to put it in'.

Rio Tinto insists that its 'partnership' arrangements be done in a 'business-like manner' and is formalised in a written contract. Should the WWF Australia – Rio Tinto contract to open to the public? Initially WWF's Butcher agreed. WWF Conservation Director, Ray Nias, thought he should check with Rio Tinto before releasing the document. After checking with Rio Tinto, he rejected the request for a copy of the document.[14]

It is not the first time that corporate agreements with WWF have sparked controversy. Leaked internal papers from WWF New Zealand revealed an even more extraordinary example of how corporate sponsorship can erode the independence of community groups. As part of a $500,000, three-year sponsorship program, Shell sponsored full-page advertisements featuring a group of children wearing WWF T-shirts and Shell sunhats. The advertisement encouraged individuals to take out membership with the organisation. However, shortly after the campaign kicked off, internal documents revealed that at a board meeting the chairman of WWF New Zealand, Paul Bowe, had canvassed the possibility of Shell being made a trustee of the organisation. 'The chair suggested consideration be given to whether Shell New Zealand, due to their great commitment and contribution towards the WWF education programme, should have a place as a trustee', one document noted.[15]

Bowe told the journalist from the NZ *Sunday Star Times* there was no link between sponsorship and board members. 'Any idea that you're trying to put into your head or the readers' ideas that we sponsor board members here because they give us something is wrong', he said. 'I think it is very valuable to have . . . a couple of sponsors [on the board] to ensure that the business ethic of their business and our business . . . is followed correctly', he said.

Lending a Hand with a Little Legislation

Another 'partnership' Rio Tinto established was with an Australian human rights group that has the potential to see Rio Tinto staff help draft human rights, environmental and corporate legislation in Indonesia. After several years laying the groundwork, Rio Tinto developed a formal 'partnership' with the Australian Legal Resources International (ALRI), a human rights group affiliated with the Australian Council for Overseas Aid (ACFOA) in 2000. The project, developed with the support of Rio Tinto and the Australian Embassy in Jakarta, aimed to provide assistance for 'legislative drafting and comprehensive legal and judicial reform'.[16] Part of the project was to involve legislative drafting of 'environmental law, human rights law, constitutional law, bankruptcy and corporate law'.

While ALRI is a small organisation with a handful of staff and a budget of approximately \$750,000, it has an impressive list of backers. ALRI's list of patrons features many respected people in Australian legal circles, including former Justice of the High Court, Sir Ronald Wilson, and the former Governor General, Sir William Deane. ALRI's current Chairman is former Federal Court judge, Justice Marcus Einfeld.

Instead of funding a project at arm's length, Rio Tinto insists on 'a high degree of involvement' in the 'partnerships' they fund, including participation of their staff in the project work. Underlying the partnership is Rio Tinto's insistence on selecting projects that have 'strategic relevance' to the company and 'the opportunity for direct involvement of Rio Tinto people and operations'.[17]

Rio Tinto's head of External Affairs, Dr Tim Duncan, is candid about Rio Tinto's role in encouraging ALRI to take an interest in legal reform work for post-Soeharto Indonesia. 'What we wanted to

117

do was bring to the attention of ALRI a close focus…We felt that if we could encourage them to focus on Indonesia, which they wanted to do … you could see there was an enormous need for basic legal infrastructure in Indonesia', Duncan said.[18]

Rio Tinto has major mining interests, including the Freeport mine in Indonesian-controlled West Papua, coalmines in Kalimantan and the Kelian goldmine, which have all been subject to criticism over labour, environmental, or human rights issues. Duncan agrees that a partnership with a legal NGO gives the work legitimacy that would otherwise be lacking if a corporation were doing it by itself.

Should corporations be helping write legislation that affects their own operations? Duncan concedes that 'it's not their business' to be working on legislation. However, 'If we think there is an opportunity and if we think there is a significant section of Indonesian opinion that thinks it is in their national interest to do that, we can act as brokers. We can through our own influence attract resources, we can put people together, we can run programs and we can to some extent begin to do work that contributes', he said.

One step in the partnership would be an exchange of staff with one or two Rio Tinto staff with a legal background helping them on a project. ALRI's Executive Director, John Pace, acknowledged that Rio Tinto staff could be involved in the project drafting legislation in Indonesia. 'We would be using them for expertise they could help us with … wherever there is experience that would be useful such as on civil and political rights in a constitution', he said. He insisted however that Rio Tinto would not be involved in a determining role.

Concerns about the close relationship between ALRI and Rio Tinto were further fuelled by a six-month secondment of ALRI's former Executive Director, John Hall, to the PR section of Rio Tinto, working on partnerships with NGO groups. In the end, Hall opted to work permanently with Rio Tinto and resigned from ALRI.

While publicity about the nature of the Rio Tinto 'partnership' with ALRI resulted in some sensitivity within the organisation about the project, it is proceeding none the less.[19] ALRI have, however, provided more information on their website about their project work in Indonesia.[20]

At the time ALRI were trying to work with Rio Tinto, Indonesian villagers who had protested against the activities of a 90 per cent owned Rio Tinto subsidiary, PT Kelian Equatorial Mining (PT-KEM) were attempting to have longstanding human rights grievances addressed. After a series of protests and blockades by community members, PT KEM agreed in January 1999 to an independent investigation into allegations that staff had sexually harassed and raped women and perpetrated other human rights abuses. The report, completed in February 2000 after a nine-month investigation, supported claims of a number of cases of sexual abuse over a ten-year period to 1997. It also investigated claims that two mine opponents had died in mysterious circumstances.[21] The head of the inquiry, Mr Benjamin Mangkoedilaga, told the *Australian Financial Review* in June 2000 that employees who reported sexual abuse were threatened with dismissal while others were given money or promise of a job at the mine in return for sex.[22]

In its Statement of Business Principles, Rio Tinto states it is 'committed, both in principle and in practice, to the maximum level of transparency consistent with normal commercial confidentiality'.[23] However, at no point has the investigation or its findings been referred to in any of the subsequent quarterly or annual reports produced directly by Rio Tinto. Rio Tinto's voluntary 1999 Social and Environmental Report, which was finalised in February 2000, devoted only three short paragraphs to human rights without making any reference to the Kelian investigation.

To overcome scepticism at the value of these voluntary reports some companies are ensuring they are subject to external auditing. Rio Tinto's 1999 report was audited by the US based auditing company, Arthur D Little, which verified the results of the report based on a sampling of information which it said, 'is sufficient in our judgement to support virtually all of the statements made'.[24] Neither Arthur D Little nor Rio Tinto would respond to inquiries about the report or the auditing process.

The Industry Responds to a River of Cyanide

On the morning of Monday 1 February 2000, the global mining industry had every reason to be confident that it was slowly regaining control of the public policy agenda. It was a confidence that was shattered over the following week when cyanide-laced tailings spilled from a breached tailings dam of the Baia Mare mine, operated and part-owned by the Australian company, Esmeralda.

As the tailings caused a massive fish kill, global pressure for increased regulation of the mining industry, and cyanide in particular, mounted. After initially ducking for cover, the industry considered its best chance to shape the nature of any reaction would be if it pro-actively supported voluntary rather than mandatory measures.

The International Council of Metals and the Environment (ICME), the global mining industry's peak organisation, proposed a partnership, not with an NGO but with the United Nations Environment Program. ICME suggested to UNEP that they jointly sponsor a two-day workshop in Paris in May 2000 to promote the development of a voluntary code of conduct on the use of cyanide in the goldmining industry.

Fish killed from cyanide poisoning resulting from an overflow of cyanide into the Tisza River in Romania from an Australian owned mine, Esmeralda Exploration.

Photo by Tibor Kocsic

It was a proposal that neatly dovetailed with the increasing enthusiasm for 'partnerships' between companies and UN agencies after the UN Secretary General, Kofi Annan launched the 'Global Compact'. The Global Compact advocates that UN agencies develop partnerships with companies in the areas of environment, human rights and development. Rio Tinto was one of the companies that endorsed the Global Compact.[25]

Forty delegates from around the world, with nearly half from major mining companies, attended the joint UNEP – ICME workshop. Only three non-government organisations (NGOs) – the World Wildlife Fund for Nature (WWF), the Sierra Club and US Mineral Policy Center – attended.

According to the workshop minutes, a consultant to WWF, Frank Almond, said, 'there is a need to shift the public's perception of industry, including mining, as a cause of environmental degradation.'

Almond distanced WWF from the views of other NGOs. 'NGOs are well-regarded but many of them have not come to terms with the need to reconcile environmental protection with economic activity', the minutes record Almond as telling the workshop.[26]

The meeting suggested the need to review a suite of mining codes including those relating to the use of cyanide, emergency responses, tailings management, the role of government regulators and the response of financial institutions. There was a catch, however. UNEP, which had virtually no resources, could only take on the workload if it could raise funds and recruit some staff.

Gold companies and cyanide manufacturers, who had most to lose from any binding regulations, were willing to fund the process of developing the cyanide code. Rio Tinto was willing to help too, offering the services of its Chief Environmental Adviser, Ms Kathryn Tayles, on a nine-month secondment to UNEP to oversee the reviews of the various codes.

Researcher for the NGO, Corpwatch, Kenny Bruno, was appalled. 'Without leverage to monitor and enforce codes of conduct, the UN feels it must bring business on board voluntarily. Yet business will not write guidelines it feels are burdensome, nor will they accept them as binding.

121

The secondment of corporate personnel, especially from a mining giant like Rio Tinto, to UNEP, is part of 'a very disturbing trend toward corporate influence at the United Nations', Bruno said.

Happy with Half a Loaf?

When mining companies talk amongst themselves about 'engagement', it it is usually from a fear of effective public advocacy that is independent of a process they can control. Headlines, they confide to each other, all too often drive a legislative agenda that damages their interests.

'Engagement', as the mining industry uses the term, is about shifting the forum of debate away from open public spaces to smaller more private venues where social pressure can be subtly mobilised to moderate more critical views. It is about subtly shifting debates away from conflict between fundamental values to discussing the 'common ground'. It pursues a lowest common denominator approach that seeks to shift debate away from 'should we mine uranium against Aboriginal wishes in a National Park' to 'how would you like the uranium mine to operate'. 'Engagement' as the industry uses it, is about converting optimistic activism to the passive fatalism of 'oh, if we can't prevent it going ahead, we can at least mitigate the impact'.

The growing level of engagement is also crystallising debate about the values of community groups. Should NGOs enter into secret sponsorship agreements? Should NGOs accept invitations to participate in advisory committees without even discussing it with other organisations working on the same topic?

Participants in corporate committees or who benefit from sponsorship often defend their participation to irritated NGO colleagues on the grounds that they are simply part of a 'good cop, bad cop' strategy. It is, however, a false analogy. When police adopt the 'good cop, bad cop' strategy it is part of a coordinated strategy designed to extract sufficient evidence to enable a successful prosecution and conviction. Unless this strategy is already established with NGOs, this approach will not necessarily work

The reason the public support watchdog groups is the belief that they are fearless and independent advocates for the public interest, yet it is this independence that 'engagement' erodes. Whether for financial reasons or growing personal ties to likeable corporate executives, those enmeshed in 'engagement' become more inclined to believe the best of a company. Often NGOs don't notice, or worse turn a blind eye, to the dual corporate game of speaking nicely to NGOs while lobbying behind the scenes to weaken existing regulations or undermine other campaigns.

Once engaged, few NGOs have clear benchmarks to judge the merit of continued involvement in the process. Withdrawal would be to admit a mistake or risk marginalisation. Others develop a financial dependency on ongoing participation, irrespective of outcomes.

Corporate PR people and some NGOs commonly argue 'engagement' is essential, given the weakening role of the state. Accepting this argument requires a level of political amnesia in assuming that the weakening of state regulation mysteriously happens, rather than being the deliberate outcome of corporate activism. Worse, while NGOs generally see 'engagement' as a supplement to regulation, industry sees it as a substitute. If NGOs help create the 'caged beast' with voluntary measures, who needs stronger regulation, they ask?

Much of the advocacy for 'engagement' is surprisingly apolitical, ducking the basic questions of whether corporations have too much power in society or even how community groups achieve, maintain and extend change. If watchdog groups bark less and settle for low profile technical discussions, isn't it inevitable that public pressure for change will decrease? If the external pressure necessary to drive change fades, where is the incentive for companies to grant even the incremental concessions sought by the financially-rewarded 'good cops'. Isn't greater engagement by more groups likely to change the character of NGOs from feisty agenda-setters to corporate consultants?

For consultants, such as Peter Sandman, a source of frustration is finding groups willing to accept the concessions that companies are prepared to offer. 'There is sometimes a risk', he says, that a company 'is willing to give up half a loaf but can't find anybody to take half a loaf. All it can find is people to accuse it of hypocrisy because it's half a loaf ... It is useful that there is someone saying "no it is only half a loaf, you asshole", but there has got to be someone saying "Wow, half a loaf!"'.

Settling for half a loaf might keep the company happy, but Sandman acknowledges that it causes problems for NGOs. Those

NGOs that accept half a loaf are sometimes hard to find because they 'risk loss of the integrity of [the] group, risk loss of membership, risk loss of media credibility, maybe risk loss of self-esteem', he says.

And maybe you'd still starve if you settled for half a loaf.

PART THREE: CHALLENGES

8 Mining, self-determination and Bougainville

Moses Havini and Vikki John

A Lament: 'White Man and Mungkas Barter System'

('Mungkas' means 'black' in Buin, a South Bougainvillean language)

White man bible he brought, Mungkas prime land he owned
Now white man prime land he owns, While Mungkas bible he owns.
White man booze he brought, Mungkas shell money he owned
Now the white man money he has,
While Mungkas you get drunk on booze.
White man tool box he brought, Mungkas copper mine he owned
Now white man Bougainville copper he owns,
While Mungkas you are the tools.

Matubuna Tahun,
June 1998.

Overlooking the abandoned Bougainville Copper Mine.

Photo by Francis O'Neill

'The Bougainville mine started in 1972. At that time PNG was under the administration of Australia, so basically the agreement signed was between the government and CRA [now Rio Tinto].

When it happened, the landowners were women because in Bougainville the women have the custodian right of the land. When the mine was beginning operations, the women fought against CRA to try to stop the mine from operating. They placed themselves in front of the bulldozer – they even put their babies when in front of the bulldozer to try and stop CRA from operating. But then the police riot squad walked in, abused a lot of women, and also abused the men. This happened in 1972 and again in 1987-88. In 1989 it ended up in a full-scale war that has lasted for five years and has continued until now.

There was no consultation with the landholders. There was no concern given to women landholders by the government in that time to list their right to the land over CRA. There was never any consultation in any way when during the operation of the mine the landholders got together and wanted to negotiate the Bougainville Copper Limited agreement. In two instances where the [landholders] wanted to renegotiate that agreement the government basically backed down to the company, and the company refused to listen to the defences, so the agreement was never reviewed.

During the course of the operation of the mine there was a whole lot of issues of environmental damage. Dumping from the mine site into the Jaba River made it highly polluted. The siltation and the overburden from the waste flowed down to Augusta Bay in West Bougainville. If you travelled on the Kawarong River you would see that on the side the siltation built up was very big. During the dry season dust blew everywhere. The fish and other river life living in the river were virtually dead.

The landowners started raising these [environmental] issues with the company because they basically lived on the protein that the river could provide and they were no longer getting this protein from the river. They then started raising the issues with the government but no one was willing to listen to them or try to review the agreement.

The company was giving royalties to the landowners but what is this royalty compared to that environmental destruction? The mine cost the life of the river and the whole environment that people were living in. Even though CRA provided housing for landowners, it wasn't enough. The suffering of the people continued every day.

There is a fear [that the mine will open up again], and that is why the landholders in Bougainville are fighting to at least be given some recognition and to run their own affairs. I think from what has happened and what has been learnt about the central government taking charge of our fate in the provinces is that it does not really fulfil the need that people want to take control of their own life. They felt the government of PNG negotiated on behalf of Bougainvilleans instead of Bougainvilleans negotiating for themselves. So there are still fears that CRA is definitely intending to return to Bougainville and I think that from what Bougainvilleans have seen so far, they do not want CRA to return to Bougainville.'

Ursula Rakova, 15 February 2000. Ursula is a Bougainvillean, and is the coordinator of the Environmental Law Center, Port Moresby, Papua New Guinea. In 2001 she plans to return to live in Bougainville.

Introduction

Mining conglomerates and indigenous cultures are worlds apart. The first is the product of western industrialisation with an obsession to mine the entire planet of its natural resources. The second are the world's indigenous nations who have sustained their natural resources since time immemorial. Mining companies keep exploiting minerals on this earth, and in some cases go so far as to breach environmental regulations to keep afloat and to please their shareholders. This race to exploit resources has now been further enhanced by the push for globalisation.

Mining companies are champions of a free world market, open and free national boundaries, where such 'giants' can operate with less accountability for their actions. Mining corporations also have the enviable ability to influence politics and governments with 'cheque book' politics. They have played a major role in changing governmental policies, regulations and legislation to suit their own aims, one of the many characteristics of the politics of globalisation we see today.

Whilst the rich West is getting richer and more powerful, many Third World Governments and indigenous nations are getting poorer and poorer – and being coerced into unconscionable agreements and treaties with the West. Having exhausted mineral deposits in their own regions, especially within the last two decades, transnational corporations are now aggressively targeting the remaining world mineral resources. Most of these are within indigenous nations' ownership, custodianship and care.

This chapter focuses on the people of Bougainville, and how their fight against the Rio Tinto-owned Panguna Copper mine has an integral connection to a wider struggle for self-determination. It covers the Bougainville people's struggle against the neo-colonial environment of Papua New Guinea and their struggle for their right to self-determination. This co-joined struggle led to the closure of the Panguna Copper mine. The insurrection against Rio Tinto and the Government of Papua New Guinea place hold in 1989, eventually leading to a war for independence.

Historical Setting

Bougainville is the biggest of the seven islands of the Solomons Archipelago. Prior to the war (1989–1998), the population was 200,000. It is estimated that in the ten years of war, about ten per cent of the population perished from fighting as well as from preventable diseases unable to be treated as a result of the blockade. Bougainville is on the perimeter of Papua New Guinea approximately 1,000 kilometres from the capital Port Moresby, and just 8 kilometers from the border of the Independent State of the Solomon Islands. Bougainville is not part of the landmass of Papua New Guinea, but is separated by 550 kilometres of ocean from the nearest Papua New Guinean town of Rabaul, in East New Britain Province.

The first recorded European contact was with French explorer Captain Louis de Bougainville. He commanded two French vessels *La Bourdeuse* and *L'Etóile* during his tour of the Pacific in 1768. From 1870 onwards many Bougainvilleans were victims (along with Solomon Islanders and natives from Vanuatu) of a thriving blackbirding slave trade operating out of Townsville, Queensland. These people became slaves to work in the sugar cane fields of Queensland and in plantations of Samoa and New Britain.[1] During their second scramble for colonies in the Pacific during the 19th century, Western powers (namely Holland, Great Britain and Germany) claimed different parts of the Pacific as their territories. The Dutch claimed the western half of New Guinea (Dutch New Guinea) in 1828 as part of their East Indies Empire. In 1884 Great Britain claimed the Southern half of New Guinea,[2] whilst the following year Germany laid claim over the Northern half of New Guinea.[3]

Thus, until 1884, Bougainville and Buka islands remained outside of European influence. Germany's main interest at this stage was purely in the exploitation of the island for its mineral resources and other raw materials for their motherland. This led to the recruitment of labour gangs to work in their plantations in the New Guinea Islands and elsewhere. Bougainvilleans were generally sought after as plantation foremen (Boss-Boys), cooks, policemen and security guards because they were viewed as 'hardworking, honest and trustworthy'.[4]

In 1886, Germany formally annexed Bougainville and parts of Northern Solomon Islands in a separate proclamation.[5] Germany and Great Britain then further rearranged the Northern Solomons between themselves, with Bougainville continuing to remain as part of German New Guinea while the Northern Solomons (Shortlands, Choiseul and Isabel Islands) south of Bougainville fell within the British sphere of influence. This new boundary was once again drawn arbitrarily without the knowledge or consent of the Chiefs of Bougainville and Northern Solomons, and in so doing cut across ethnic and economic ties of a people of a common region.

In 1906, Britain handed over British New Guinea (Papua) to the new Commonwealth of Australia. The 'fear campaign' commenced by Queensland against Germany's possession of German New Guinea came to an end at the outbreak of World War I in 1914, when Britain requested Australia to send in an Expeditionary Force to neutralise the Germans at their headquarters in Rabaul. The Australian Government took over the supervision of Australia New Guinea Army Unit, which had taken initial responsibility over the 'conquered territory'. The formal approval of New Guinea's placement under Australian Administration was agreed to in a Trustee Agreement passed by the UN General Assembly in 1946.[6]

It was at this point in the progression towards PNG independence that Bougainvilleans stopped cooperating with the political machinations to ask why their territory and persons were just a subject of political 'horse-trading'. For the sake of political control and economic gain the people of Bougainville were displaced. Once such a grievance is implanted, it becomes part of the psyche of successive generations of a people. The words of Bougainville's first martyr, Theodore Miriung, the wartime Premier of Bougainville who was assassinated in October 1996 by PNG Defence Forces, describes this case in no uncertain terms: '...As in most cases in which serious armed conflicts of a political nature are involved, there has been a breach of faith, or a denial of a basic human right at some point of time in the history of the countries or states concerned. Similarly, there has been a breach of faith or a denial of a basic right in the case of the crisis on Bougainville. At no stage during the [annexation of Bougainville by Britain and Germany], did we ever yield, concede or accede to any foreign takeover of any of our rights, our power or sovereignty as happens in normal cases of similar nature. We were traded like sheep or cattle without our knowledge and consent. We, therefore, consider this as a serious breach of faith or a denial of a basic right of freedom of choice at the threshold of colonial history of

Bougainville. Both the [League of Nations and UN Trusteeship] entrusted with the care of non-self-governing peoples, failed to take any action to remedy the situation. Similarly, the Australian Colonial Administration failed to remedy this problem. Instead, it took every step to ensure that Bougainville remained with PNG, right through to the eve of PNG's independence in September 1975.'[7]

The people of Buka and Bougainville were free-thinking people who were always confident enough to question the actions, behaviour, practices and policies of their 'custodians'. Their protestation reached a heightened phase on Buka Island with the emergence of the 'Hahalis Welfare Society Rebellion'. Between 1954 and 1962 the first nationalist movement against both the Australian Government and the Papua New Guinea Administration was undertaken. The so-called 'rebels' refused to pay their 'Head Tax' to the Port Moresby Administration. The people of Buka protested that they were not getting the benefit of their taxes. They looked at the condition of their roads and lack of promised health and education services and wondered where their tax money had gone. The Hahalis Welfare Movement agreed on a united stand not to pay their taxes to Port Moresby, but rather to their own organisation. These people preferred to rely on their own initiatives to find a better alternative for their social and economic development.

After three years of overdue Head Tax from the Hahalis Welfare Society and obvious 'recalcitrance', the PNG Administration and Australian colonial authorities found enough excuse to launch their first government-sanctioned operation on Bougainville in February 1962. Sir Paul Hasluck, then Australian Minister for Territories, justified using force in Buka by stating in Canberra that, 'Hahalis had already refused a part in the democratic self-government, the government set up Buka Council. Therefore Hahalis was still liable to head-tax to central government and for the sake of prestige, Australia would have to collect the money as best it could'.[8] An additional 500 police from all over Papua New Guinea were flown in to face more than 1,000 men, women and children on Buka. The battle that ensued resulted in serious injury to 40 Hahalis followers and 25 policemen, 306 persons being jailed for riotous behaviour, 272 for obstruction, eight for refusing to pay head tax and two for escaping from custody.[9]

In the early 1970s, the United Nations placed increasing pressure on Australia to step up its preparation for Papua and New Guinea's movement towards self-government and independence. Papua New Guinea attained 'self-government' in 1973, an initial step towards independence, which was achieved on 16 September 1975 when the Constituent Assembly adopted its National Constitution. PNG became a sovereign and independent state causing the Trusteeship Agreement to cease due to obsolescence.

In the build-up to PNG independence, the secessionist fever was building up in Bougainville. This 'fever' was permeating all Bougainville strata, from its political leadership and educated elite through to students and the grassroots level. The 'Secessionist Movement' was running in parallel with the debate in Papua New Guinea for its nationhood. Bougainville students at universities and other tertiary institutions coordinated the campaign through the '*Mungkas* Association', and stepped up the debate for a separate political entity from Papua New Guinea. *Mungkas*, meaning 'black, or the black skin' (in one of the Bougainville languages), was an all-Bougainville political association based on Bougainville, but with several branches in PNG. A UN resolution, mainly supported by Asian and African delegates, was put through for Australia, 'to fix an early date for self-determination and independence for New Guinea and Papua, in accordance with the freely expressed wishes of the people of the territories'.[10]

Continuing with the pressure and building the momentum for Bougainville's independence, Bougainville leaders in the PNG House of Assembly, university students and senior Bougainville public servants took another significant step on Sunday 1 September 1970 in Port Moresby. All concerned condemned the Australian CRA mining corporation on Bougainville. Moses Havini, co-author of this chapter, was the youngest member of this group of 25 who met in the home of Paul Lapun, Member of House of Assembly.

In this most significant step in moving the independence issue of Bougainville into the international arena, they issued a statement. They called for Australia, Papua and New Guinea to allow Bougainville 'to go it alone'; or failing that, they called for a plebiscite or referendum to be held to conclusively establish Bougainvillean views on, 'whether Bougainville should: a) form an independent nation on its own, or, b) leave PNG and unite to form one nation with British Solomons to the south of Bougainville, or, c) remain with Papua New Guinea'[11]. The motion was defeated on the floor of the House of Assembly on the basis that it would be too expensive to conduct a referendum on Bougainville. However, in an independent localised referendum conducted by the Kieta-based Napidakoe Navitu Association in the same year, it was conclusively found that 99.9 per cent of the people supported an independent Bougainville.

In July 1973, the PNG Constitutional Planning Committee was given the task of gathering the views of all Papua New Guineans, including Bougainvilleans, on the creation of a new Constitution in preparation for independence in 1975. The talks on a separate government and autonomy for Bougainville were also in progress. The leaders undertook this opportunity whilst the PNG Constitution was being formulated, and, to strengthen their call, submitted a comprehensive submission on autonomy and independence for Bougainville. The Committee's Chairman, Mr. Michael Somare, promised that Bougainville would be guaranteed recognition and security under the new constitution.

Although a political framework in the form of a 'Provincial Government System' was being discussed for Bougainville, the real test to its ability to function was to be seen on the 'devolution' of 'powers and functions' to a Bougainville Government.[12] A deadlock arose in the on-going talks between Bougainville and Port Moresby on issues of financial and taxation powers.

The Bougainville leadership believed these to be gravely inadequate for a self-sufficient government, as Bougainville was already producing more than 51 per cent of PNG's Gross National Product, 43 per cent of its foreign earnings and 17 to 20 per cent of its internal revenue. Without adequate financial and taxation powers to the new proposed 'Provincial Government', Bougainville would just simply continue to be a beggar of its own wealth.[13]

Unilateral Declaration of Independence and Civil Disobedience

On 1 September 1975, 15 days before Papua New Guinea's independence, Bougainvillean nationalism and dissent finally came to a climax. The people and their leaders unanimously rejected the sovereignty of Papua New Guinea and declared themselves the new

'Republic of North Solomons'. The immediate reaction from the newly-created independent state of Papua New Guinea and the out-going Australian colonial administration was to suspend all services to Bougainville within weeks of the Unilateral Declaration of Independence (UDI). For twelve months the new 'Republic of North Solomons' continued to run all its services uninterrupted from makeshift offices.

Towards the end of 1975, Papua New Guinea carried out its first threat of war by flying police troops to Bougainville. However, troops were unable to land at the Aropa airport in Kieta, as the Aropa airport had been dug up the night before by protestors. In Buin, several attempted landings were aborted because of hundreds of 44-gallon drums dumped on the runway and strategically parked trucks. Port Moresby however, managed to land police troops flown from Rabaul to Buka where 20,000 Buka men, women and children, under the leadership of Moses Havini, were peacefully demonstrating at the PNG government sub-district headquarters at Hutjena. During this confrontation, Havini and three other young men were fired on by riot police and injured with rubber bullets. Nevertheless, the demonstration had been very successful in conveying its strong message to the Papua New Guinea government.

Amidst this explosive situation and on the brink of a real war, negotiations were resumed after twelve months with PNG, and an acceptable form of autonomy was agreed between the parties. This led to the establishment of the North Solomons Provincial Government in July 1976. Bougainvilleans saw this only as the first step towards full independence. Papua New Guinea, however, assumed this to be the end of the matter. The Port Moresby government had gravely misjudged the deep-seated political awareness that had developed within the Bougainvillean psyche since colonisation.

The Panguna Copper Mine, Bougainville

A significant feature of colonisation in Papua New Guinea and Bougainville was resource extraction by transnational corporations. German and Australian control over Papua and New Guinea established a platform of resources and economic exploitation, including gold and copper.

In 1961, the Australian Bureau of Mineral Resources released a report on the 'Panguna copper investigations', just as Britain's

Conzinc Rio Tinto was looking for low-grade copper in Australia. Serious prospecting began in the mountains of Panguna in 1964. By May 1965, Conzinc Rio Tinto of Australia Exploration (CRAE) located a huge copper ore deposit in the Panguna valley that proved to be economical for an open-cut mine. Bougainville Copper Pty Limited was incorporated in 1967, and Bougainville Copper Proprietary negotiated with the then Administration of the Territory for the development of a copper mine on Bougainville.[14]

Children have suffered the harshest impacts from the sanctions imposed on Bougainville following the popular rejection of the Panguna copper mine by Bougainvilleans.

Photo by ICEM

One of the biggest disadvantages for Bougainvilleans at this time was their complete lack of knowledge and concept of what a 'mega mining developmental project' entailed and to what extent it would soon destroy not only their social fabric, but also up-turn their customary laws. A people still content with their egalitarian way of life were soon to be rocked by the full impact of mining, never before experienced in their lives since time immemorial. The landowners resisted the taking of their land, but against the biggest 'mining giant' and its powerful government allies, this 'David and Goliath' duel was soon be lost to 'Goliath' and friends.

In Bougainville, it was the then colonial administration of Australia in collusion with the PNG Administration who would make the 'momentous' decision to develop the Panguna mine, at the expense of Bougainvilleans. Being pushed by the United Nations Decolonisation Committee, Canberra saw this as a timely answer. Until this opportunity presented itself, the Papua and New Guinea economy was in static mode. It was not growing and in no way fit to run an independent country. This mineral discovery which would ensure a viable economy for Papua and New Guinea would finally encourage Australia to proceed with the decolonisation of Papua and the Trust Territory of New Guinea in earnest.

The decision made in distant Port Moresby without the knowledge of the landowners in Bougainville was based on the *1928 Mining Ordinance*. Under the terms of the Ordinance, 'access to native land could be granted by the Administration – without reference to the [traditional] owners'. A Prospecting Authority (PA) or such a license was granted for a specified area on 'traditional and customary land' where the miners would prospect. A Prospecting Authority in turn directed the company to pay an annual fee to the Administration (i.e. the government) but not to the traditional landowners.[15] Prior to the construction of the Panguna mine, there were no environmental impact studies carried out, as there were no laws governing such evaluation.[16] Before the amendment of the Mining Ordinance in 1966, the customary landowners were not paid occupation fees for the land covered by the prospecting authorities, except for compensation for crops and other properties destroyed or damaged by the prospectors.[17]

CRAE experienced opposition and resistance from the customary landowners right from the very beginning. Fundamental issues that were held right throughout Papua New Guinea on customary land rights ownership were raised by Bougainvilleans for the first time during these ensuing confrontations. Bougainvilleans could not understand Australian mineral laws about sub-surface ownership, and that the people owned only what was on the land yet the government owned whatever was under it. In accordance with the tenets of their Customary Land Tenure System, the people own what is on the land, what's under it, the reef, and the sea extending from the reef and beyond.

In a meeting with prospecting geologists in 1967, opposition to land acquisition by transnational corporations was clearly articulated by one of the leaders, Andrew Erenaru of Darutue village, saying 'I do not recognise Australia's rights to make laws for the Territory . . . The people of Bougainville do not wish to give their land in this manner. We are aware of what happened to Nauru. There the white people have destroyed all the ground and have left the place bare. All the old people of my place are determined to hold the ground as it is our custom'.[18] Another landowner, Keni Maia of Idobua village reiterated, 'All the ground on top and underneath the surface belongs to the owners. There is now an increase in the birth rate in Bougainville. If we give the ground to CRA we will have no land for the children'.[19]

Tambu ('No Trespassing') signs sprung up in the Panguna and Kupei area while resistance grew by the day. Company workers were forced back by landowners in other parts of Panguna and Kupei area. The traditional landowners in Bougainville are women and the culture of the people is entwined with the land. Mothers put babies on survey pegs to stop the pegs being hammered in and a village leader publicly threatened to cut his throat in protest.[20] Drilling sites were destroyed by the landowners – but prompt actions were also taken by the Kiaps (colonial officials) and police to put these men in the Kieta gaol for, 'destruction of property'.

In an attempt to better inform the people, a group of Bougainville leaders and customary landowners were sent to Australia in 1965 to learn about mining. In a meeting in Canberra with then Minister for External Territories, Charles Barnes, the landowners raised the issue of 'direct financial benefits'. But the 'Minister did not answer or directly reject' this request. The landowners took it as a 'tacit approval of their requests'.[21]

The situation deteriorated when Minister Barnes visited the exploration in Bougainville in 1966. The Minister told a meeting on his arrival at Kieta that they would not personally benefit from the Panguna mine as, 'the development would be for the benefit of PNG as a whole'. The next day, the Ministerial Party met a number of the Guavas at the Panguna Camp, and, 'when old Oni (Chief) plaintively asked if there were not a silver shilling in it somewhere for them, the Minister then said "NO"'.[22] After this dissatisfying visit, the PNG Administration was concerned that CRAE could possibly be stopped at this stage so they decided on rough justice and strong-arm tactics by establishing a Police Station on site at Barapinang – for the protection of the company and its workers.

The local people stepped up their hostility by refusing to work for CRAE, which immediately led to a shortage of manpower. At this point, CRAE started to recruit an unskilled labour force from other provinces of Papua New Guinea.[23] This created another unwelcome problem with 'illegal immigrants' from mainland PNG flocking into Bougainville seeking work at the new mine. This directly led to the beginning of what would be another problem of an ever-increasing squatter settlement of unemployed PNG Highlanders in the ensuing years. CRAE nevertheless stepped up its drilling program and mine construction.

In order to find answers to landownership and occupation issues, the outdated *1928–1966 Mining Ordinance* was amended to create new provisions for land occupation, compensation and other mining related issues. Inclusion of a five per cent (5 per cent) royalty to go to Bougainville was made based on 1.25 per cent of the value of ore at shipment. The percentage would not change whether the price of metal rose or fell. Royalty payment was previously paid to the government, but at a much higher rate. This amendment was approved quickly, as CRAE had confirmed, 'a massive low-grade ore body in the Panguna area; and they were seeking prospecting and mining leases of a kind which could not be issued by the Administration under the terms of the existing Ordinance'.[24]

The Mining (Bougainville Copper Agreement) Bill, 1967

In 1967, Australian senior colonial officials in Port Moresby introduced the *Mining (Bougainville Copper Agreement) Bill*. The Bill allowed Bougainville Copper Limited (BCL) extension of prospecting authorities, mining and land leases. The equity shares were also decided during this time between CRA 53.6 per cent, PNG 20.2 per cent and the remaining 26.2 per cent to private shareholders mostly in Australia. No shares were given to the landowners in Bougainville. Further concessions given to the company included a three year tax holiday, an 84 year lease, and exemption from major stamp duty.[25]

This Bill enabled fast-tracked construction of the CRA mine at Panguna to production level. This included other ancillary facilities, such as port facilities at Loloho and a mining town in the former Arawa plantation.[26] Under the same agreement, the landowners would just receive an occupation fee, bush compensation, physical disturbance compensation, crop compensation, property damage

138

compensation, river and fish compensation, village relocation compensation, social inconvenience and nuisance compensation, condolence compensation and footbridge construction.[27] This compensation would never make up for the irreversible loss of land, property, sacred sites, gardens and economic crops. The landowners were still not happy with these offers, but with the Administration, Canberra and CRA in control and allied to the House of Assembly (with passage of legislation and policies), Bougainvilleans just simply did not have the power to push their case more strongly.

In early 1969, CRA mining company wanted to take more land owned by the Rorovana people to build a port, roads and townships, displacing hundreds of villagers. The mining company offered the Rorovana people a derogatory $105 per acre, plus $2 per felled coconut palm in compensation. The Rorovana people refused to sell their land and soundly rejected the offer.[28]

On 1 August 1969, 75 riot police (equipped and trained by the Australian government) were flown in from Port Moresby to take possession of the land that CRA mining company wanted. In the early morning, a hundred police carrying rifles, shields, batons and gas masks marched through the coconut groves onto Rorovana land with the mining surveyors. The women led the protests and resisted the police, pulling out the survey pegs. Three helicopters hovered above. By 4 August, CRA had completed its surveying and moved in the bulldozers to clear the jungle and knock down the coconut trees.[29] The Australian Colonial Administrators and CRA mining company insisted that the mine proceed despite the protests of the landowners. On 5 August around 65 villagers lined up in front of the bulldozers. Some of the women landowners lay down with their babies in front of the bulldozers in an attempt to stop the taking of their land. The police fired a barrage of tear gas canisters at them, and then charged at them with batons, clubbing both men and women, forcing them off their land.[30]

In 1972, the CRA mine commenced commercial production. With a three-year tax holiday and the value of metals on the world market exceptionally high in the first years of commercial operations, CRA more than recouped its establishment costs from profits resulting from such high metal prices for copper, gold and silver. Bougainville Copper had become a successful and a profitable mine for CRA, its first mine in the Pacific region. It had also provided a viable economic platform, which would now smooth the way to independence for PNG within three years.

For the Bougainville landowners, the mine was an environmental disaster. According to Paul Quodling, who became the General Manager of Bouvainville Copper Limited (BCL), working with Rio Tinto Mining Company from 1956 to 1987, 'This land is lost for ever, being replaced, most likely, by a man-made crater lake'.[31] Mr. Quodling states that, 'some 50 per cent of the solid waste is systematically stacked in a nearby valley and these waste dumps add some 300 hectares of flat land for the extension of mine facilities, but destroy the valley slopes' potential as traditional garden sites'.[32]

Over a billion tonnes of poisonous tailings from the mine were dumped straight into the Kawerong and Jaba Rivers. Alternative methods of dumping the poisonous tailings such as tailings dams were considered by CRA but ruled out because of the high seismic activity in the area. A pipeline transport was also considered by the company to dump the poisonous tailings into the sea but was rejected on technological and financial grounds.[33]

The tailings contained heavy metals such as copper, zinc, cadmium, mercury and molybdenum – these washes are also high in sulphur, arsenic and mercury.[34] The systemic effects of cadmium include fatal illness, severe breathlessness, lung and kidney damage, anaemia and adverse reproductive effects. The early symptoms of mercury poisoning include psychological and emotional disturbances, tremors, kidney disease, nerve degeneration and also adverse reproductive effects.[35] Before the mine even started, hundreds of hectares of forests were poisoned then chopped down and burnt. Whole forests died. Birds, flying foxes and possums disappeared. The Panguna valley was turned into a huge crater. By mid 1971 the naturally clear rivers were already silted, had increased in size and intensity and widened, causing blocked stream flows in many places, flooding and new swampland.[36] The toxic wastes were carried down the Jaba River to the coast, leaving a trail of death 35 kilometres long.

The Banoni people lived on the coast near the mouth of the Jaba River before the river widened. The poisonous tailings sediment flowing from the Jaba River into the bay increased the size of the delta from 65 to 900 hectares and spread silted water far out from the shore, with some known or suspected lethal effects on marine life up and down the coast.[37] Fish in the rivers developed ulcerations and died.

The first political group set up to defend land rights and depredations of the mining company was Napidakoe Navitu in 1972. This group demanded that all royalties from the mine be returned to the province of Bougainville. Their demands were not met. The Australian Administrators ignored them, as it was feared that financial independence could lead to assertions of political independence.[38]

By mid-1975, the Bougainville provincial assembly requested the same demands as the Napidakoe Navitu but it was only offered a quarter of what was demanded. This infuriated the Bougainville people all over the island. They retaliated by attacking government offices. They tore up the airstrip and invaded the mine site. Police and paramilitary forces were called in to quell riots.[39] The Bougainvilleans voted to secede and on 1st September 1975 they raised their flag, just two weeks before Papua New Guinea celebrated its own independence from Australian control.

The mining company argues that Bougainville has profited from the mine. Apologists for the mine imply that Bougainville, before the mining company arrived, was backward and impoverished. The mine sought to use local labour – primarily to minimise costs. The Employment Relations Manager at the mine, Colonel Kenneth McKenzie, was full of praise for the skill of the Bougainville workers. He said, 'Now, we wouldn't think of employing Europeans – who are paid three times as much as the natives for doing the same job'. Colonel McKenzie continued, 'Morally, politically and economically it's a proper and sensible thing to do. Now two-thirds of the company work force are black, which is helpful economically'.[40] However, neither the landowners nor the Bougainville provincial government benefited from the mine. They received 1.3 per cent and 4.2 per cent respectively of the mine's profits.[41]

The landowners received little, while losing everything – their subsistence culture and their land, their birthright. Of course in 1972, the landowners never had a comprehensive understanding of the absolute destruction, degradation and pollution of their land, sea and air environment that was yet to follow. The Bougainville Provincial Government was also paid a pittance compared to the earnings received by the Papua New Guinea National Government.

By 1988, a decade and a half later, the worst fears of the Bougainville people had been confirmed. Perpetua Serero, a leader of Bougainville's matrilineal landowners told a visiting reporter: 'We don't grow healthy crops any more, our traditional customs and values have been disrupted and we have become mere spectators as our earth is being dug up, taken away and sold for millions. Our land was taken away from us by force. We were blind then, but we have finally grown to understand what's going on'.[42] The people of Bougainville have experienced one of the worst human-made environmental catastrophes of modern times.

Philip Hughes, Head of Environmental Science at the University of Papua New Guinea, described Panguna in 1987 as 'An economic godsend – and an environmental disaster'. Ken Lamb, Professor of Biology at the University of Papua New Guinea called the Bougainville experience 'disastrous'. 'All aquatic life in the Jaba Valley has been killed', concluded another scientist, M R Chambers in 1986. In 1988, the Environment Minister, Perry Zeipi, found the pollution 'dreadful and unbelievable' and that the Jaba River was 'full of all kinds of chemicals and wastes' and that 'the people had been forced to abandon traditional fishing'.[43]

In mid-1988, in response to escalating agitation from the landowners, a consultancy firm from New Zealand, Applied Geology Associates Limited (AGA), was commissioned by the mining company to determine the past and future social and environmental impact of mining operations at Panguna. At a meeting on 18 November 1988, the AGA expressed the view that although environmental damage from mining operations was substantial, there was no direct evidence of significant levels of chemical pollution. The AGA implied that it was unlikely the Bougainville copper mine operations were responsible for the loss of wildlife, declining agricultural production or a range of human illnesses. Landowners present at the meeting disagreed violently and declared the environmental enquiry to be a 'whitewash'.[44]

Numerous attempts by the landowners to obtain redress for their grievances through gentle persuasion, petitions, lobbying and attempts to negotiate an equitable agreement with CRA and the Papua New Guinea Government all fell on deaf ears. After 17 years of trying to negotiate with the mining company and the Papua New Guinea government for better terms and more efficient environmental control, the people of Bougainville saw no other avenue but to mobilise.

On 22 November 1988, four days after the AGA meeting, explosives were stolen from the mining company. A group of dissidents, led by Francis Ona, the Secretary of the Panguna Landowners Association and former surveyor with the mining company, burned down mining company buildings, and destroyed a helicopter as well as vital communications and electricity installations, thus closing the mine. Desperate to force the mine open again, Papua New Guinea sent in the Riot Squad in December 1988 and then the Army in an attempt to crush the militants – the Bougainville Revolutionary Army. Australia then supplied four Iroquois helicopters ostensibly for 'non-military' purposes. This perfidious action was to cost thousands of innocent lives, as the aircraft, kitted out with machine guns, strafed villages and terrorised women and children, in sorties which were compared to those of US forces in Vietnam, a decade earlier.[45]

A 'State of Emergency' was declared and the Papua New Guinea Military deployed in March 1989. Anti-company activities escalated, rendering the mine and its employees unsafe, and inevitably led to the full closure of the CRA mine in May 1989.[46] What had originally appeared to be a social and economic issue had now developed into a full-blown declaration of war. Bougainvilleans were at war with the PNG State over land, the environment and political freedom. Civilians were attacked, tortured and killed by the Papua New Guinea Army, which routinely burnt villages in an attempt to flush out the Bougainville Revolutionary Army. These abuses turned Bougainvilleans against Papua New Guinea and ignited their smouldering desire for independence. The fight against the mine grew into a full-scale struggle for self-determination with the creation of the Bougainville Interim Government and the raising of the Bougainville flag once more on 17 May 1990.

Around the same time in 1990, a land, sea and air military blockade was imposed around Bougainville. All government and social services were suspended, schools closed and medical staff withdrew from the entire island. The blockade prevented medicines, food, fuel, humanitarian assistance, and journalists from going to Bougainville. The purpose of the blockade was to increase the hardships of the people in an attempt to turn them against the Bougainville Revolutionary Army. The governments of Australia and Papua New Guinea waged a prolonged and brutal war against the people of Bougainville with the purpose of re-opening the Panguna copper mine and avoiding secession. Australia was heavily involved in the war on Bougainville through training, equipping and financing of the Papua New Guinea Defence Force operations on Bougainville. Australia supplied Papua New Guinea with patrol boats, speed boats, pilots, Iroquois helicopters and aircraft, which were used to maintain and enforce the deadly blockade around Bougainville.

The people of Bougainville experienced most degrading violations at the hands of the Papua New Guinea Defence Force (PNGDF) and its pro-PNG Resistance Force, and many thousands of Bougainvilleans lost their lives. Many were forced to live in so-called 'care centres', effectively 'concentration camps' where human rights abuses and food shortages were severe. In spite of these horrors, and the total destruction of all developed infrastructure, the people of Bougainville remained strong in their conviction that only when the Papua New Guinea Defence Force withdrew from Bougainville would justice prevail.

Both governments of Papua New Guinea and Australia have admitted that the war on Bougainville could not be resolved by military means. Despite this, in January 1997, the government of Papua New Guinea, under the direction of Prime Minister Sir Julius Chan, hired the British-based mercenaries, Sandline International, to wage its war against the people of Bougainville. The Papua New Guinea Government engaged the mercenaries from South Africa and from Britain as their final option for crushing local resistance. The mercenaries were contracted for $36 million dollars by the PNG Government and were preparing to bring into PNG, for deployment into Bougainville, some of the most lethal arsenals ever seen in the Pacific before. These were purchased from the former Soviet Union and Eastern Europe, and included: four Russian helicopters, six rocket launchers, 1,000 rockets, 5,000 mortar bombs, 2,000 grenades, and 100 AK47 assault rifles.

The Attack Force for what was called 'Project Oyster' was to include more than 30 mercenaries with all the commanding posts held by mercenary commanders, a Special Force Unit (SFU) especially trained by the PNGDF and Bougainvillean Resistance Forces included for their local knowledge. The operation embroiled the PNG Government in unusual financial dealings and contracts that caused local disquiet that ultimately forced the Government to cancel the operation. From the start there were tensions between the PNGDF and

Sandline International. There was a sharp disparity between payments to the mercenaries ($11,000 per month) and payments to the Special Forces ($750 per month). The 'below standard' training provided by the mercenaries to the PNGDF also became a cause for concern. There was no clear line of communication between the mercenaries and the PNGDF. It seems the mercenaries were withholding vital information from the PNGDF, and that the question of leadership was unresolved.

When the operation became public knowledge, it quickly became unviable. The US$36 million contract signed between the Papua New Guinea (PNG) government and the mercenary company, Sandline International, indicated that the PNG Government and the mercenary company agreed to take 'appropriate steps ... to prevent media reporting, both nationally and internationally'. Fortunately, the international media were tipped off and news of the Sandline deal became known.

Pressure was applied by international NGOs, some governments (including Australia, New Zealand, South Africa and the United States) and PNG civilians. With non-co-operation from key elements of the PNGDF and mounting opposition from ordinary Papua New Guineans, the PNG Government was overthrown and Project Oyster started to crumble.

The anti-climax of Operation Oyster came with the PNGDF counter-operation Operation Rausim Kwik with the arrest of Sandline leader Tim Spicer and his senior henchmen on 16 March 1997. This move was headed and led by General Singirok, Major Walter Enuma and other PNGDF Officers. Upon the arrest of the mercenaries General Singirok publicly called for the resignation of Prime Minister Sir Julius Chan, and the Prime Minister was eventually forced to suspend the Sandline contract and establish a Commission of Inquiry.

By mid-March 1997 all the mercenaries had been rounded up and deported – including Tim Spicer, who was eventually allowed to leave the country after he had appeared before the Commission of Inquiry. The PNG government was left with a debt of US$23 million.[47] Clearly, the incident highlighted the extent to which the PNG government was willing to go to force the mineral-rich island back under its control. Rio Tinto, now lacking government allies, has announced its intention to sell the Bougainville copper mine.

Conclusion: Mining and Self-Determination

Bougainvillean experience with successive colonial powers and transnational corporations has helped to create and strengthen a Bougainvillean common sense of identity, and a strong desire to separate themselves from the rest of Papua New Guinea. Bougainvilleans were already unhappy at the time when CRA, fully supported by the then colonial Administration, began its exploration. The people were concerned over the establishment and operation of CRA and the fact that massive profits would be diverted from Bougainville. This solidified their separate identity and struggle for independence. Bougainville's fight for independence is totally central to, and inextricably part of, the whole issue of mining, land rights, resource developments and the right to be self-determining as a people.

The people of Bougainville are known throughout the world as the only indigenous people to have shut a mine owned by Rio Tinto, one of the world's most powerful mining companies.[48] They have faced exploitation, plunder and the defrocking of their sovereignty – all in the name of modernisation and 'development'. The ecological damage caused by mining on Bougainville was the price paid for development. Confronted with state injustice and the power of the multinationals with their aggressive development policies, and in the absence of any acceptable solutions to the grievances of the Bougainville people, the Bougainvilleans had no other option but to mobilise and face the 'aggressor' head on. The people of Bougainville closed the mine and are determined to keep it closed.

9 Corporate imperialism in the Philippines

Antonio Tujan Jr.

Like many Third World countries, mineral production in the Philippines has been colonial in character, characterised by the large-scale extraction of minerals for export mainly to the colonising country at dirt-cheap prices. This chapter will seek to show how a grand effort to liberalise Philippine mining in the 1990s was thwarted through a nationally coordinated campaign by a broad movement involving grassroots activists, indigenous communities, Church workers, environmental activists and others. This campaign resulted in a decline in production and the departure of many transnational corporation (TNC) investments that had originally been attracted by the liberalisation policy. This campaign lasted more than three years and achieved an unprecedented victory in the Philippines against imperialist corporations mining operations.

History of Philippine Mining

Large-scale mining was instituted by foreign corporations since the turn of the last century, prompting American colonial administrators to pass the Mining Code of 1905 which took over tribal lands and allowed extensive corporate control over mining areas. This pattern of exploitation was continued even after independence and took the form of neo-colonial economic domination and exploitation mainly through the transnational mining corporations. Thus mineral production in the Philippines has traditionally been dominated by large mining corporations such as Benguet Consolidated, Philex Mining, Marcopper, and Atlas Mining. Typically, these corporations trace their history to American colonial times, with strong equity and financial linkages with transnational mineral interests in Japan, the US, Canada and Australia. Through such corporations, the Philippines mining industry became enmeshed in a global network of giant mining and metals corporations. Non-economic factors such as political domination were translated into super-profits in the production of ores. Costs were held down as corporations are able to underpay mining workers, minimise royalty payments for the non-renewable resources of Third World countries, and benefit from the relative lack of environmental controls.

In spite of a general decline from the 1980s, speculative activity in the Philippines mining industry continued, and global production in copper, gold, silver, chromite and nickel increased (see Figure 1, from *Metals Week*). However, depressed international metal prices combined with declining productivity (due to outdated machinery and labour problems) resulted in an overall decline in Philippine mineral production and export (see Figures 2 and 3). This decline would seem unacceptable to imperialist corporations considering the great potential for profits from Philippine mining.

Despite its relatively small land area, the Philippines is second only to Indonesia in terms of geological prospectivity and was second only to South Africa in gold production per square kilometre; it is also ranked third globally in copper reserves and sixth in chromite. While the Philippines has been a major global producer of ore, at least until the 1980's, the country has been assessed to be producing only ten per cent of its potential.[1] Mineral production, especially in gold, copper, chromite and nickel, reached its peak in the early 1980s. Gold production peaked between 1980 and 1990.

Globalising Philippine Mining

Recognising the great potential for the mining sector to earn foreign exchange through incoming investment and ore exports, mining was made part of a comprehensive program of corporate globalisation implemented by former President Fidel Ramos. In 1993 he launched 'Philippines 2000', a comprehensive economic development program which promised to industrialise the country by promoting corporate investment and aggressively implementing structural adjustment. This five-year program covered 1993-1998 and was premised on the Philippines' accession to the General Agreement on Trade and Tariffs (GATT) Uruguay Round.

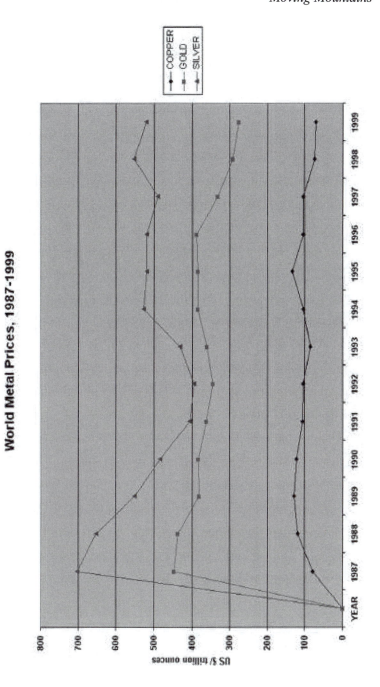

World Metal Prices, 1987-1999

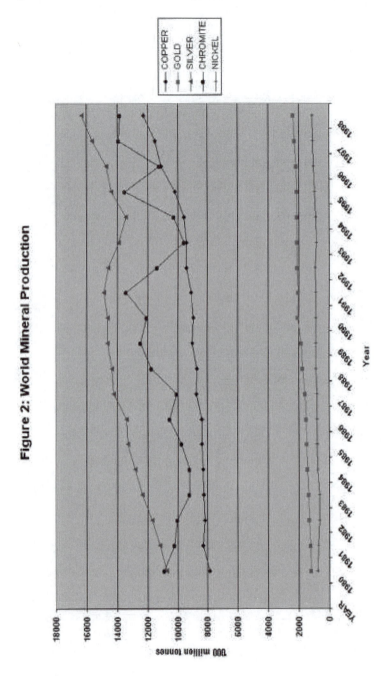

Figure 2: World Mineral Production

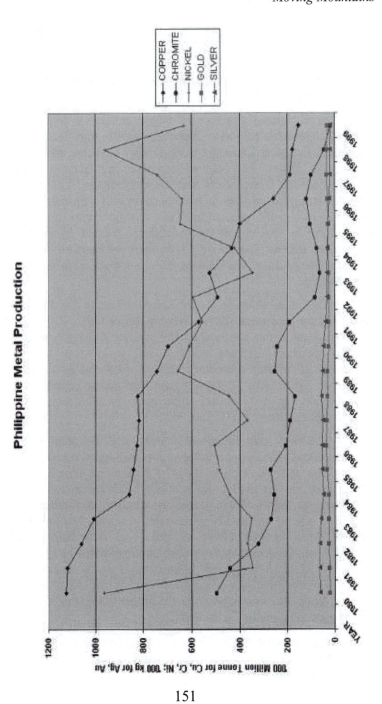

Philippine Metal Production

The 'Philippines 2000' blueprint systematically liberalised finance, trade and investment, and saw the privatisation of state utilities, social services and other assets. This succeeded in attracting investment similar to its then-touted Asian tiger cub neighbours until the Asian financial crisis of 1997.

In the mining sector in the 1990s, the Ramos administration sought to respond to corporate complaints, mainly from the American, Australian and New Zealand Chambers of Commerce and Industry, pointing to factors that hobbled corporate investment in mining. Foremost among these factors was the constitutional prohibition on majority foreign ownership in mining companies. Foreign investors were also wary of increased activism among environmentalists as exemplified by the opposition to tailings disposal by Marcopper Mining, indigenous peoples as in the case of open-pit mining by Benguet Consolidated and militant trade unionism as in the case of Atlas Mining.

The main strategy in the Ramos blueprint for the mining sector was the enactment of a new Mining Act of 1995. This new law was significant in that it permitted 100 per cent foreign ownership of mining operations, skirting constitutional prohibitions to foreign ownership of mining companies through Financial and Technical Assistance Agreements – FTAAs – and Exploration Permits (EPAs). The Act also granted Mineral Agreements for Philippine majority equity corporations.

The deal was sweetened dramatically by granting FTAA holders various rights similar to those provided under the US Colonial Mining Law of 1905. Besides rights to explore and mine the ore, the law granted foreign mining corporations water rights, timber rights and easement rights. These corporations were also offered fiscal incentives beyond the already preferential treatment they enjoy under the 1987 Omnibus Investment Code. Slicing-up of the Philippines like a mining pie, the country was divided into meridional blocks. These were offered on a first-come first-served basis to mostly foreign mining corporations, reminiscent of the Spanish and American colonial eras. The meridional block system disregards the actual activities of communities on the surface.[2]

The response to the Mining Act exceeded expectations. A total of 62 FTAA applications were received by 1996, and 84 by 1998, mainly from the major global mining concerns like Rio Tinto,

Newmont, Climax, and Western Mining. In fact, corporate interest was so high that 17 of these applications were actually filed before the Act was passed into law. Even before the law was passed, President Ramos approved the FTAA applications of Arimco (Climax) in Nueva Vizcaya, North-Central Philippines, and Western Mining Corporation straddling the former Cotabato provinces of Mindanao, Southern Philippines.

The Mining Act is a clear example of how the current neo-liberal economic paradigm is translated into the wholesale opening up of Third World natural resources to corporate exploitation, especially by global monopoly corporations. Not only does it remove investment controls for foreign exploitation of mineral resources, but the Act provides more privileges and incentives over the welfare of the country's environment, its rural communities and its indigenous peoples.

The People's Fight

The Mining Act or Republic Act No. 7942 was signed into law on 6 March 1995 without much fanfare and opposition. As previously mentioned, the mining industry had been on the decline and consequently most protests against mining companies had also declined. The World Trade Organisation and other issues under the Philippines 2000 program of the Ramos administration occupied the attention of most activist organisations.

This situation changed dramatically after the accident at the Marcopper mine in Marinduque province, Western Philippines, an accident of unparalleled proportions in Philippine history. Marcopper, a subsidiary company of the Canadian-based multinational, Placer Dome, had become the largest copper mining operation in the country. It had already been in the public eye after a series of environmental controversies mainly involving the release of mine tailings directly into Calancan Bay. On 24 March 1996, millions of tons of mine tailings stored in its old open-pit mine were accidentally released into the Boac and Makulapnit rivers. It took four months before the leak was plugged. In the meantime, the four million tons of mine tailings released had destroyed ten million hectares of agricultural lands and affected a total 126 million hectares of land around the rivers. A twenty six kilometre stretch of the river was declared biologically dead five days after the accident.[3]

153

The Marcopper labour union, MELU-NAMAWU, reported that the spill affected 14 villages and initially isolated more than a thousand families, and threatened to swamp another 20 villages. Damage was estimated to be US$700,000 worth of marine life and US$200,000 worth of milkfish fry. Catching milkfish fry through crude nets in the shallow coastlines is a major source of livelihood of poor fisher folk who do not own fishing boats and nets.[4] The waste exuded hydrogen sulphide and nitrous oxide vapours and residents complained of cases of skin irritation and respiratory problems, and a number of people were hospitalised after drinking water and eating fish contaminated by the spill.

Unprecedented in scale in more than a century of large-scale mining in the country, the Marcopper accident shocked and traumatised the Philippine nation. Previous community and environmental battles against mining had already highlighted such risks. Furthermore, since Marcopper had a long-running conflict with the Marinduque residents and the Department of Environment and Natural Resources (DENR) over environmental issues, there were suspicions that the tailings were intentionally released

Beyond the issues of extent of damage and remuneration, the attention of the public readily shifted to the newly enacted Mining Act. At the time, the IBON Foundation published an expose on the Mining Act that pointed out the greater danger of environmental disasters from large-scale mining as well as issues of indigenous people's rights and national patrimony.[5] National outrage at the Marcopper mine disaster was quickly transformed into a nation-wide campaign against the Mining Act, and against large-scale mining by transnational corporations in general. The issues were taken up by many of the political forces in the Philippines, and various avenues of protest were utilised, from the streets and pickets, to the media and the Congress.

As a result, the government was forced to delay approval of pending FTAA applications – all except the two initially approved by Ramos. This was a significant victory, but it was not sufficient. People's organisations wanted the Act repealed, and many wanted large-scale corporate mining ended altogether. A sustained campaign was necessary.

In the network of the militant political organisation, Bagong Alyansang Makabayan (Bayan or New Patriotic Alliance), the initial protests were consolidated into regional conferences which firmed up the people's understanding and analysis of the issues. Action plans were drawn up and protest coalitions created. Similar processes were implemented by some indigenous and environmental networks and coalitions, as well as church social action networks. The following action was taken:

- In April 1996, a People's Regional Mining Conference was held in the Cordillera region, a traditional centre of large-scale mining in the Northern Philippines. This was organised by Bayan and the Cordillera People's Alliance, and attended by 130 delegates representing 87 grassroots organisations and coalitions. Besides rejecting of the Mining Act of 1995, the conference resolved to resist any exploration work done by mining companies.
- In September 1996, a similar conference was also convened for all the Visayas islands in the central part of the country. This was spearheaded by the National Council of Churches in the Philippines. Following this conference, protest actions were held in various Visayan Islands, including a rally on Negros island on October where more than 15,000 mobilised.
- In October 1996, another conference was held, gathering various indigenous peoples in Mindanao, Southern Philippines. This focused on the impacts of the Western Mining Corporation (WMC) FTAA in Cotabato. A conference was also held in Nueva Vizcaya, gathering representatives from all communities covered by Arimco's FTAA operation.

Throughout the archipelago, grassroots and community-based organisations, environmentalists, civic organisations, tribal communities, churches and other religious organisations started researching the corporations that had applied for FTAA, MPSA and exploration permits in their province or region. They launched information and education campaigns drawing on existing publications such as the IBON Special Release and produced their own materials.

The widespread and sustained protests calling for the scrapping of the Mining Act had immediate effects on the government. Besides the unofficial but effective freeze in the granting of new FTAAs, a Bill was filed in Congress for the repeal of the Mining Act.

However these were only temporary victories, as the WMC and Arimco FTAAs were still being developed. It was not yet certain that the Mining Act would be repealed. As the dust settled, the Mines and Geoservices Bureau (MGB) or the President could potentially resume awarding FTAAs. In the meantime, numerous exploration permits and Mineral Production Sharing Agreements (MPSAs) were being awarded as a number of foreign FTAA applicants withdrew in favour of exploration or joint production.

Unprecedented Mobilisation

The nationally coordinated campaign against the Mining Act, and all operations of mining corporations which was launched in 1996, continues up to the present. This includes a sustained campaign for the repeal of the law and a freeze in the awarding of new FTAAs through coordinated popular mobilisation. It includes protests at the WMC and Arimco mining operations and protests against exploration activities, protests against operations of other large-scale mining operations existing before the Mining Act or under the MPSA.

Mining Bans

Large demonstrations were held intermittently from 1996 to 1999. In March 1998 more than five hundred representatives of indigenous peoples, church people, and farmers and others went to Manila, travelling from Pampanga, Zambales, Aurora and other provinces in central Luzon and Southern Tagalog regions. They demonstrated at government offices demanding the scrapping of the Mining Act and the withdrawal of all FTAAs, MPSAs and EPAs granted by the Ramos government.[6]

Between 1996 and 1999, campaign caravans were used to ensure maximum participation of activists and to take the campaign to various towns in a large island or a province. Caravans were held in the Cordillera region, Negros Island, Panay Island and in the provinces in the far south of Mindanao and served to dramatise the call to scrap the Mining Act and end existing mining operations. In these caravans more than 100 vehicles moved from one town to the next, campaigning along the way. At every stop, rallies were held which mobilised local townsfolk.

Reflecting these mobilisations, local victories against mining corporations have been quite dramatic. In the province of Capiz in

Panay Island, environmentalists and militant activists led by the Madyaas Environment Coalition campaigned against the granting of Australian Company, Minera Mt Isa's, application for a 80,919 hectare FTAA. The Coalition conducted sustained lobbying with the support of progressive members of the Capiz Provincial Board. Government approval of MPSA applications for a joint venture created by Mt Isa, and for its initial exploration work in Capiz, resulted in widespread protest. In response, the provincial government banned commercial mining in the province for 15 years. [7] This campaign was supported by research provided by the Australian NGO, the Mineral Policy Institute.

A mural depicts the Cordillera peoples' struggle for the right to control development on their land.

Photo by the Mineral Policy Institute

A similar measure was passed in neighbouring Iloilo province where residents had previously barricaded roads leading to the mines operated by Malampay Mining Company, a subsidiary of Phelps Dodge Philippines.[8] These provincial laws contravened the Mining Act and existing national legislation, but effectively put a stop to exploration activities by transnational corporations. These have never been overruled nor questioned before the Supreme Court.

A more significant achievement than local legislation banning corporate mining is the departure of Climax Arimco and Western Mining Corporation from their mining development projects on separate occasions in 2000. After pouring US$30 million into mining development in four years, WMC decided to withdraw its operations in its South Cotabato FTAA in February 2000, acknowledging social and political challenges posed by the project – the result of a combination of advocacy from anti-mining activists, sustained protests from B'laan indigenous communities and solidarity action by Australian activists.

Climax Arimco also proceeded with its mining development in spite of intense opposition from local residents, mostly belonging to the Kankanaey, Ibaloi, Bungkalot and Ifugao tribes. Besides petitions and rallies, the residents also undertook a people's initiative in July 1999, a referendum that is guaranteed by the 1987 Constitution and several laws. Although an Environmental Compliance Certificate was issued to Climax Arimco on 11 August 1999 which allowed it to proceed with its gold/copper mining project, drilling and exploratory activities were halted and its employees were retrenched later in July 2000.

In October 2000, the Regional Development Council rejected Climax Arimco's operation in the region, on the grounds that the target area was a watershed and that mining was beyond the development priorities of the region. National economic and mining government agencies lobbied for the reversal of the decision but a subsequent meeting on 23 February 2001 upheld the previous decision in the midst of counter mobilisations by anti-mining organisations. In the meantime, residents continue to press the demand to close the Climax Arimco FTAA and the Mining Act through a series of protest actions.

Victories in Contesting Corporate Mining

The victories notched up by the Filipino people's struggles against corporate mining can be traced to various factors, but mostly to the firm resolve of a people who did not want a repeat of the Marcopper disaster. This brought out their creativity in launching protests and other struggles, and by linking up strong local movements with environmentalist movements. A rapid process of capacity building ensued among indigenous peoples who were now confronted not only with fear of the 'new white man in helicopters', but also the potential permanent loss of their ancestral domain to him.

The campaign against corporate mining also transformed the environmental movement, which had been focused on environmental protection and biodiversity conservation. Through the campaign, the issue of environmental degradation was clearly linked with neo-colonial corporate exploitation and its direct impact on the livelihood and physical displacement of rural communities.

This 'horizontal' networking was also strengthened with 'vertical' networking. Besides linking and consequently developing various interest groups and issue-based organisations, networks linked local groups with provincial and national entities. Conferences and fora provided effective venues for creating linkages that eventually led to coordinated actions. International networks and solidarity provided crucial support through research, increasing pressure through protests and policy advocacy such as shareholder action in the home countries of the global corporations.

Protests were grounded in respective constituencies, and as a result became concrete and effective rallying points for popular consciousness raising and action. Local struggles touched mainly on loss of rural livelihood and negative effects of environmental degradation of land, air, river and coastal areas, and loss of ancestral domain and sacred sites. The negative environmental impacts were interpreted in terms of the dislocation of livelihoods of upland and lowland farmers and fisher folk.

Another important factor was that the people relied on their own militant struggle through pickets, rallies, caravans and barricades, and combined this with various forms of engaging government through petitions and lobbying. This created a synergy that made their militant action even more effective. Government offices and officials from the local level up to the national level became targets for petitions and protest actions. Legal processes such as issuance of clearances, official permits, hearings, legislative processes and judicial processes were all used to highlight the opposition in conjunction with militant protest actions. These protests were sustained and remained viable even after three years.

Mine-affected community members from the Cordillera region of the Philippines perform traditional dances to highlight their plight.

Photo by the Mineral Policy Institute

As a result of the people's determination and persistence there have been concrete victories. The national government's Mining Act has been neutralised in spite of the power and influence of the existing and incoming global mining corporations. Taking advantage of this neutralisation, there have been victories at the local level with the enactment of laws prohibiting corporate mining, and the perhaps permanent delaying of the two flagship mining projects.

Finally, the Filipino people have come out of this campaign even stronger in terms of their resolve and capacity to fight corporate mining, and are now vigilant against all forms of encroachment by global mining corporations. The protests have caused the continued decline of corporate mining in the Philippines. The Philippines is no longer anywhere among the global top mineral exporters. In 1992, Philippine ore production was considered in its lowest decline but still held the 13th global rank in gold and 16th in copper production. By 1998, it had dropped to 20th in global gold production, 23rd in copper, and improved to 11th from 14th in nickel in 1997.[9]

There has been stagnation and even decline in the mining industry. This decline is most dramatic in exports and foreign investment. Instead of increasing the number of large-scale mines as expected from the Mining Act, total mines in operation have actually declined in 1998 and 1999.

This decline in the mineral ore production (as well as the continued decline of timber exports) has been greeted with satisfaction and pride by Filipinos who know only too well the consequences of corporate mining.

National Patrimony and Imperialist Globalisation

The nationally coordinated campaign against corporate mining in the Philippines was sustained over several years because it was founded on struggles that sprang from or focused on specific issues against mining. However, the overarching theme in the Philippine struggle against corporate mining is the issue of national patrimony which in the Philippine context defines natural resources as commonly held national treasures entrusted to the state for safekeeping.

This concept has been taken up by the various political groups and grassroots organisations, as well as churches and other institutions that took up the cause of the Mining Act.

With the Mining Act, the government is seen as directly destroying the Filipino people's patrimony and betraying their trust. Their only option is to stand up and fight.

As then Bayan Secretary General, Nathaniel Santiago, stated, 'We have surrendered our national patrimony. The Mining Act restores the economic and political colonial set-up under the guise of liberalisation and globalisation. There is nothing left to do but scrap [this law] and fight [this government]'.[10]

It has been generally recognised by all sectors along a broad front sympathetic to the campaign against the Mining Act, that neo-liberal globalisation is behind this renewed corporate interest which has meant the opening up of an important natural resource for unbridled exploitation by global corporations. While direct negative effects on livelihood and the environment are the immediate concerns of the protests, these have been placed in the context of corporate power and profits.

Global mining corporations realise super-profits by reducing operating costs through cheap wages mineworkers that are still below the already low decent living costs, and are obscenely lower than wages in industrialised countries. They also reduce operating costs by scrimping on measures necessary for reducing environmental degradation such as building and maintaining effective tailings dams and instituting non-polluting measures for disposal of wastes. For example, open-pit mining has become the favourite method because it reduces labour costs and is generally cheaper – yet it is environmentally degrading.

Even more difficult to cost than the environmental degradation is the loss of non-renewable mineral resources and the impacts of mining operations to the ancestral domain of indigenous peoples. In this respect, the issue of super-profits for imperialist mining corporations takes on a different aspect. The overwhelming unity of indigenous peoples against the entry of mining corporations mirrors campaigns in defence of the national patrimony of an underdeveloped Third World country such as the Philippines.

The Mining Act, though unrepealed, now remains un-implementable because people have become empowered and vigilant. Mining corporations have been constantly pressured and forced to introduce more effective measures of waste disposal and management.

Deception, subterfuge, PR activities, harassment and even outright military intervention have all failed to subdue an enlightened and empowered Philippine people. Global corporations are now wondering how attractive an investment site the Philippines is, considering the social and legal concerns they now have to face if they enter, or if they stay. New entrants are finding that the Philippines is not exactly heaven for global mining corporations as even exploration activities are subjected to protests. For many people this is a significant victory in the campaign against the continued environmental degradation of the Philippines.

The problem of mine tailings disposal remains unsolved, partly because of technical difficulties, especially with the volume of tailings produced by open-pit mining. But this lingering problem is also due to the lack of commitment from profit-conscious corporate mining with the collusion of government. In the face of this situation, many people would rather end corporate mining altogether, even at least temporarily, until such time that the environmental issues are resolved convincingly.

For many people, this campaign is a significant victory for democracy, especially for the economic and political rights of the marginalised rural sectors such as the small peasants, fisher folk and indigenous peoples whose subsistence agriculture is dependent on the wellbeing of the environment. As Joan Carling, chairperson of the Cordillera People's Alliance declared, 'The victory of the Cordillera people against Climax Arimco, as well as the victory of the "lumads" or Aborigines of Mindanao against Western Mining Corporation, is a significant victory in our people's struggle for self-determination, for our ancestral domain, for democracy in our country, and for our very existence.'[11]

For many people, this is also a significant victory for national patrimony and sovereignty against a subservient Philippine government and against imperialist mining corporations. It is a victory in the national struggle against foreign domination, a victory founded on the people's assertion of their sovereignty. Putting the Philippines outside the global map of top mineral producers is a significant victory of the Filipino people's struggle against imperialism in the form of the global mining corporations.

What the Philippines has lost by way of new corporate investment and foreign currency earnings from mineral exports is insignificant compared to what the country has gained. The Filipino people have preserved their natural resources and national patrimony, protected their environment from extreme degradation, secured their people's livelihood from irreparable damage, prevented the genocide of its indigenous communities, and achieved national and democratic power.

10 Mineworkers on the offensive

Jean McSorley and Rick Fowler

Introduction

In 1997, a corporate campaign against Rio Tinto – at the time the world's largest mining company – was launched by the Australian Trade Union, the Mining & Energy Division of the Construction Forestry Mining and Energy Union (CFMEU), and its international affiliate body the International Federation of Chemical, Energy, Mine and General Workers' Unions (ICEM). Over the three years preceding the campaign, Rio Tinto had been aggressively de-unionising its workforce, making many workers redundant and deliberately isolating those who represented the workers' interests through the union structure. Within Australia, Rio Tinto was openly acknowledged to be at the vanguard of the conservative Federal Government's 'workplace reform'. Changing work practises in the coalmining sector was seen not only as priority, but an ideological goal for Rio Tinto and the government, which perceived that sector as being one of the last bastions of strong trade unionism.

Internationally, ICEM affiliates believed that without united action not only would collective bargaining disappear from negotiations on pay and safety, but that whole communities would be irreparably damaged. In particular, they were concerned that the company was allowing the drive for shareholder dividends to guide all operational criteria. As an integral part of the company's operations, the workers felt their interests as stakeholders to be as important as financial shareholders in determining company policy. The union also felt a responsibility to safeguard the communities in which its members lived. For those communities it was the collective damage being wrought by the company policies, not the potential for individual gain, that was uppermost in their minds. For the miners and their families, however, this was a desperate battle for survival – not an opportunity to the line the wallets of investors. It is worth remembering that most executive directors have a direct financial interest, as salary packages invariably include large parcels of shares and bonuses linked to cost cutting.

Rio Tinto and the Australian government chose to portray the campaign as a conflict between a union and an employer: one vested interest fighting another. The company claimed the Mining and Energy Division of the CFMEU was simply stuck in a backwater of industrial relations, hanging on to wage structures and work practises that no 'forward thinking' organisation could tolerate. The company rejected claims that it was following a pattern set by it and other multinational corporations around the world.

Research revealed that the company's attempts to de-unionise its workforce was one more manifestation of a corporate strategy that was trampling human rights and environmental concerns. The union knew that for the campaign to succeed it had to look beyond union concerns alone and publicise company practices on a range of issues. In particular, human rights in the broadest sense – and how workers were entitled to recognition under international conventions – became crucial to the campaign. The campaign was not about one group of workers in one sector of its operations. The company had already been engaged in disputes across Australia, with workers at the Weipa bauxite mine, the Bell Bay smelter, as well as at the New South Wales and Queensland coalmines. Internationally, it had also clashed in recent years with unions in Norway, Namibia, Portugal, South Africa, the US and Zimbabwe. Rio Tinto was facing campaigns over human rights, compensation cases and environmental damage in Canada, Chile, New Zealand, Madagascar, the UK, Indonesia, West Papua and Papua New Guinea. The campaign drew these issues together and exposed Rio Tinto as a repeat and unrepentant offender in a number of areas. Rio Tinto was not the good corporate citizen it liked its shareholders to believe.

Indeed, the realisation that the union had to expose the totality of the damage done by the company and the knowledge that it was not alone in its struggle led the CFMEU to propose establishing a network with environmental and human rights non-government organisations (NGOs) in order to allow the full picture on Rio Tinto to emerge and the harm caused to workers and their families could be put in the context of a broader movement fighting to curb the excesses of a major multinational corporation.

A representative of communities affected by Rio Tinto's Kelian goldmine in Indonesia addresses protestors through a translator outside the Rio Tinto Annual General Meeting in Brisbane, 2000.

Photo by Nina Lansbury, Mineral Policy Institute

Global Capital, Privatised Power: The Broader Issues.

The union campaign did not spring from ill-informed opposition to corporate reform. As with many other organisations representing sectors of society, unions are not isolated entities dealing only with their own problems. Unions represent millions of workers at a national or international level. They are all too well aware of the power of global enterprises to influence national government and interstate organisations and how, in turn, the social justice agenda is determined by the corporate drive for profits.

As other chapters in this book highlight, the ability of such corporations to empower themselves through the accumulation of financial resources and interaction with political systems, is reaching truly frightening proportions. Unions feel this pressure. Under the guise of globalisation and international competition businesses are restructuring, contracting out, downsizing, retrenching, and sacking in order to generate unreasonable, and possibly unsustainable, profits. Within this system workers, their families and communities become little more than an asset to be moved around the balance sheet to feed the bottom line. The multinational corporations' (MNCs) expansion strategies do not aim to create secure full-time employment with a decent living wage, a comprehensive welfare system and a system that recognises workers' rights.

The mindset that puts the power of the company over that of elected government and neglects the role of unions, views the worker as totally dependent on corporate largesse. Without an officially recognised and working system of collective bargaining, workers are left to deal with the company by themselves. The notion of a direct relationship between a company and workers, one of the key tenets of Rio Tinto's industrial policy, places the individual worker in an untenable and unwinnable bargaining position.

Rio Tinto's antagonistic stance towards unions is not unique. A recent survey produced by the International Confederation of Free Trade Unions (ICFTU) shows a growing movement to curtail trade union activities through both legal and illegal means. Among the many disturbing statistics, the report reveals that during 1997, within the 116 countries surveyed there were:

- 299 trade unionists killed;
- 1,681 reported cases of violence against trade unionists;
- over 50,000 trade unionists who lost their jobs due to their activism;
- 450 strikes fiercely repressed;
- 80 governments which placed obstacles in the way of freedom of association; and
- 79 governments which directly interfered in trade union affairs.[1]

The ICFTU reports that trade union activists are no more protected now than 50 years ago and concludes with the opinion that today we are living in a world, 'where many governments have abdicated responsibility, leaving trade unions as the last bulwark against social injustice.'[2]

It is within this setting that the Rio Tinto campaign emerged. The campaign did have other examples to draw on, for organised labour has not been inactive or ineffective in challenging multinational corporations – the steamrollers of global capital. For example, ICEM has been involved in the struggle by Korean workers who fought hard for their democratic unions to be legalised. They were successful, but business and the government, under the direction of the World Bank and the International Monetary Fund, have now launched a new attack on Korean workers. This has led to over 100 officials being arrested, including the leadership of the Korean Confederation of Trade Unions, and leaders of the larger and more militant unions, such as the Metalworkers Federation.[3]

The union movement has also shown its capacity to act locally. Within Australia unions have been able to organise massive community support against unfair business practices. A good example is the Oakdale workers' victory, where retrenched coalminers won a campaign to be put at the top of the creditors' list when the company went broke. This campaign also resulted in the Federal Government being forced to allow access to worker superannuation to mitigate against financial hardship for redundant workers – setting a precedent for similar campaigns around the country.[4]

Effective in their own way, none of these campaigns have derailed the corporate agenda. For example, there have recently been closed-door talks where the leading MNCs are demanding quasi-membership of the United Nations. Their argument is very simple: many MNCs have greater assets and revenues than many countries, and employ more people than many national governments. They believe therefore that they have the right to have more representation and direct input into UN policy-making.

For organised labour this is a disturbing development, as very few corporations have positive attitudes to unions and many have sided with conservative national governments in arguing whether the world needs institutions such as the International Labour Organisation (ILO). The ILO, as the UN's oldest committee, is central to overseeing the core labour conventions that protect workers globally.

Disgruntled Rio Tinto coalminers demonstrate their frustration with the company outside the Rio Tinto Annual General Meeting in Brisbane, 2000.

Photo by Nina Lansbury, Mineral Policy Institute

Why Rio Tinto? Why Us?

Although not the wealthiest MNC, Rio Tinto does hold a special place within global industry, and is viewed as the company that sets the benchmark for behaviour in the mining sector. Now the third largest mining company in the world, it employs approximately 51,000 people directly and through associated companies. Many more are employed as sub-contractors or derive their living from company activities. Rio Tinto operates over 60 mines and plants in 40 countries. It has a long reach and many friends in high places.[5]

Much has been written about Rio Tinto over its 127-year history. The company has been aptly compared to a modern day Dutch East India Company. Rapacious in its drive to seek massive profits, the company has used many tactics to undermine environmental, human rights and worker organisations. Driven by what it terms the 'geological imperative', Rio Tinto has bulldozed its way across communities, using workers as resources to be exploited and expended in the same way as the minerals it mines. As with latter day companies of the 17th and 18th centuries, Rio Tinto has often enjoyed the support of national governments in pursuing its goals.

In recent years the company has used some clever ploys in de-unionising its workforce. It has appealed to the sense of individualism of some workers, claiming it is best for a company to have a direct relationship with an employee rather than having to work through a third party such as a union. This situation is 'conducive' to a flexible arrangement that not only serves the company, but (so the claim is made) also allows the employee greater freedom to realise their true potential. In the case of the workforce at Hammersley Iron in Western Australia the majority of miners chose individual contracts, the appeal being higher wages for those agreeing to give up union membership.

For some union members at the Weipa Bauxite mine in Queensland, the offer of worker-company contracts was not attractive. These workers refused to take up the company offer, preferring instead to stick with the union system. To pressure the remaining union members into leaving the CFMEU, Rio Tinto paid non-union workers at Weipa more for doing exactly the same work as those represented by the union. After a long battle, the company was found guilty of discrimination against union members at Weipa by the Australian Industrial Relations Commission.[6]

Other strategies used by the company have been more devious. In 1997, Rio Tinto allowed one of its senior executives to work on secondment to the right-wing Liberal/National coalition government in Australia to draft new Federal legislation on workplace reform. That legislation was subsequently found to breach core conventions of the United Nations' International Labour Organisation. In this move Rio Tinto curried favour with the government and furthered its own objectives by changing the regulatory processes.

The impact of cost cutting and de-unionisation in some regions in Australia has been devastating. Rio Tinto cut a swathe through coal-mining communities in the Hunter Valley. Only 28 per cent of Rio Tinto's workforce survived the first six years of Rio Tinto ownership of the Hunter Valley mines. When Rio Tinto acquired Coal & Allied's mines in the Hunter Valley there were 1,695 employees at five mines. By 1999 the workforce had been decimated down to 487 employees at two mines, a cut of 1,208 jobs.

This had a significant impact on the local economy. It is estimated that for every one job lost in a coalmine, two to three were lost in the local economy. Lack of money in the community has led to a lowering of house prices, closure of small businesses and staff laid off. In general, the financial wellbeing of the whole community was undermined. Many of the workers in coalmines are semi-skilled or unskilled. Those who lost their jobs found it very hard to sell or even rent their homes in what had by then become a depressed area, thus making moving to another area for work all the more difficult.

Long term, the financial impact of social dislocation in the Hunter Valley was borne by the State government and taxpayers through social security and community employment projects. Those enjoying the profits – the executives, the individual shareholders and the investor corporations, escaped paying the social cost of Rio Tinto's industrial policy. The company claimed to help, putting $3 million AU$ over three years into a community trust fund – but which was operated and controlled by Rio Tinto. This was not meaningful compensation. Compared to the annual salary of the company Chief Executive Officer (AU$876,000 in 1997), and the tens of millions lost in workers wages, the company's voluntary donation was woefully inadequate. The Hunter Valley was not alone in suffering from Rio Tinto's approach. Negative impacts have been felt by many other communities.

In Indonesia, small-scale gold-miners lost their livelihoods when the Kelian goldmine was bought by Rio Tinto. Fishermen and subsistence farmers were forcibly removed by the company from land surrounding the site. Pollution from the operation made locally produced foodstuffs too contaminated to eat. Often the local water supply, used for bathing and drinking, was polluted by siltation resulting from mining operations, or contamination from toxic chemicals such as cyanide. All of this was having a direct and indirect impact on the health of the local community. Community Aid Abroad campaigned in Indonesia and Australia to get the company to clean up its act, pay compensation and make redress where possible, such as providing water pipes for villages. While some issues have been settled, others remain to be dealt with, in particular the contentious issue of human rights abuses linked to the mining operations.[7]

Here are two examples of very different communities confronted with different problems, but united on one issue, with the common factor in their problems being Rio Tinto. Examples such as these highlighted the need for an information exchange system, based on a network of those faced with dealing directly with the company, whether in Australia or overseas. That network later expanded to include many organisations which, although not immediately concerned with Rio Tinto's operations, were concerned at the publicity being distributed by the company as it sought to present itself as an 'ethical' corporation. For example, whilst it was attacking unions in Australia, Rio Tinto made much of its signing of the Universal Declaration on Human Rights (UDHR) in 1998 – the 50th anniversary of the convention. Rio Tinto also refers to the UDHR in its Statement of Business practice, *The way we work,* although it also took pains to note the document was *not* a Code of Conduct for which it could be held to account. However, in even this non-binding document the company took care not to mention unions, despite the fact Article 23.4 of the UDHR states, 'Everyone has the right to form and to join trade unions for the protection of his/her interests.'[8]

In a stinging rebuke to Rio Tinto's Statement, and its signing of the UDHR, the International Conference of Free Trade Unions (ICFTU) sent a critique to the company pointing out where it had failed to recognise over 20 international labour and human rights conventions. In the three years since the ICFTU wrote to the company's Chairman, the company has not made any effort to amend its Statement of Business Practice to reflect the concerns of the ICFTU critique.

The Campaign

The above gives some idea of the issues that form the backdrop to the campaign network which was established in early 1998. This kicked off with a visit of campaigners from the Indonesian Environmental Forum (WALHI), Community Aid Abroad (Oxfam in Australia) and village representatives from the Rio Tinto-controlled Kelian goldmine in Kalimantan, Indonesia. These representatives met with striking miners and other trade union members from the Hunter Valley collieries in NSW at a major Stop Work meeting. Over the following months, a number of one-to-one meetings were held with NGOs as well as informal networking meetings, to discuss what measures should be taken to highlight problems associated with the company. Out of these meetings came a landmark stakeholders' report *Tainted Titan,* a fully-referenced, 60-page report containing case studies on the human rights, worker rights, and the health and environmental impacts of a range of Rio Tinto operations.[9] *Tainted Titan* also contained a section on the economic situation of the company, explaining the unsustainability of its practices. To accompany the report, a short video was produced that explained the background to the campaign. Much to Rio Tinto's annoyance, this video contained some damning historical footage of the company's overseas activities. With these initiations, the foundations for an information campaign were laid.

For the union, an especially important aspect of the campaign was to show that some company operations were profiting not through *real* gains in efficiencies, but simply through cutting back on environmental protection and through refusing to properly compensate for health and financial damage resulting from company activities. Down sizing the workforce was also shown to be a short-term first measure which was failing to make the gains that the company had said it would. A company can only sack so many workers before its operations become untenable. In the case of Rio Tinto, they were driving very hard, very fast to the lowest number.

Not surprisingly, Rio Tinto's response to *Tainted Titan* was to claim that some of the issues raised were irrelevant, particularly to discussions about industrial relations policy. Rio Tinto also said that NGOs should only deal with the company as single groups, not as coalitions. If a coalition did exist it had to be around a single theme, such as environmental issues. Thus, while Rio Tinto was busily building lobby networks within the national and international mining industry it was attempting to impose an altogether different model on those who were critical of it. The company steadfastly refused to accept that its behaviour as a whole should be under scrutiny.

Most of the groups involved in *Tainted Titan* felt they did benefit from exchanging information and from the opportunity to undertake joint work even though there were many different views within the network. For example, some of those involved wanted to stop Rio Tinto undertaking any more mining projects, while some just wanted the company to have proper community consultation processes for all its projects. Others were seeking compensation for past activities of the company, and others still wanted the company to set down and implement broad principles on issues such as human rights conventions.

What Rio Tinto failed to appreciate in attacking the network as a whole was that no individual or organisation involved in the network was under the illusion that the network was working towards a set of commonly held goals, or that all the motives were the same. The main objective was to work strategically and opportunistically to force Rio Tinto, first and foremost, to acknowledge its responsibilities and begin to negotiate appropriately with various stakeholders over their concerns. In its attacks on the network, the company succeeded in bringing the network members closer together.

However, it cannot be ignored that within the network there were different approaches – for example, what was the best way to communicate with the company, if at all? Some groups believed one-to-one dialogue was appropriate, although all agreed that collective discussions would also prove useful. The call was made for a round table meeting with Rio Tinto management and stakeholders from within Australia and the region.

The company had already held meetings with some NGOs in London and Australia. Most of the NGOs that attended these meetings had no direct involvement in Rio's operations, or had only a tangential interest in its activities.

The agenda for these meetings was set by the company and very closely controlled by the management. Rio Tinto had invited very few organisations that had been critical of it, and because of this the first UK meeting was boycotted by a number of groups. Most noticeable was that no union had been invited!

The question of how to address these issues was something each organisation had to deal with itself at different levels and for different issues. For the unions, their main responsibilities lay in servicing and protecting their members, regardless of whatever other action it might have liked to undertake within the network, such as exposing corporate greed in general. The unions exist to represent their members and workers in getting the best conditions possible on wages and safety. This places an over-arching obligation on them to meet with companies and enter into negotiations even when other organisations might have refused.

For the CFMEU, this proved to be something of a dilemma as the union has a long history of supporting social justice issues. As a key player on the industrial and labour scene over the past 100 years in Australia, the CFMEU's views have helped shape government and trade union policy on a number of issues, including Australia's response to apartheid South Africa. In relation to Rio Tinto, the union was keenly aware of the violent repression of the indigenous people in West Papua by security forces guarding Freeport and Rio Tinto's Grasberg mine (see chapter 4). Likewise, the union was acutely aware of the failure by Rio Tinto to reach a settlement with the Aboriginal people from the Weipa district. Local representatives of both the traditional owners and union knew each other well; there was a common bond. Indeed, through involvement with the Weipa issue, CFMEU officials have become directly aware of the company's 'divide and rule' tactics. This included the way the company has controlled discussion on (now settled) payments to the traditional owners through a confidentiality clause that stopped anyone from talking about the negotiations.

This tactic was also employed by Rio Tinto in its dealings with NGOs. Many people reported back after discussions with company representatives that they had been told if they spoke openly about the company, or exchanged information, they would become part of the 'outer circle' of groups which Rio Tinto would refuse to meet. Similarly, the legal representatives of the unions were restricted by the protocol of the legal system from fully discussing negotiations with Rio Tinto. Those most closely involved in discussions with Rio Tinto, whether in unions or NGOs, did not believe that every piece of information should be made publicly available or the subject of a press release. However, they recognised it was essential that as many as possible knew what Rio Tinto was saying and doing, and that a very discrete information exchange system was needed. It was equally important that the company was aware that information was being exchanged not just at a national level but internationally, and that its 'gagging orders' had not worked in stopping the flow.

While courting relatively uncritical NGOs, Rio Tinto refused to establish round table talks with the contributors to the first stakeholder report. When *Tainted Titan* was issued, Rio Tinto fought back by issuing a reply shortly after, that failed to address the substantive issues of the stakeholder concerns. The company then appeared to decide to avoid any interaction with the network, choosing the tactic of 'no reply' as more revelations came over the following months. The company retreated, invariably making little or no response to accusations over worker right abuses, legal cases from indigenous people or environmental damage. Meanwhile, the campaign was starting to have a political impact. For example, the union utilised Parliamentary support by getting Early Day Motions tabled in the United Kingdom's House of Commons for two years in succession. These criticised the company over its record on workers rights and its operations in West Papua. Several Members of Parliament signed up to the first motion. This was not a huge number, but enough to surprise Rio Tinto, which has always guarded its reputation in the UK more jealously than in other countries.

Publicly, Rio Tinto may have been silent, but it was far from inactive. The company made every effort to gather support for its operations, particularly in the UK, where the understanding of ethical investment and corporate practices was more advanced than in Australia. It seemed particularly keen to reinforce its image in its homeland rather than deal with criticism from overseas. There were good reasons for this, as hearings in front of the European Parliament had resulted in recommendations that mandatory codes of practice be enforced for European-based companies operating overseas. Rio Tinto had got wind of the fact that it had been suggested as the ideal test-case company for a European Parliament investigation.

Campaigners kept up the pressure. In 1999 the second stakeholder publication, *Behind the Façade*, was published to coincide with the Rio Tinto Annual General Meeting (AGM). Presented as a report back, it detailed how Rio Tinto had failed to move on key issues despite the 'concerns' expressed by some company executives

177

at some aspects of the company's operations. For example, in early 1999, Leon Davis, then chairman, had attempted to distance the company from the Soeharto regime in Indonesia – one of the worst (and most recent) examples of the company's liaison with a government known for human rights abuses.

For the workers in the Hunter Valley, despite the occasional win in the Industrial Relations Commission and a dogged determination by sacked workers to keep the pressure up on the ground, and apart from strike action in the Australia coalfields, very little was making the company rein in its managers. The company had claimed individual managers made decisions on industrial policy based on their individual operational needs. However, no one in the union campaign was so naï ve as to think that individual managers were acting alone and not following company orders.

In late 1999, the international trade union movement was finally in a position to consolidate work on the campaign that had been building for two years. The union organisations taking part included the Australian Construction, Forestry, Mining and Energy Union (CFMEU), the Australian Council of Trade Unions (ACTU), the American Federation of Labor and Congress of Industrial Organisations (AFL–CIO), the Trade Union Congress (TUC), the International Federation of Chemical, Energy, Mine and General Workers' Unions (ICEM), and the British Trades Union Congress (BTUC).

Through lobbying with financial fund and company law experts, the campaign gained the backing of investors with over £28 billion (A\$73 billion) in assets to give support to two union-initiated shareholder resolutions at Rio Tinto AGMs. In 2000 these resolutions demanded that the Rio Tinto Board of Directors become more accountable to its shareholders through the appointment of a single, independent, non-executive Deputy Chairman, and that the company adopt the International Labour Organisation's conventions on human rights. The aim was to bring pressure to bear from financial quarters, rather than rely on the moral arguments to change Rio Tinto's approach to workers' rights. Not surprisingly, Rio Tinto knew it would be under greater pressure through a campaign exploiting financial clout, rather than just moral arguments. The resolutions attracted a remarkable level of support from financial institutions in the UK and internationally.

Suddenly, the criteria by which key shareholders judged the company were bought into sharp focus. None of those approached to support the union campaign had ever had the issues of workers' rights raised with them, but were open to discussing them further. Unfortunately, the environment issue did not rate much mention, for despite promises they would produce an environment report in time for the 1998 or 1999 AGMs, the company did not. Rio Tinto, like so many other companies, had never had to put this type of issue before its shareholders. This is because they are not required to under corporate regulations and had never been challenged by major shareholders over the lack of information.

As one of the few dual-listed companies in the world, Rio Tinto faced an unexpected hurdle by having to face protests and resolutions at both its Annual General Meeting in the UK, then in Australia. Decisions made by the largely UK-based executive also had to be faced in Australia, where the potential for stakeholders from the region to participate is much greater. Media attention was sought in Australia as well as in the UK. These are aspects of 'globalisation' that international companies would rather live without.

Conclusion

While some companies talk of the double bottom line of profits and environment, few talk of the triple bottom line: profits, environment and community/social impacts. The companies claim that shareholders have a right to expect high rates of dividend regardless of the environmental or human rights costs of an operation. It is for this reason that multinational corporations work hard at keeping the stakeholders and shareholders in enmity, or at a distance.

No one single action or stakeholder brought about the change in Rio Tinto's awareness to address the triple bottom line. Before the shareholder action and resolutions could be used, the campaign relied on the interests and support of a variety of organisations and individuals. This helped keep up the pressure at the time when the union needed support. The additional input from superannuation companies assisted to put much of the political lobby work into a form the shareholders could understand and to which they could respond.

The most important role in this campaign was played by the union membership. No organisation as controlled by the rank and file as the CFMEU can mount such an enormous campaign without the full support of the membership. The membership of the CFMEU, especially those employed by Rio Tinto, contributed enormously to the campaign in numerous ways – through financial support to the campaign, through taking industrial action (with some cases lasting over 12 months), and through disciplined action at the sites.

The campaign would not have lasted without the support of the members' families and friends. When a worker goes on strike or is wrongfully dismissed, the dispute is taken home from the worksite to the family home, where support is crucial. The community supported the campaign because they knew the drive to protect communities and families from corporate giants was central to the campaign.

Those most intimately involved in this campaign in the union are all too well aware of the enormous hardships that families endure during a protracted dispute. Lack of money, facing a harsh media, and a divisive corporate campaign is not easy. It is perhaps this aspect that makes a union campaign very distinct from many other campaigns.

Without united action in the mining industry, collective bargaining would disappear from negotiations on pay and safety, damaging whole communities irreparably. Ironically, despite Rio Tinto's persistence to de-unionise the Australian coal industry and weaken this unity, union membership has actually increased following this campaign. Additionally, Rio Tinto has concluded collective agreements at all CFMEU mine sites in the past year and dropped a major damages claim against unions. These successes demonstrate and reinforce that workers' interests as stakeholders, and their surrounding social and natural environment are as important as those of financial shareholders in determining company policy.

11 Engagement or confrontation?
Ruth Phillips

Introduction

Advocacy efforts of many social movement non-government organisations (NGOs) have traditionally focused on the state and inter-state institutions to monitor and change the behaviour of multinational corporations (MNCs). However, in the context of globalisation, they are now turning their advocacy efforts towards corporations. The global mining industry has long been the focus of NGOs established specifically to monitor, research, analyse and protest against mining activities. In the current context, even the most critical NGOs are now being faced with the prospect of engaging with corporations. The global mining industry is actively seeking out NGOs for dialogue, negotiation and in some cases, partnership. Additionally, NGOs are initiating engagement with corporations as a strategy for change in some of their advocacy campaigns and wider activities. These new relationships are described as 'corporate engagement'.

In a discussion about emerging relationships between social movement NGOs and corporations, the broader context of globalisation must be considered. Globalisation is best thought of as sets of processes – technological, financial, economic, social, environmental and cultural. Globalisation has become central to ideas about the contemporary world and is important in this discussion as a site of resistance and change for social movements and the NGOs that identify with, or are directly attached to, those movements. It is also important as an operational context for mining MNCs. Controversial issues in the extractive industries have been drawn to the attention of a wider public, thereby expanding corporations' perceptions of their responsibilities, highlighting the need to review operational behaviour.

The ways that NGOs choose to operate within the globalised context mirror the complexity of the processes of globalisation and can be seen to play a part in democratisation and the strengthening of a global civil society through empowerment and capacity building of local communities affected by mining activities. The growth in developing relationships between NGOs and MNCs is part of that complexity.

This chapter explores ideas of corporate citizenship and corporate engagement and reflects on the process of engagement. The discussion draws on case study research into Oxfam Community Aid Abroad's Mining Campaign. By focusing on the early part of the campaign, the discussion highlights key issues for consideration when corporate engagement advocacy is adopted as a strategy for change.

Engaging the Corporate Citizen

The idea of 'corporate citizenship' appears to have emerged from corporate vulnerability to attacks on 'reputational capital'.[1] It is a widely discussed idea about how contemporary corporations should behave, socially, environmentally and financially. It relies on a view of corporations having a significant role in the global context and encourages a strong sense of responsibility for the effects and impact of their activities. This is particularly the case for high profile MNCs. Part of being a corporate citizen is the ability to communicate with and 'work' with all the 'stakeholders' in the communities in which the corporation operates. Stakeholders are generally thought of as the constituencies affected by decision making. Corporations have traditionally limited stakeholders to shareholders (and perhaps workers), but now broadened this concept through efforts of 'corporate citizenship' to include all groups, organisations, governments and communities with an interest in the activities of the company.[2]

In 1998, the global mining giant Rio Tinto produced its own corporate citizenship script in the form of a publication entitled *The Way We Work*. This policy statement sets out a formula for ensuring

Rio Tinto's reputational capital. On the topic of human rights, for example, it states:

'Rio Tinto supports and protects the dignity, well being, and rights of those with whom it is directly involved: its employees and their families, and the local communities, which are neighbours of its operations ... employment and communities policies commit operations to making a positive contribution to their development through a relationship based on mutual respect. Infringements of their rights by others will be opposed, through dialogue and, where it will be helpful, in public ... [Rio Tinto] is guided by the values of the international community that human rights should be protected and promoted everywhere.'[3]

This policy document was produced in the UK and is used for all Rio Tinto operations. According to a Rio Tinto executive, one of the reasons it was produced was due to the negative reputational experiences of large British-based oil companies, Shell and BP, part of an extractive industry group with whom Rio Tinto identifies.[4]

For many with a history of struggling with Rio Tinto either as activists, advocates, workers or affected peoples, this rhetoric is surprising and possibly engenders scepticism. The International Confederation of Free Trade Unions (ICFTU), in a response to *The Way We Work*, pointed out the corporation's failure to, 'refer to two of the most authoritative, internationally-agreed definitions of responsible behaviour for multinational companies, that is, the International Labour Organisation's Declaration of Principles and the Organisation for Economic Cooperation and Development's Guidelines'.[5] They also noted the statement lacked transparency and was not accompanied by a plan for implementation, thus appearing to be little more than a public relations exercise.

A key question relates to how the new rhetoric is reflected in changed practice. Is there a perceptible change in the behaviour of Rio Tinto or other corporations with their new 'citizenship' profile? This is not only a vital question for corporations choosing to reconstruct themselves but also for the NGOs who are drawn into it via the engagement process. Is *believing* in the potential capacity of corporations to change their practices an important precondition for engagement with them? According to the advocacy framework of two key Oxfam UK members, NGOs can be motivated by a strategic approach to advocacy that dictates starting with the 'target' rather than the 'typology'. This means that NGOs embarking on advocacy for change should aim to 'understand' what would influence the 'target' (the corporation) to change. As the application of advocacy to corporations is relatively new, it leads to an 'engagement first' approach before moving to confrontation.[6] In other words, without entering into some initial engagement with corporations it is impossible to know or understand whether engagement will result in the outcomes sought by the advocacy strategy.

For corporations, corporate citizenship is a means to draw NGOs into engagement because corporations believe either that they *can* change and behave better socially or environmentally, or that engagement in itself will improve the reputational outlook for the corporation. This is evidenced by the, now common, references in corporate annual reports that list 'dialogue' or engagement with NGOs as a measure of social or environmental contributions to community development.

A key argument for NGOs initiating corporate engagement is based on the notion that corporate power outweighs the power of governments. The global dominance of neo-liberal economic policies, the global push for deregulation and the increased dependence on private investment as aid for development is an argument for the inevitability of corporate engagement.[7] This is particularly the case for development or social justice NGOs, where poverty and the redistribution of wealth are central issues.

For NGOs to be motivated to engage, there needs to be a belief that people running corporations want to see their corporation act with 'civility', with the objective of changing their practices. NGOs also have to confront the issue of whether their influence can override the structural logic of corporate power, the corporate necessity to accumulate capital, and the drive for profit. This is critical in arguments against any form of engagement with corporations, as market capitalism challenges the redistributive and equity principles pursued by many social movement NGOs.

NGOs have become key figures in 'corporate citizenship' discourse and debates.[8] For some NGOs, new corporate citizens are simply 'wolves dressed in sheep's clothing'. Underneath the rhetoric, they are just as naked in their greed and exploitation as they have ever been. MNCs are seen as part of a global corporate structure that controls the world's resources, dictating agendas for inter-state institutions (such as the World Trade Organisation) and nation states.[9] For other NGOs, however, there is a belief that corporations do have the capacity to change and this is played out in their responsiveness and efforts to behave differently. Evidence is available to demonstrate better, sensitive corporate behaviour.[10] However, there also continues to be extensive documentation and protest about current activities and poor behaviour of corporations that contradict 'corporate citizenship' discourse and aspirations. Recent Australian research showed that there is a very low level of embedded corporate citizenship amongst Australian corporations. Although aware of trends overseas, few had prioritised issues such as environment or social impact in their corporate objectives.[11]

Mining MNCs

Mining corporations have specific characteristics that limit their capacity to act as 'good' corporate citizens. For example, they cannot transform themselves as the global chemical corporations have, now calling themselves 'life sciences corporations' and focusing their efforts on seeds and biotechnology.[12] Neither can they adopt the stance of major oil companies now claiming to be injecting massive amounts of capital into alternative, 'greener', energy development.

Mining is simple, it occurs at a certain site or it doesn't. Mining MNCs cannot avoid the fact that wherever they operate, it will have a devastating impact on the surrounding environment and communities. Therefore, the only way to do mining better is to ensure that the impact of mining is kept to a minimum and the reparations of damage – environmental, social, cultural and economic – are addressed in some way.

The mining industry is concerned with its long-term commercial sustainability, as evidenced by its collective effort to address its own sustainability with campaigns such as the Global Mining Initiative, a project led by the major international mining corporations. However, the broader, more crucial question of whether mining is a sustainable activity in terms of a viable global ecology is dismissed as the 'no mining stance' by mining corporations.

Challenging mining as a sustainable practice has been the objective, for many years, of numerous environmental NGOs concerned with a sustainable future. Anti-mining campaigners have found a relatively recent alliance with indigenous peoples' movements against mining. Because most of the world's remaining mineral and metal resources are located in developing countries and in remote regions occupied by indigenous peoples, these concerns have become the focus of a number of environmental, human rights and development NGOs.

Lipschutz describes an increasing linkage between human rights and environmental organisations arising out of the concern, 'that large-scale, environmentally destructive projects often displace large numbers of the poor and disempowered, whose rights to land are routinely ignored'.[13]

These new linkages of solidarity social movements have forced issues onto 'global' political agendas, and become a major factor behind corporate citizenship. It has become impossible for MNCs to ignore the popularity of such movements. This politicisation has materialised around specific cases that have publicly revealed damaging corporate practices.

The role of Shell Corporation in Nigeria and the opposition they face from the indigenous Ogoni people, and the environmental and social devastation created by BHP's Ok Tedi mine in Papua New Guinea, are examples from a long list of high profile, internationally publicised cases that have motivated corporate executives to take a hard look at their own 'reputational capital'.

Shell Corporation has not only attempted to reconstruct its image in Nigeria but has had a global advertising campaign under way for some years to build a green, human rights friendly, reputation. In 1996, BHP was forced to make a $150 million out of court compensation pay out for people living along the Ok Tedi and Fly rivers who were adversely affected by their mine.[14]

Since acknowledging the extent of the environmental and consequential social and local economic damage in 1999, BHP engaged in a frenzy of 'dialogue'/consultation with a wide range of NGOs in Australia, in an attempt to proceed in the least damaging way. However, BHP's intentions to rid itself of responsibility for the mine by selling its majority share became clear in 2000. The PNG Government, affected local communities and Australian NGOs are fighting this move, as they believe that, by withdrawing from the mine, BHP will withdraw from its long-term responsibility for the extensive damage created by the mine.

Corporate Engagement

Corporate engagement can take a number of possible forms. Engagement that merely seeks to gain the attention of a corporation, for example, can be limited to the well-practised confrontational form. It might be argued that confrontation is not engagement and it is better described as a form of protest. However, as the case study discussed later demonstrates, it can be effective as a first step in an engagement. It is suggested that confrontation is located at the 'least involved' end of a continuum of forms of engagement that include confrontation, negotiation, collaboration, partnership and sponsorship.[15] This is important for NGOs aiming to maintain integrity and credibility when contesting corporate power. Sponsorship is the 'most involved' form of engagement, and often reflects a fixed, co-optive relationship between a corporation and an NGO, implying a lack of critical independence for the NGO. It is suggested that confrontation and negotiation are strategic forms, and that consultation and collaboration are constructive forms of engagement. There is overlap in 'real life', however, as different issues will generate different demands on both parties.

A major question that arises from a polarised debate within the NGO community about the appropriateness of corporate engagement, is whether or not it can be an effective strategy for social change or democratisation or whether NGOs are simply being seduced and silenced by MNCs. NGO participation in corporate engagement is also part of what might be considered an emergent role in international relations. NGOs are clearly visible on the world stage, involved in processes of mediation, advocacy, negotiation, policy development and protest. This is part of an improved, technologically assisted effort in making a difference in the context of globalisation. The role of NGOs must not be underestimated, as they have managed in the last two decades or so to wield influence in contexts and situations that have previously been out of bounds to them.

Primarily driven by the failure of the modern era to address issues of environmentalism, poverty and social injustice, cross-national social movements have emerged as a new form of 'democracy', representing the 'voices' of many beyond the confines of the nation state. This idea is epitomised by Korten's ideas for a 'post-corporate world' where he envisages 'life after capitalism', a place where the people have defined, 'a new core culture, a new political centre and a new economic mainstream'.[16] Korten views new social movements and the NGOs that have emerged from them as a global democracy movement and as a key force in the future transformation of capitalism away from corporate dominance. Here, social movements and NGOs acting as transformative agents can clash with the more accommodating NGOs seeking to work with the corporate sector. Why are the latter, 'self-appointed stakeholders',[17] taking this approach?

The Engagement Experience: The CAA Mining Campaign

Oxfam Community Aid Abroad (CAA) is a development NGO with a long tradition as a non-secular organisation that has attracted broad support for its diverse, unconventional approach to its project work and its willingness to campaign on key political issues. This includes its early, and ongoing, support for East Timor and Australian indegenous land rights.[18]

In 1997, CAA launched its Indonesian Mining Campaign. This was prompted by a shift in CAA towards rights-based advocacy campaigns and requests from mining affected peoples in Kalimantan, Indonesia. There was also a growing awareness of the role of Australian mining MNCs in the South-east Asian region and the impact it was having on local peoples. These included human rights violations, displacement from land, destruction of natural resources vital for local people and the cessation of access to traditional mining.

The campaign evolved into what is now called the Mining Campaign and employs a range of approaches, including protest and confrontation, negotiation, dialogue, collaboration on codes of conduct and the promotion of regulations and legislative measures.

For CAA, the campaign's most tangible success was its support for peoples affected by two mines in Kalimantan, namely Rio Tinto's Kelian mine, and Aurora Gold's Indo Muro Kencana mine. Initially, CAA worked with and funded the Indonesian umbrella environment group, WALHI, and other Indonesian NGOs, to bring local Dayak people and other local peoples to Australia for a month to conduct a publicity tour highlighting injustice and damage caused by the mines.

This visit was significant as it saw CAA orchestrating engagement with mining corporations. After the publicity tour, CAA and the Dayak people met with Rio Tinto, with the objective to get

Rio Tinto to direct their Kelian mine management to meet and negotiate with community representatives. The outcome was a series of meetings that continued throughout 1997 to 1998. By mid 1998, Rio Tinto agreed to pay close to $1 million compensation to 440 families they had evicted in 1991.

Following this compensation, Rio Tinto at Kelian continued to negotiate the supply of a clean water supply, the sealing of roads and other infrastructure needs. A key CAA actor in the campaign observed:

'From the community's point of view, they see it as the company at last fulfilling what was promised back in 1991. The company just sees it as spending money on community relations. Whatever the reasons, it is keeping both sides happy. It was only when NGOs started creating a problem for them, that [Rio Tinto] started looking for a solution.'[19]

An executive from Rio Tinto confirmed that CAA's participation had drawn their attention to the need to act, describing their action as a 'wake up call' and commenting it was: '... a painful beginning, from our point of view, but in the end a useful process because it made us re-engage in the compensation issues there. And without CAA, would we have focused to the extent that we had at the time? I think we would have. At least we would have here – but would we have got the attention of our colleagues in Indonesia at the same level? Probably not as fast but, ultimately, I still think we would have because I don't think they understood the extent to which the company had opened up. It might have been a bit of a surprise to CAA. They thought they were fighting against a closed door and it was much more open than they thought it was.'[20]

There were two key elements in CAA's advocacy approach that brought about an initially successful outcome. The shock value of taking confrontational action as a first step probably precipitated the positive response from Rio Tinto. The publicity generated by the jointly organised 'protest' tour got the attention of the company. CAA's follow-up attempt to establish negotiations between the local people and the Kelian mine managers through dialogue with the Australian head office executives of the company was a successful strategy. Clearly, there was a positive outcome in this early experience of corporate engagement.

This single positive outcome did not mean that all problems and conflicts were solved in the Kelian community. Many injustices remained unresolved and the relationship between the local community and mine management resumed a high level of discord and tension.

For example, in 2000, the mine was temporarily closed due to protests against the mine, suggesting that the conciliatory approach of mine management was short-lived.

The campaign targeting Aurora Gold was not successful. It was eighteen months before the company even sat down and talked with local people in July 1999. CAA was not directly involved in any of the meetings with the local people but, along with other groups, helped to bring the company to the negotiating table. They achieved this through meetings and telephone calls with Aurora executives in Australia and in July 1998 had obtained a written agreement from the company that it would act to resolve some of the Dayak's grievances.[21] Three years after the written agreement was made, most issues remain unresolved.

The dispute at Aurora Gold's Indo Muro Kencana mine with the local Dayak villages of Siang, Murung and Bekumpai, began with the opening of the mine in 1987. There was no consultation with local people and the company deeply offended the Dayak people by removing graves at the mine site. The local community considered the mining company responsible for the condemnation of traditional mines by use of force, claiming house burning, destruction of traditional mining apparatus, and the imprisonment of hundreds of traditional miners for illegal mining. There was also the loss of an entire village and the displacement of 8,000 people from their homeland due to deforestation of surrounding land.

At Aurora Gold's first meeting with CAA, the company, 'held on to their fundamental principles of their operations in Indonesia, rejected any responsibilities for any loss that occurred in the past [having taken over the mine in 1993] and refused to ever acknowledge the existence of the indigenous lands of the people'.[22] The company claimed it was being restrained in its response by Indonesian laws that don't recognise indigenous land rights and an agreement with the Indonesian government that stipulates no sharing of their lease with another party.

From the Indonesian NGO perspective, Aurora Gold demonstrated a lack of flexibility in their approach, especially in their refusal to acknowledge the adverse economic and cultural impact the mine had on the Dayak people. The following summed up the community reaction:

'After being kept waiting for more than ten years, the community discovered that their problems remained unsolved. When the company agreed to meet them, they thought that their problems would soon end. On the contrary, the company's response towards their claims has truly and deeply hurt their feelings.'[23]

There was no demonstrated willingness on the company's behalf to compromise or look for alternative solutions to the problems, and their response created more hostility. An acknowledgment of the impact of the mine may have engendered a sense of understanding and created common ground. For companies attempting to build positive linkages with communities affected by their operations, acknowledgment of their responsibility is important. Aurora Gold claimed it wanted to work 'in partnership' with the local community.[24]

However, they were unwilling to negotiate with the Yayasan Bina Sumber Daya (YBSD), an NGO made up of 34 representatives with the authority to negotiate on behalf of 2,292 Dayak families. The company did not believe YBSD represented the people living around the mine despite the fact that they were endorsed and supported by national Indonesian NGOs and were the key contact for CAA in the mining-affected community.

Although CAA has continued to maintain 'dialogue' with Aurora in Australia, there has been little success. The current status of the Dayak/Aurora engagement, three years later, is that the local people are considering legal action, having reached no satisfactory response from the company.[25] The engagement strategy that worked well initially with Rio Tinto did not precipitate the same response from Aurora Gold. There are many likely reasons for this, but clearly, the physical distance and the lack of personal contact between Aurora executives and CAA had some impact.

Rio Tinto is based in Melbourne and CAA had some advantage through personal networks and physical co-location. Personal contact can be the 'critical element' that makes NGO/business 'partnerships happen and produce results'.[26] Another 'failure' in the Aurora/CAA relationship may be the lack of local research on CAA's part. According to an Aurora Executive, CAA never sent anyone to visit the mine or its local community.[27]

This was partly due to CAA's position of not accepting any financial assistance for travel (or any other purpose) from the companies they were engaging with. A danger in being involved in relationships from a distance highlights one of the broader dangers of a developed/developing country NGO-advocacy relationship, and suggests that effective advocacy requires an in-depth understanding of local issues from the people involved.

Advocacy work is time-consuming and expensive.[28] This can mean, in a broader sense, that corporate engagement ends up being exploitative for the NGO. Corporations have a tendency to utilise their new found stakeholder NGOs as free consultants, always ready to exploit the expertise of NGO workers. Part of the paradox of competing agendas between NGOs and corporations is that corporations are very good at exploiting all resources available to them, placing NGOs in danger of becoming another resource.

Conclusion

In discussing the details of only two examples in a long-term CAA campaign, this chapter opens up a small insight into the complexity of corporate engagement as an NGO advocacy strategy. It is not a fair examination of CAA's efforts in a campaign that has taught them and other NGOs many lessons. However, the CAA Mining Campaign reflects a controversial direction for NGOs in a context that challenges all NGOs to consider the role of MNCs in the global political economy.

Corporate engagement may bring about real, improved outcomes for some people affected by mining or other industries, but it is a risky and not always fruitful strategy. Through the Mining Campaign and other concurrent campaigns, CAA has widened its advocacy role in recognition of structural and institutional barriers to development. But as grassroots and local NGOs develop the capacity to conduct their own development strategies, CAA, like many international development NGOs, directs its efforts towards wider advocacy processes. This goes beyond strategies focused on state and inter-state institutions. The corporate sector, in the global context, looms large in issues that directly affect poverty, human rights and development.

The Aurora Gold and Rio Tinto engagement examples illustrate the many factors that can affect the corporate engagement advocacy process. The willingness of companies to address demands made by local communities is in direct relation to their initial approach and their capacity to respond to those demands. The principle of recognising issues specific to indigenous people as a human rights issue is central to good corporate citizenship, management and practice. If this requires corporations to influence contractual agreements with states unwilling to recognise land rights, like Indonesia, there would be significant advantages for those corporations in avoiding ongoing conflict and disputes as in the Aurora Gold case.

A key objective in CAA's campaign was to support indigenous and local people to create a more level negotiation process. Maintaining dialogue with, and pressure on, Australian based corporate executives may bring about longer-term transformations in the way the mining sector behaves in remote, developing country mines. However, demonstrating solidarity with communities that seek to resist mines being imposed on their communities, is crucial. Partnerships between better-resourced, developed country NGOs and their developing country counterparts are critical in countering the imposition of cultural, environmental and local economical impacts from mining.

Finally, corporate engagement is an increasingly popular strategy for change. There are many documented examples of success,[29] however there are also failures and evidence of exploitation through NGO/business partnerships.[30]

How engagement is used is vital for both parties. Increasingly, the global mining sector is acknowledging its social responsibility, through pressures from a growing corporate citizenship culture and the effective campaigns of social movements and individual NGOs. The growth in corporate sensitivity and responsibility to demands like human rights and indigenous rights offers opportunities for NGOs. There are clearly many risks on the engagement path, most importantly that the well-resourced mining sector may take over key agendas and work them to their own advantage.

Engagement or confrontation?

This risk can be minimised by the active diligence of NGOs that stay outside the corporate engagement process, and by a diversity of approaches for those that choose to pursue it. NGOs need to maintain an ongoing role in generating publicity and counter-publicity, pushing for transparency and contributing alternative expertise to debates. The NGO role of scrutinising corporate behaviour in the global political economy is more vital than ever before.

12 Mining uranium and indigenous Australians: The fight for Jabiluka

Jacqui Katona

Introduction

The Mirrar People of northern Australia are the traditional owners of land under the Ranger and Jabiluka uranium mineral leases within Kakadu National Park, 250 kilometres east of Darwin. Kakadu is one of less than 25 sites worldwide listed by UNESCO's World Heritage Centre for both natural and cultural values. These values are intrinsically linked to the living tradition of the Mirrar and are currently under direct threat from existing and proposed uranium mining operations. Although the Mirrar are legally recognised as the traditional owners of the area, the European economic imperative of mining has meant they cannot enjoy their rights as traditional owners.

This chapter provides background to the Mirrar's long struggle against uranium mining on their land and is largely based upon their 1998 submission to the World Heritage Committee Mission to Kakadu. Following its visit to Kakadu in October 1998, the Mission recommended that Kakadu be declared as 'World Heritage in Danger', and that uranium mining at Jabiluka not proceed.

Overview: Campaign Against Jabiluka Uranium Mine

The Mirrar have achieved a great deal of success in their public campaign against Jabiluka. In 1998, a major non-violent direct action blockade near the Jabiluka mine site was conducted in conjunction with anti-uranium and environmental organisations.

The eight-month blockade directly involved over 5,000 people and saw more than 500 arrests as people from across Australia and around the world undertook non-violent action to highlight the human and environmental impacts of the mine plan. Along with speaking tours, legal action and national and international lobbying, the blockade helped make Jabiluka a household word in Australia and created attention throughout the world.

Apart from significant public and political attention, the campaign was also recognised in 1998 when the Mirrar Senior Traditional Owner Yvonne Margarula received the Friends Of the Earth International Environment Award. In 1999 Ms Margarula and myself, Jacqui Katona, were jointly awarded the US Goldman Environment Prize.

The development of Jabiluka has been stalled since September 1999 due to the weak international uranium market and ongoing Aboriginal and community opposition. In August 2000, Rio Tinto, one of the world's largest mining companies, acquired the majority shareholding in Energy Resources of Australia (ERA), the operator of Ranger and Jabiluka, as part of a broader corporate takeover. Since then Rio Tinto has stated that it does not support the development of Jabiluka in the 'short term'. Rio Tinto has not committed either to selling or developing the Jabiluka project.[1]

Differing Concepts of Living Tradition[2]

The living tradition of the Mirrar is integral to the cultural values of the Kakadu World Heritage Area and is directly affected by mining activities in the Jabiluka Mineral Lease enclave. It is important to note that those accustomed to European (*Balanda*) notions of heritage, tradition, cultural landscape and land ownership need to adjust to very different Aboriginal (*Bininj*) understandings of such concepts when examining living tradition in the Kakadu World Heritage Area.

One of Australia's most respected heritage experts, Professor D J Mulvaney, has provided some important guidelines for *Balanda* when considering *Bininj* concepts of living tradition. He states, 'expressed succinctly, their traditional world is a humanised landscape which is indivisible and immutable, and every natural feature has a name and meaningful mythological association. Place and person are inseparable, while past and present form a unity of ongoing creation.'[3]

Mulvaney also makes an important point with regard to sacred or spiritual sites, stating: 'European legal agreements assume the disclosure of all relevant information. Yet Aboriginal custodians may

196

withhold secret cultural information because much esoteric data normally is revealed only to appropriate clan elders upon ritual occasions. Awareness that ceremonial pathways of Dreaming ancestors or some adjacent dangerous sacred site may be impacted upon by proposed development may only dawn later . . .

A further complication is that those persons standing in a custodial role to Dreaming localities and stories may place themselves or their clan in danger by divulging information to inappropriate persons. So there exists a reluctance amongst elders (who alone are entitled to divulge information) to disclose all their knowledge to Europeans . . .

To ignore these realities of Aboriginal custodianship and to assume that elders act like Europeans in legal matters is to place undue pressure on them.'[4]

Mulvaney is widely respected by the Mirrar as a *Balanda* with considerable experience of talking to *Bininj* and the Mirrar drew on his interpretations when asking the World Heritage Committee to examine the dangers to Mirrar living tradition posed by the Jabiluka uranium mine.

Administrative Borders Versus Traditional Boundaries

Mirrar country is defined by both *Bininj* law and *Balanda* law as encompassing the Ranger and Jabiluka mineral leases, the mining town of Jabiru and parts of Kakadu National Park. *Bininj* have verified the extent of Mirrar country on countless occasions. In the early 1980s this was 'formalised' through the claims process of the *Aboriginal Land Rights Act 1976 (Northern Territory)*. The Mirrar were successful in demonstrating under Australian law their claim to land by satisfying the legislative requirements for proof of connection to their country, through *Bininj* law and custom, and that other *Bininj* continue to respect the extent of the Mirrar estate. The Mirrar proved to the satisfaction of the Commonwealth that they had a common spiritual affiliation to their country; that they exercised primary spiritual responsibility for their country; and that they had the right to forage on their country.

The Mirrar exercise their rights as Traditional Owners under two Aboriginal Land Trusts and benefit from *fee simple* title to most of their estate. The town of Jabiru and surrounds were excluded from the Kakadu Aboriginal Land Trust and are currently subject to a native title claim lodged in the Federal Court by the Mirrar.

The enclave boundaries of the Jabiluka and Ranger Mineral Leases are not recognised under *Bininj* law. The mineral leases do not concur with any 'borders' established by the Mirrar or other *Bininj*. This was reiterated in discussion between senior *Bininj* at a meeting held in Kakadu where it was stated: 'A lot of argument is caused by *Balanda* making lines on maps to show how Aboriginal land ownership is represented. It isn't like that . . . Arguments are forced on us when we are forced to make decisions in the interest of some group of *Balanda* or government . . . we are continually forced and harassed until they get what they want.'[5]

The concept of administrative borders is inimical to the Mirrar relationship with country and other *Bininj*. Furthermore, the Mirrar do not believe that any *Balanda* have a legitimate right to carry out activities on country without Traditional Owner consent. No such consent exists for the Ranger Lease. The Mirrar veto over development of Ranger, as provided for in the *Aboriginal Land Rights (Northern Territory) Act 1976*, was removed by special Commonwealth legislation.

The Mirrar believe that no legitimate consent exists for the Jabiluka Mineral Lease. Under both *Bininj* law and *Balanda* law the Mirrar are the only clan group with ultimate rights and obligations to the land within the Jabiluka excision. Other clan groups are affected by activity in the area, and the Mirrar owe responsibilities to these groups. These *Bininj* would also be the beneficiaries of any royalties generated by a mining project. There are some non-Mirrar individuals who have important rights and obligations to this land as Custodians by virtue of Mirrar instruction to them.

Mirrar Responsibilities for Country and People

Mirrar have rights and interests that arise from country and flow from Mirrar law and custom. These rights are recognised under the *Aboriginal Land Rights Act*. In exercising these rights and interests, Mirrar are guided by their obligations and responsibilities to other *Bininj* affected by Mirrar decisions about Mirrar country.

There are two main approaches to the way Mirrar view their responsibilities – looking after country (*gunred*) and looking after people (*guhpleddi*). *Gunred* encompasses control of country including the prevention of both destruction of country and desecration of sites.

It is also the recognition, assertion and promotion of cultural rights and the carrying out of living tradition on country. *Guhpleddi* is intrinsically tied to *gunred* because *Bininj* and country are as one. It encompasses an extremely complex set of relationships between Mirrar, other *Bininj* and country.

The Mirrar and other *Bininj* have dreaming tracks that traverse country. These dreaming tracks cross both the Jabiluka and Ranger Mineral Leases and the World Heritage Area. The Mirrar and other *Bininj* have many sacred sites within the Jabiluka and Ranger Mineral Leases. Customary Aboriginal law is inextricably linked to country and ceremony and these sites are interconnected with the spiritual and cultural significance of the entire Mirrar estate and to other *Bininj* country, including the World Heritage Area. These spiritual connections to country should only be described by particular Traditional Owners and Custodians to particular people at particular times.

Some of the sacred sites on the Jabiluka Mineral Lease, including rock art and ancestral living areas, are recognised under *Balanda* law inside the large areas of the lease registered by the Australian Heritage Commission (AHC). There are no current plans to mine in these AHC areas, but the Mirrar believe these areas are nevertheless affected by mining activity. The entire Jabiluka Mineral Lease was covered by AHC listing until objections by mining companies saw the AHC areas reduced.

There are also sacred sites that are not afforded the 'protection' of the AHC areas. One that has been publicly identified by the Traditional Owners and Custodians is the Boywek–Almudj site that is very close to the proposed Jabiluka uranium mine. There are many other sites on the Jabiluka excision that have not been identified by *Bininj* for a range of cultural reasons. Some of these sites are at present being directly and severely impacted upon by the proposed Jabiluka uranium mine.

The importance of sites of significance to the cultural values of Kakadu National Park was confirmed by the Australian Government in its 1991 World Heritage renomination document, stating ' ... a major aspect of the past that affects the present and future is the creative behaviour of beings said to have travelled across the landscape when it was flat, featureless and lacking the presence of ordinary men and women. These beings are said to have moulded the landscape into its present form and to have established people's languages and social institutions. Aboriginal people hold as significant features of the landscape that mark the temporary or permanent abodes of these beings. This system of beliefs gives Aboriginal people vital links with the land; the links continue through membership of a clan or local descent group.'[6]

The Mirrar and other *Bininj* have traditionally hunted, gathered, held ceremonies, lived and died at places all over the Mirrar estate, including the Jabiluka Mineral Lease. *Balanda* scientists have 'proved' this by discovering ancient remains and rock art all over Mirrar country, including the Jabiluka Mineral Lease. The Australian Government believed one of the archaeological sites inside the Jabiluka Mineral Lease (Malakananja II) to be so important that it specifically referred to it when seeking inscription of Kakadu National Park on the World Heritage List.

Mirrar Country in Danger – Living Tradition in Danger

The Mirrar believe that mining activity on the Jabiluka Mineral Lease presents a genocidal danger to their living tradition and therefore a specific and imminent danger to the World Heritage values of Kakadu National Park. The Mirrar base this belief on their knowledge of land and culture inherited from ancestors since time immemorial and from their experiences of the Ranger uranium mine over the past 20 years.

When the Mirrar have questioned the mining company's release of contaminated water into the wetlands where they hunt and fish, their concerns have been treated as naïve. Mirrar cultural knowledge appears irreconcilable with the scientific justifications used to achieve commercial outcomes. The Mirrar people hold great fears about the cultural and physical health of future generations.

To fully comprehend the significance of these dangers, it is imperative that the living tradition of the Mirrar people is not understood as just the source and support of Kakadu's cultural values – as simply the 'infrastructure' for rare sites and cultural practices. The World Heritage Convention, in this instance, must be seen as protecting one of the few remaining islands of traditional culture from the relentless forces of development.

The Mirrar and other *Bininj* believe that culturally significant sites would be damaged by the construction of the Jabiluka uranium mine. Mirrar are less likely to go to the area of the Jabiluka Mineral

Lease because it is country that has been taken from them and damaged in a way that makes the country dangerous. In this way the mine effectively prevents access to a much wider area than is demarcated by *Balanda*. Damage to these spiritual sites not only destroys living tradition from a *Balanda* anthropological viewpoint – the Mirrar believe that damage to these sites will have actual cataclysmic consequences. Descriptions of these consequences can only be explained by Traditional Owners and Custodians to particular people at particular times.

Social Destabilisation by Mining

The Mirrar believe that their living tradition has sustained an extreme attack as a result of the process by which industrial development has taken place. This attack lies in the refusal by the Australian Government to recognise fundamental Mirrar rights to land and the exercise of those rights by the Mirrar. This attack is most clearly manifested in the extinguishment of the Mirrar's right to say 'no' to the development of the existing Ranger Uranium Mine and the duress applied to the Mirrar to gain their consent for development at Jabiluka. The consequences of this attack have exacerbated the poor social and economic conditions experienced by the Aboriginal community. Unemployment, social discord, health, housing and education problems plague the Kakadu Aboriginal community.

Against the backdrop of national controversy about legislating land rights for Aboriginal communities in the Northern Territory, the mining industry and governments were well aware of the potential for social destabilisation in the Aboriginal community as a result of uranium mining at Ranger. In the 1970's the Federal Government commissioned the Fox Report that highlighted the poor social and economic conditions of the Aboriginal people of Kakadu at the time. It said, 'personal incomes depend ... largely on social service payments such as age pensions and family allowance payment, contributions from relatives who are earning wages and the sale of artefacts ... '[7] This is still the case.

The Fox Report went on to say that 'Excessive consumption of alcohol by a large proportion of the Aboriginal people in the Region will have a deleterious effect on their general welfare; their future will depend in a large part on removing or substantially reducing the causes of this problem.'[8] These causes have never been identified. Alcohol is still an inescapable problem. The Fox Report concluded, 'the Aboriginal people of the Region are a depressed group whose standards of living are far below those acceptable to the wider Australian society. They are a community whose lives have been, and are still being, disrupted by the intrusions of an alien people. They feel the pressures of the white man's activities in relation to their land. In the face of mining exploration, and the threat of much further development, they feel helpless and lost.'[9] This continues to be the case. Mirrar believe that since the Fox Inquiry in 1977, a continuing cycle of cultural genocide has taken place.

Damage or restricted access to spiritual sites by *Balanda* mining projects contributes to disempowerment and a general pessimism amongst *Bininj* that complete loss of culture is imminent. This historical, psychological and sociological impact is one of the key reasons for abandonment of traditional living culture by many *Bininj,* and is recognised in symptoms such as alcoholism and other socio-economic indicators of cultural decline.

This loss of cultural significance extends to all aspects of Mirrar living tradition, including food collection, ceremony, customary law, spiritual connection and socio-political systems.

Mining Impacts on Traditional Management Practices

Contemporary patterns of living tradition include decision making about the management and use of the landscape in accordance with Aboriginal traditions. A sense of hopelessness is created if Traditional Owners believe that fundamental decisions about management of their land are ignored or violated.

This fosters abandonment of traditional management practices that are integral to living tradition, to continuing cultural practice, and to the World Heritage values of the Kakadu National Park.

Balanda political systems and notions of jurisdiction are usurping traditional political systems based on the living tradition of *Bininj.* The systems of committees, action groups and other bodies designed by *Balanda* industry and governments to replace traditional political systems have nearly always failed due to exhaustion and/or disinterest resulting from cultural inappropriateness. The Mirrar believe that the continued presence of mining in the region will complete this domination.

The traditional cultural system of relations between clans in the region is based on co-operation, mutual obligation and respect for Traditional Owner decision-making. The development of the Jabiluka uranium mine, and the associated promises of financial benefit for people other than the Traditional Owners, has created social fragmentation that is destroying the traditional methods of maintaining harmony and equality.

The Jabiluka uranium mine project cannot be viewed in isolation from other social impacts on *Bininj* in the region, including the cumulative impact of the operating Ranger uranium mine. The Mirrar do not argue that mining is the only threat to living tradition, but do maintain that mining and its associated social, economic and political impacts poses the single greatest threat. An additional mine would push *Bininj* culture beyond the point of cultural exhaustion to genocidal decay.

So important is the issue of *Bininj* control over country and so dire is the position of the Mirrar living tradition that the Senior Traditional Owner of the Mirrar, Yvonne Margarula, has indicated that she would have no choice but to enter into self-imposed exile from her country if the Jabiluka uranium mine proceeds, and her clan's authority is usurped by Government and the mine proponent ERA. The Senior Traditional Owner is the main repository of knowledge that allows for Mirrar living tradition to continue and exercise jurisdictional power. Ms Margarula's exile from country would deliver a fatal blow to the survival of Mirrar culture.

The Mirrar Perspective: Lessons from Jabiluka[10]

There are several broad lessons that need to be drawn from the involvement of ERA in Kakadu. It is the responsibility of each and every member of any community to make their views known, and to teach the lessons, because we all have to live with the consequences.

1. Mining companies should never proceed without informed Aboriginal consent

There is a problem when no doesn't mean no. This is a violation of Aboriginal consent at the most basic level. It might take place because of "legal reasons" or it might take place in the "national interest" but it will always be a violation. Added to this there is the continuing insult of ignoring the consequences. Rewriting history or attempting to sanitise the reality of environmental, cultural and human rights abuses, and present them as "negative social impacts" is an exercise in gross deception.

The Mirrar have been repeatedly told that the removal of the right of veto over the Ranger project is an unpleasantness best forgotten and that it is the future that is all-important. The reality is that the problems suffered by our people in the past are what we must take responsibility for now. Why should Aboriginal people be expected to put the interests of a private company before the interests of their children and grandchildren? A dramatic change is required in the terms on which Aboriginal people are expected to negotiate around mining issues. There is a demand currently being made on government and industry that Aboriginal people in Kakadu be assisted to manage and control their own affairs. So far this fundamental aspiration has been consistently ignored.

2. Mining projects should facilitate economic and political independence and not merely transfer welfare provision and political control from the white public sector to the white private sector

A major Social Impact Study completed in the early 1980s clearly documented the absence of government action to assist the Mirrar community in dealing with the effects of a series of major industrial developments. The most recent social impact study, completed in 1997, has simply recommended an increase in welfare programs. In effect this approach is little more than turning up a kind of a drip feed. The study failed to recognise the most fundamental traditional owner rights, it marginalised traditional owners as "stakeholders", and again denied indegenous people the right to exercise control over their future.

Studies, reports, inquiries, assessments and the like are increasingly industry-driven processes that have become an end in themselves. They are touted as the solution, conveniently crafted and promoted as justification for further abuse of indigenous and environmental rights. Too often, such mechanisms exist to entrench the dominance of government and industry, and facilitate the ambitions of a privately owned company.

ERA's answer to the existing social problems created by the mining operation at Ranger is for Traditional Owners to condone more mining by saying 'yes' to Jabiluka. The company believes that if this happened all the problems would be solved and mine money would be there to right the wrongs of the past. For the Mirrar this is like taking a gunshot wound to the chest, leaving the wound open, while increasing the amount of blood supply to the patient, through a drip. This is not an acceptable solution. Wounds must be allowed to heal and the mistakes of the past must not be replicated.

Yvonne Margurula, traditional elder of the Jabiluka mine site, with members of her clan

Photo by Sandy Scheltema

3. There must be recognition that mining projects have irreversible impacts that destroy aspects of culture forever

There is a point when a community can take no more. Jabiluka cannot go ahead for this reason. One enormous uranium mine, combined with little concern for social impacts over 20 years, is surely enough in anyone's language. There is a point at which the development of the community by the community at the community's own pace must take priority over external pressures and imperatives. In the case of the Mirrar and Jabiluka that point is now.

Conclusion: An Appeal from the Mirrar People[11]

If you have not been to our country, you would have only an image in your mind of what the country looks and feels like. Maybe this image would contain bright sunlight, birds and animals, paperbark swamps with flowers that smell like a baked potato. *Marrawutii*, the sea eagle, swooping low over Mohla billabong. Cool green grasses on hot days, glorious fires where embers burn low in cool night temperatures. Maybe you can imagine what it's like to see tens of thousands of magpie geese feeding on lush floodplains.

These lands give to us our identity, our history, and our future. We are obligated to take care of this country not only because of what the country provides for us, but because our law requires it. It has been a sustainable economy for thousands of years.

Land rights were supposed to protect our people and help to rebuild our communities, but in north Kakadu land rights never arrived. Instead, our people's lives have been dominated by a uranium mining company driven by narrow financial imperatives and with little regard for the future of the Aboriginal community.

PART FOUR: ALTERNATIVES

13 An international regulatory framework?

Geoff Evans, Gabrielle Russell, Rory Sullivan

Transnational mining corporations have resources that dwarf those of many countries and the communities in which they operate. Community campaigns have emerged in both the Global South and the Global North to challenge the lack of accountability and the poor environmental, human rights and labour standards of these mining corporations. The focus of these campaigns has varied. In the South, where the people who have suffered most at the hands of mining transnational corporations (TNCs) are those who are poor, have comparatively little power and education, and little or no expertise in western approaches to the law. Many of their campaigns are focused on stopping encroachment and exploitation by mining transnationals. In contrast, the campaigns of many organisations and communities in the North (where most of the largest mining transnationals have their corporate headquarters) have tended to concentrate on forcing accountability and regulation.

This chapter discusses the strategies that have been adopted by communities and NGOs in the North and South and canvasses the links and commonalities. One of the objectives of the chapter is to synthesise these strategies into an *and* rather than an *either/or* model for future campaigning activities.

The chapter is divided into three parts. The first is a review of the history of efforts to regulate and control multinational mining companies. This history provides an of the problems faced in regulating multinational enterprises as well as an indication of possible future directions. The second is an assessment of what, if any, is the appropriate role for the self-regulation regimes preferred by corporations and many governments. The third is an overview of the strategies and approaches that can be used to ensure that the mining industry operates in a socially and environmentally responsible manner.

A depiction of commitment by corporations to codes of conduct.

Cartoon by Heinrich Hinze

The Regulatory Environment: Overview and Context

To date, national governments have proved unwilling, or unable, to control the activities of TNCs. The primary reasons appear to be the risk of limiting foreign direct investment as well as the increasing constraints on national governments arising from the international trade and investment regime.

In fact, many national governments have legislated to weaken laws protecting the environment, local industries, labour and indigenous peoples in order to actively encourage TNC investment. In the Philippines, for example, prior to the 1995 Mining Act, only four mining projects involved foreign corporations. Today mining concession areas, mostly taken up by TNCs either singly or in partnership with Filipino companies cover most of the Philippines. Governments also offer mining TNCs a range of incentives from tax holidays to the granting of extensive land, water and other concessions and state protection against community opposition.[1] Furthermore, TNCs can (and do) exert enormous influence on domestic legislation. A relevant example is in Papua New Guinea (PNG), where, in response to landowner concerns about the environmental impacts of the Ok Tedi mine, which is majority-owned by the Australian-based BHP, the PNG government passed a law to prevent PNG plaintiffs from suing an Australian company in an Australian court. It was reported that lawyers from BHP assisted in drafting the law.[2]

In addition to the pressures on domestic governments to allow mining TNCs to establish a presence in their country, it is increasingly clear that the international trade regime, in particular the trade rules developed by bodies such as the World Trade Organisation (WTO), can act as a barrier to the development of effective domestic regulatory regimes.[3] The WTO rules do not permit discrimination against traded goods on the basis of their source or method of production. While the boundaries between WTO rules and national regulatory regimes have yet to be fully defined, cases such as the complaint brought to the WTO by the European Union (EU) and Japan against the Massachusetts *Burma Law* point to future tensions. The EU and Japan claimed that the Massachusetts law which, when awarding government contracts, created a 10 per cent preference weighting in favour of companies which avoid doing business with the military junta of Burma, actually constituted a tax and therefore breached WTO rules on government procurement.[4] Many NGOs consider that the focus of the WTO on narrowly defined trade issues has resulted in broader issues associated with human rights and environmental protection being ignored, weakened or compromised, in particular given the tendency for governments to consider international trade law as having primacy over human rights and environmental law.

These problems are compounded by the failure of efforts to develop a regulatory framework for TNCs. The only multilaterally endorsed code that governments have committed to promoting are the Organisation for Economic Cooperation and Development (OECD) Guidelines on Multinational Enterprises.[5] Although non-binding, the Guidelines have acquired stature simply by virtue of their broad acceptance, at least by the member countries of the OECD. However, the Guidelines' effectiveness is undermined by their lack of compulsion. Perhaps the most damning praise of the Guidelines comes from the Business and Industry Advisory Council (BIAC), an industry group which has consistently lobbied for the Guidelines to be weakened and to be retained only as non-binding guidelines. The BIAC in its statement on the revised Guidelines stated:

'The Guidelines were and are voluntary in fact and effect and this has been confirmed in the new texts. What is expected from multinational companies is good corporate citizenship, leadership by example to promote the effective use of the Guidelines as a tool.' [6]

That is, the OECD governments have agreed, at the behest of business interests, that the Guidelines will not be binding or mandatory. The fact that the Guidelines are voluntary means that they are unlikely to deliver concrete safeguards to those communities most adversely affected by the activities of transnational enterprises.

Another development in the regulation of TNCs is the European Parliament's 1999 Resolution on standards for European enterprises operating in developing countries. [7] The Resolution requires the European Commission to establish binding requirements on European TNCs, to ensure that these corporations comply with international law relating to the protection of human rights and the environment when operating in developing countries. While the Resolution is not yet fully implemented, it does require the European Commission to respond to every point contained in the Resolution within six months and to hold annual hearings where good and bad corporate practices can be highlighted.

Approaches of International Law

International law is only binding on national governments and does not bind TNCs, except where the national government implements and enforces international law through domestic legislation. Under international law, States do have an obligation to give effect to human rights conventions between private parties. [8] However, this 'horizontal' application does not mitigate the fact that there is generally an absence of suitable vehicles for action to be taken in situations where human rights are violated or where gross environmental damage is caused by TNCs.

Specifically, there are serious constraints on the ability of communities and NGOs to access justice in domestic courts, in particular in developing countries. This problem is compounded by the difficulties associated with taking cases to seek injunctions and/or compensation in a corporation's home country (or country of incorporation). Even where international conventions and resolutions are incorporated into national law, this legislation is of no value if the mechanisms available to ensure compliance (e.g. ability to monitor, inspect, gather evidence, take cases, impose penalties) are not available.

Foreign Direct Liability

As foreign direct investment increases, so too does the threat of 'foreign direct liability' whereby companies are subject to legal actions brought by foreign citizens claiming damages for negative environmental or health impacts resulting from their foreign direct investment.[9]

To date, legal approaches have been dominated by the *forum non conveniens* doctrine (i.e. that the available court is not the appropriate forum to bring the action). In the context of this chapter, this issue frequently arises because local communities are unable to take domestic action either due to an absence of appropriate legal mechanisms or because of fear that their lives, family or well-being will be harmed as a consequence. The US *Alien Tort Claims Act 1989 (ATCA)* allows, 'US district courts to exercise extra territorial jurisdiction with respect to claims by aliens of torts committed in violation of international law.'[10]

The Act has been narrowly interpreted to apply, in the main, only to violations of *jus cogens*. These are the peremptory norms of international law that are recognised by the entire international community of nations and from which no derogation is permitted and include the gravest violations of international law, such as slavery, genocide, murder and torture.[11]

The most comprehensive example, to date, of the manner in which the *ACTA* operates is the case of *John Doe I, et al. vs. Unocal, et al.* In 1997, a US Federal District Court in Los Angeles agreed to hear a case brought against Unocal and Total by fifteen victims of alleged human rights abuses arising out of the Yadana gas pipeline project in Burma.[12] The court stated in this case that, 'private actors can be state actors if they are wilful participants'.[13]

The plaintiffs alleged that Unocal was engaged with the state officials in using forced labour and committing human rights abuses. According to the court this allegation was sufficient grounds to support jurisdiction under the *ATCA*. In September 2000, the court dismissed the case (despite finding that Unocal was cognisant of the crimes committed by the Burmese military) as the Court did not find that the corporation exercised control over the military's decision to commit the abuses and did not engage in a conspiracy to commit the crimes.[14]   While the case establishes the precedent that private actors can be held liable for human rights abuses, it is also clear that the evidentiary thresholds are extremely high and that demonstrating explicit links for human rights violations between companies and the state can be virtually impossible to prove in a court of law.   In this context, arguments such as 'proximity' or 'circumstantial evidence' are unlikely to constitute sufficient proof of complicity.

The UK's House of Lords also tested the *forum non conveniens* doctrine when it gave leave to several thousand South African plaintiffs to take action in England against an English company, Cape PLC, for personal injuries. Cape operated asbestos mines in South Africa, but the appellants made their claim against the parent company, located in the UK, claiming that Cape was negligent in its duty to ensure that proper occupational health and safety standards were employed throughout the group.[15] The House of Lords concluded that the absence of legal aid in South Africa to fund the litigation and the absence of a suitably experienced law firm who would be willing to take the case on a 'no win, no fee basis', if the case was heard in South Africa, meant that there would not be sufficient access to justice.[16]

Domestic Legislation

There are increasing signs that national governments are at least considering how to exercise legal control over the activities of TNCs. Recent examples have been the McKinney Bill[17] introduced into the US House of Representatives, and the Corporate Code of Conduct Bill 2000 tabled in the Australian Senate by Senator Vicki Bourne.[18]   Both Bills address areas such as occupational health and safety, freedom from discrimination on the basis of race, gender, religious affiliation, pregnancy (or potential for pregnancy), the right to organise, and minimum wages. They also address environmental standards as well as requiring that organisations comply with core ILO standards.

The key aspect of these bills is their extraterritorial application. That is, they seek to regulate the activities of TNCs beyond national boundaries. Both Australia and the USA have previously enacted extraterritorial legislation in areas where the activity is seen to be of sufficient import to justify extending jurisdiction overseas, for example bribery and corruption. The passage of these Bills into legislation is by no means assured. However, these initiatives provide a vehicle for public debate and campaigns to convince governments that public opinion expects that TNCs should be controlled.

Furthermore, the review and assessment processes for these Bills will enable the barriers to regulating TNCs to be critically assessed and practical, effective solutions to be found to many of the issues that are currently dismissed as 'intractable' or simply 'too hard'.

Self-Regulation

Recent years have seen a range of initiatives at the national and international levels to define codes of conduct for the mining industry and promote the concept of responsible industry self-regulation. These include the International Council of Metals and the Environment's (ICME) Sustainable Development Charter[19] and the Minerals Council of Australia's (MCA) Code for Environmental Management.[20] Individual mining companies (such as Rio Tinto and Shell) have also promoted the concept of self-regulation by developing their own corporate codes of conduct or policy statements on issues such as human rights and the environment.

In 1999, the Global Mining Initiative (GMI) was launched by Chief Executive Officers of some of the world's largest mining companies. The GMI's sub-project, Mining, Minerals and Sustainable Development, aims to 'identify how mining and the minerals industry can best contribute to the global transition to sustainable development'.[21] Many mining-focused NGOs are sceptical of the MMSD project and other engagement strategies of the industry, seeing them as, at best, ill-conceived and, at worst, 'greenwashing' designed to promote the industry's self regulation agenda. However, it is important to consider whether (and how) self-regulation could fill the void in ensuring the performance of the global mining industry.

Benefits of Self-Regulation

The supporters of self-regulation cite benefits such as speed, flexibility, sensitivity to market circumstances and lower costs. It is argued that, because industry sets the standards and is responsible for identifying breaches, this will lead to more practicable standards that can be more effectively policed. It is argued that industry peer pressure offers the potential for improving the rate of compliance over traditional regulatory regimes. It is also frequently suggested that self-regulation, through the adoption of standards beyond legal compliance, may significantly raise standards of behaviour and environmental performance.

Self-regulation may also provide a range of intangible benefits such as raising awareness of specific issues and developing an industry-wide normative framework (i.e. a set of principles that defines 'right' conduct in the context of the industry's behaviour and operations).

Limitations of Self-Regulation

Self-regulation often fails to fulfil its promise and is regarded with scepticism by local communities, environmentalists, consumer organisations and other interested parties.[22] Self-regulation is seen as lacking many of the strengths of conventional regulation in terms of credibility, accountability and compulsory application.[23] A specific concern of NGOs is that self-regulatory regimes are also designed to give the appearance of regulation and thereby ward off government intervention or regulation.[24]

There are a number of specific limitations associated with self-regulation, namely the emphasis on process rather than outcomes, regulatory capture, lack of access to third parties, limited enforcement processes and 'free riding'. Each of these is considered briefly below.

Target-based or Process-based Regulation

Self-regulatory regimes may either define the specific targets to be met, 'target-based', or the means whereby external targets are to be met, 'process-based'.[25]

The experience with target-based regimes has been many organisations' policies and objectives on issues such as human rights and the environment are believed by critics to be extremely limited, contain few concrete commitments and often represent little more than 'business as usual'. The targets that are set are alleged to be generally far lower than those that would have been set by government. It is claimed that industry-defined targets tend to take into account only the interests of the industry rather than the public interest in general.

Where the self-regulatory regime is process based, the meeting of the process specifications is taken as ensuring the success of the regime. For example, the signatories to the Australian Minerals Industry Code for Environmental Management[26] are required to implement the Code, produce an annual public environment report, complete an annual code implementation survey and have the survey results verified by an accredited auditor at least once every three years. No specific performance obligations are imposed on Code signatories beyond complying with statutory requirements and continuous improvement in environmental performance. While the Code does refer to terms such as sustainable development, these terms are not defined nor are specific performance measures defined for these. The consequence is that, even though companies may comply with the requirements of the Code, this compliance says nothing about their actual social or environmental performance.

Regulatory Capture

Industry is frequently suspected of using self-regulation to 'capture' (i.e. exert undue influence over) public policy. Capture may occur as a consequence of the industry being required to meet lower standards than would otherwise have been the case or through avoiding or obstructing more stringent regulations.[27]

Given these risks, the question is why do governments and regulatory bodies at the national and international level support voluntary approaches? Self-regulation may be seen as speeding up the regulatory process (through acting as a stepping stone towards more binding regulation) and saving on budget resources (through enabling some of the costs associated with the development and administration of regulation to be transferred to industry). Furthermore, the ongoing pressures from business interests for government to withdraw from many areas of social policy creates pressure on regulatory bodies to be seen to be assisting industry and not to be imposing 'unwarranted' costs on business. Through the creation of 'an impression of regulation', self-regulatory regimes are frequently used as a justification for no regulation or control.

Access to Third Parties

As self-regulatory regimes are generally developed outside the standard regulatory framework, it is often the case that some or all elements of the regime are not transparent and open to all

215

stakeholders. This raises issues in terms of the credibility of the targets that are defined, the monitoring processes that are established and the processes for reporting and data interpretation.

Many of the largest mining TNCs have actively sought to engage NGO and community critics in monitoring and verification of their environmental and social performance. While, in theory, these 'partnership projects' provide a mechanism for independent scrutiny of corporate activity and accountability to NGO and community aspirations, critics allege that the reality has been that much, if not all, stakeholder consultation is designed to legitimise the goals, objectives and process rather than lead to any significant changes in the scope or content of the self-regulatory regime.[28] Those critics believe that the reality is that most of this 'consultation' is predicated on the assumption that mining will proceed and the discussion is then *'How should such mining be carried out?'* rather than *'If such mining should be carried out'*.[29]

For under-resourced or unwary communities and NGOs, engagement in corporate controlled monitoring and verification processes is very problematic. Usually the terms of reference, selection (both of the issues to be considered and of the NGOs to be involved in the process) and resources are controlled by corporations. While an 'inner circle' of external monitors might be invited into the process of self-regulation, others who are marginalised due to geography, culture, gender or political persuasion are left outside of the process, often leading to a 'divide and conquer' situation between those on the 'inside' and those on the 'outside'.[30] The record of NGOs and community groups' involvement in monitoring and verification has been perceived by observers to have frequently been limited to rubber stamping the status quo and identifying issues that can be managed on corporate terms.

Enforcement

A critical question is what, if any, penalties can be imposed for non-compliance within a system of self-regulation? In practice, heavy sanctions, such as the withdrawal of licences, are unlikely to be available. Much of the literature on self-regulation has been critical of the role of industry associations in self-regulatory regimes.[31]

The reality is that the primary purpose of industry associations is to serve the needs and interests of their members. They are, therefore, unlikely to be able to effectively regulate their members. While industry peer group pressure can provide pressure for compliance, the reality is that there are few, if any, options available to address non-compliance with self-regulatory regimes and such regimes are all too easily open to be flouted by less scrupulous organisations. [32]

Free-Riding

A major problem with industry self-regulation is that, although each individual enterprise may benefit from collective action if other enterprises participate, each will also benefit even if it does not participate, provided that others do participate (and the 'free-rider' is not caught).[33] An example is the response of the Australian mining industry to the cyanide spill in North West Romania in January 2000, at a mine owned and operated by the Australian company, Esmeralda Exploration. The Australian mining industry has a Code for Environmental Management and many of the major Australian mining companies are signatories to the Code.

The industry was at pains to point out that Esmeralda Exploration was neither a signatory to the Code, nor a member of the Minerals Council of Australia (MCA). The industry also emphasised that the Code had not failed but that the spill was the result of an organisation that did not conform to the industry's self-defined norms of good corporate behaviour. The perception among NGOs was that industry was more concerned to protect the reputation of the MCA Code and its signatories, rather than remedying the damage caused, sanctioning the 'free rider', or moving to improve the performance of the industry as a whole. Clearly, the existence of the Code provided no guarantees regarding the performance of the industry as a whole.

Where To From Here?

In practice, in the absence of effective legislation, many transnational corporations do not even meet the minimum standards specified in international law on issues such as human rights or the environment. Both regulation and self-regulation are clearly failing. The question is how to move forward? The following section outlines seven key strategies for expanding the capacities of communities and their representative organisations to enforce corporate accountability and standards to protect the environment, human rights and labour rights and, where necessary, to resist mining corporations altogether.

217

An international regulatory framework?

1. Strengthen the Rights and Capacities of Civil Society

The first and most fundamental requirement for increasing the accountability and regulation of TNCs is to strengthen the democratic rights and powers of people, communities and civil society organisations, relative to those of corporations. Civil society includes organisations focused on community welfare, human rights, indigenous peoples, environment, religious, development assistance, labour, and consumers' rights.

As a minimum, this requires that governments delegate to local communities and their representative organisations the powers to veto and/or control development in their localities. Furthermore, communities and representative organisations and self-government bodies must be resourced and supported so that they can be fully involved, and informed through independent advice, in negotiations about development, standard setting, monitoring, and sanctioning. The special rights of indigenous peoples to self-government and self-determination must be explicitly guaranteed.

2. Standing for Communities and Civil Society

Legislation is not enough; communities and non-government organisations need expanded rights and capacities to take legal action against corporate abuse in local, national and international jurisdictions. Any limits to these rights must be removed from the statutes. These rights must be explicitly included in international law regimes. Affected communities must have the ability and the right to take cases seeking restraints, compensation and rehabilitation.

The scope of such legislation should include:

- Access to a recognised court or forum;
- The potential for full, adequate and effective compensation to be granted;
- The potential for injunctions to be granted where such injunctions are warranted (e.g. where there is the potential for grave environmental harm); and
- Effective enforcement powers for the court, including sanctions in the event of non-compliance.

3. Contesting Companies' Licence to Operate

The mining industry knows it has a crisis of legitimacy and that

218

its 'licence to operate' is being strongly challenged by mining-affected communities, NGOs and ethical investors. As Rio Tinto's Sir Robert Wilson noted: 'Unless the major players in the global mining and minerals industry can present a convincing case that their activities are conducted in line with [sustainable development] principles then their long term future is in jeopardy'.[34]

These villagers at the Mosquito camp in Daru have been displaced by the activities of the Ok Tedi mine, which severely reduced the river's capacity to provide them with their traditional food sources. State regulation could prevent such impacts occurring in the host country of mining projects.

Photo by Simon Divecha, Mineral Policy Institute

A corporate licence to operate has both the 'formal' element of maintaining a corporate entity that can legally conduct business and thereby gain legal access to land and capital, and an 'informal' element of community consent or support.

The case mounted in the US (discussed above) against the legal licence of a Californian-registered oil company demonstrates the potential threat.[35] The case sought to withdraw Unocal's right to operate as a corporate entity because of its appalling track record on human rights abuses in Burma and Nigeria. This case foreshadows the possibility that corporations could be de-registered in future (although, clearly, there will need to be a lot of strong campaigning to achieve these types of community protections).

The threat to mining corporations' 'informal' licence to operate is exactly what is driving developments such as the Global Mining Initiative. The industry is aware of its critics' charges that its bad environmental and social record means that it is unwelcome in many communities, that many financial institutions are now looking at alternative investments, and many talented workers are looking to other industries more in line with ethical values for employment opportunities. These pressures create new opportunities for tougher regulatory regimes to be implemented and enforced and to challenge the legitimacy of industry public relations exercises.

4. Cease Financing Destructive Mining

Finance is the 'oxygen' for any development project, including mining. Mining projects require large amounts of capital and long lead times and, as a consequence, financial institutions have enormous influence. In recent years, the mining industry has had difficulty in attracting finance, in part due to the rapid growth of environmental and social screening of both private and public investment funds.

The mining industry's record on human rights, the environment and social issues is subject to ever-increasing scrutiny and it is likely that investor disclosure requirements will force companies to provide much more accurate accounts of their activities and impacts than has been the case to date. These transparency and disclosure requirements will, in turn, increase the pressure on companies to take action to address their social and environmental performance.

5. Enhance Nation State Powers and Responsibilities to Protect Citizens

Corporate globalisation, and its associated weakening of the power of nation states, has obstructed struggles for environmental and social justice. The excesses of economic liberalisation require that the powers and responsibilities of nation states to protect their citizens must be re-established and strengthened. Equally, and sadly, in many cases, national governments have been the worst violators of human rights and the environment and have actively supported TNCs in their exploitation of communities and their resources. Therefore, any expansion of the regulatory role of the nation state must encompass strengthening democracy and building greater transparency and accountability of government decision-making processes.

6. Make Directors Personally Responsible for the Actions of their Corporations

The due diligence argument that is increasingly part of health and safety and environmental law must be applied to human rights and environmental activities of TNCs. Historically, common law has separated the acts of corporations from the acts of the individuals working for the corporation, making assigning liability for pollution offences problematic. In recent years, however, this difficulty has been addressed with legislation in many countries now assigning the responsibility for such offences to organisations and to the individuals working for organisations.

For example, in Australia, all of the States now have environmental legislation that imposes liability on corporate directors and managers for the offences of their corporations. The penalties that can be imposed include large fines and prison sentences.

Making the directors and managers of a TNC personally responsible (and liable) for the actions of their organisation represents a potentially powerful means of focussing the attention of corporate leaders on the environmental, human rights and social impacts of their decisions.

7. Democratise Shareholder Powers

Shareholders have enormous potential power to make corporations accountable to the wider community. This power is being increasingly used with the growth of shareholder activism by environment, human rights and labour organisations.

At the Rio Tinto 2000 AGM, held in Brisbane, Australia, an alliance of union, indigenous, church, environmental and human rights organisations, supported shareholder resolutions proposed by the Construction, Forestry, Mining and Energy Union (CFMEU) and the superannuation funds.

In June 2000, the Australian government (influenced in part by heavy lobbying from the mining industry) moved to counter this type of shareholder activism by substantially increasing the threshold shareholding required for small investors to call for special meetings, to speak at meetings and to move resolutions regarding corporate governance, ethics and investment decisions.

It may be that the negative consequences of this decision may be offset, to some extent at least, by the increasing willingness of large institutional shareholders to exercise activism, as part of their socially responsible investment portfolio obligations.

Conclusion

This chapter may be cold comfort for those who want to see mining TNCs more effectively regulated through the formal processes of international and domestic legislation. Efforts to date have been disappointing. Furthermore, it is clear that self-regulation offers, at best, a partial solution. Without credible minimum, mandatory standards of performance, credible monitoring and reporting and effective enforcement, self-regulatory regimes will not be the solution.[36]

Despite the limitations of traditional regulatory approaches, mining TNCs can be regulated and controlled. Communities and NGOs must look outside the traditional regulatory approaches and seize the range of other tools and opportunities that are presented by today's increasingly globalised and transparent world. A multitude of sites of struggle and tools are available to create pressure for change. Ease of information sharing, exposure through the media, civil dissent and popular intervention all act as driving forces for change. The seven strategies proposed in this chapter provide the framework for future action and for future campaigning efforts. Other chapters in this book provide examples of the application of these strategies.

Ultimately, the long-term survival of the minerals industry is contingent on protecting and enhancing the environment, human rights and economic, social and cultural rights of the communities and nations in which they operate. To survive and prosper longer term, the industry will need to be vastly different in its structures and practices. Those that are successful will be those that prepare best for operating in a democratic and transparent environment where communities, not corporations, rule.

14 Strategies for change: What next?
Sarah Wright

Introduction

Freedom is a word loaded with meaning. In many people's minds, concepts of freedom conjure associations of greater civil liberties, of justice, equality and the advancement of human rights. The latter part of the 20th century, however, has seen the word 'free' used to invoke a very different set of ideas. Free trade, free markets and the freedom of companies to do as they wish, unconstrained by unnecessary regulation, have become the order of the day.

The website of the World Trade Organisation (WTO), the organisation developed after the Uruguay round of the General Agreement on Tariffs and Trade to oversee a system of global rules of trade between nations, redefines peace and prosperity in terms of access to market and choice of products.[1]

The redefinition of these concepts as economic is a fundamental process that draws upon one of the dominant economic doctrines of the turn of the 21st century, namely, the doctrines of free market consumer capitalism. According to this doctrine the world is an economic one, and safe trading means safety for all its citizens.

However, the experience of an increasingly large section of the population is that economic prosperity of this unidentified consumer does not mean prosperity for them.

The growth in free trade has broadened the gap between rich and poor and hastened environmental destruction. The poorest 20 per cent of the world's people saw their share of global income decline from 2.3 per cent to 1.4 per cent in the last 30 years. Meanwhile, the share of the richest 20 per cent rose from 70 to 83 per cent.[2] These huge disparities have a strong geographical basis. Thirty-five countries in Africa, twenty-two in Latin America and the Caribbean, twenty in Eastern Europe and the former Soviet Union and fourteen Middle-Eastern States are now poorer than they were several decades ago. However, the inequality is also based on race, class and gender lines as income differences have increased within countries as well as across the First World/Third World divide.[3]

We are witnessing a global revolution. This revolution is not one fermented by grassroots activists, be they environmentalists, unionists, feminists or socialists, but by transnational companies, powerful governments and neo-liberal economists.[4] The revolution they describe is a revolution to promote friction-free global markets in the name of rationality and growth. It is the creation of an 'economically-accountable' world where nothing will jeopardise the 'freedom' of capital.

Yet is it really inevitable that our lives will be founded on an ideology that centres on free trade and neo-liberalism as the salvation for all human beings? From Brazil to the Philippines, Australia to the USA, hundreds of thousands of people have taken to the streets to demand a more equitable future and to ensure that corporate 'rights' are not prioritised over human and environmental interests. The breadth of concern speaks with fear and suspicion about the so-called 'options' associated with globalisation. Social change workers in communities throughout the world are saying they do not want a global economy in which old inequities are perpetuated by new forms of power and ideology, or industries that rely upon exploitation of land and people for their existence. What, however, do social activists want? Can there be an alternative to corporate globalisation, a path or set of paths leading to a more just and equitable future?

This chapter brings together many of the themes of this book. The first part looks at the minerals industry and discusses some paths forward. It discusses different visions of sustainability and asks what a sustainable minerals industry might look like. The second part of the chapter turns to the envisioning of broader alternatives. Social and environmental sustainability will not come at the level of a single mine, or from an isolated view of the minerals industry. We need to struggle for an alternative vision. The fight is a fight against a race to the bottom, for something beyond a rehashing of exploitation. This vision does not have as its central pillar the re-enforcement of global inequalities and the advancement of the rich at the expense of the poor.

A Sustainable Minerals Industry?

The minerals industry has been a central pillar in the process of globalisation. As the chapters in this volume attest, mining companies have been heavily involved in promoting and in benefiting from the move toward a freer, more globalised market. Like many large-scale industries, the minerals industry has profited from inequalities, and by exploiting people and environments for its own gain.

What would a sustainable minerals industry look like? Obviously this question has many answers. There are some mines that are more sustainable than others. Some mines, such as have been chronicled in this book, are unequivocally not sustainable, destroying land, cultures, ecosystems and lives. A sustainable minerals industry would not contravene international environmental agreements and treaties, International Labour Organisation conventions and International Human Rights law. It would not dump untreated tailings into rivers or oceans nor rely on military forces or excessive security for its operation. These kinds of abuses are perpetuated by the industry every day.

Yet what of cases that are not so clearly unsustainable? What if the minerals extraction or processing is undertaken with the full support of the local people, or better, is undertaken by the local people in consensus, and is done with all due care to minimising environmental effects? Perhaps it is on land already degraded, with a strong revegetation program that is put in place after the mine is finished. Perhaps the mine minimises exploitation of people and land, creates just employment and contributes over the long term to the local economy. Perhaps an equivalent number of trees are planted for every tonne of greenhouse gas that will be produced as a result of the mine's existence. Is this a sustainable mine?

The key question is what is 'sustainability' and who defines it. As Roger Moody points out in *The Gulliver Files*, 'The truth is that 'sustainability' implies something quite different for those at the sharp end of the bulldozer than it does for those in the driving seat.'[5] Today, mining companies are clambering to take the lead in defining sustainability, offering schools, and hospitals and jobs in return for the mineral wealth, supposedly extracted with minimal long-term environmental harm. However, for communities facing the bulldozer, the concept and the reality of 'sustainable mining' is not necessarily the same. Moody summarises this difference: 'Replacing the contours of ripped-up ranges may serve an aesthetic purpose, but can never compensate for the loss of part of an ecosystem, or indigenous peoples' sacred places.'[6]

The word 'sustainable' comes from the Latin *sus tenere*, meaning to uphold. Not surprisingly, given the ideas discussed above, sustaining can either mean 'supporting a desired state of some kind' or conversely, 'enduring an undesired state.'[7] A commonly used definition of sustainable development is that the needs of today's generation should not compromise the needs of future generations.[8] But what these needs are and how they are defined remain in contention. Economists look to categorising sustainability into three levels: that of very weak, weak and strong sustainability.

Very weak sustainability is primarily concerned that the overall stock of capital assets (natural, man-made, and human) should remain constant. In this case, it doesn't matter if a resource is depleted somewhere as long as the total amount of it (or a possible substitute) in the world is constant. Weak sustainability assumes that the world cannot guarantee the constant stock positions because of constraints imposed on assimilative capacity. As such it emphasises the value of safeguarding ecological processes that are irrecoverable if lost. Finally, strong sustainability takes into account the primacy of the ecosystem functioning to maintain life on Earth. Strong sustainability puts justice at the centre of the philosophy rather than as an addendum to be incorporated after the basic decisions are made.

These definitions hold a fairly clear, if harsh, answer; that a mine cannot be more than very weakly 'sustainable' as it is by nature extractive, drawing upon a non-renewable resource. To come back to the question of what a sustainable minerals industry might look like, for the minerals industry to be strongly sustainable it would not be involved in mining at all, but perhaps would focus on recycling or metal re-use.

226

The 'Three Rs' of Metal Mining: Reduce, Re-use, Recycle

There are clear paths toward meeting metal needs more sustainably. The 'three R's' of reduce, re-use, recycle are perhaps nowhere more pertinent than to the minerals industry. The demand for metals could be immensely reduced. *Factor Four*, the latest report to the Club of Rome, proposes that we can double our wealth and halve our resource use through conscientious resource efficiency and by raising energy productivity. It sets out fifty working examples, including office retrofits with 'superwindows', photovoltaic solar panels, and metal recycling. [9]

Police face crowds protesting the growth of corporate globalisation in August 2001 in Barcelona.

Photo by Barcelona.indymedia.org

This report uses the catchphrase, 'Design for Environment'. This is a practice that goes back to the drawing board where the base infrastructure can be redesigned with environmental and energy efficiency as the goal. The conventional car has been incrementally improved to be more fuel-efficient, which is, in effect, 'designing the whole car backwards'. *Factor Four* describes the design concept of the 'hypercar' which designs the car from the beginning with fuel efficiency in mind.

The result? A car which saves 80–95 per cent of the fuel and cuts 90 – 99 per cent per cent of the smog. If, in addition, the infrastructure is of higher quality, it will allow re-use of all parts.[10] By reducing demand for metals these basic ideas have huge implications for the mineral industry. Reducing and redirecting the West's huge demand for fossil fuel and nuclear power is another clear way forward. We have at our disposal many, many techniques and opportunities to reduce power demand if only we had the political, cultural and personal will to do it.

For the (vastly reduced) power needs we do have, the time has come to move from coal-based and nuclear power to alternative energy systems. Renewable energy sources, including solar-thermal, photovoltaic, wind and biomass power, passive and active solar heat exist in copious amounts. Most of these energy sources cost less than nuclear power, especially if the external costs of nuclear accident risks and contamination are internalised.[11]

A move to renewable energy systems would mean that new coal and uranium mines, and oil projects, as well as new exploration could be eliminated. Reflecting this, an immediate ban on new exploration in indigenous lands and frontier ecosystems was called for by over 200 organisations from 52 countries of the OilWatch network at the Kyoto meeting of the Climate Convention.[12]

Similarly, the Earth Day 2000 Indigenous Solidarity Statement endorsed by Ijaw, U'wa, Gwich'in, Mirrar, Karen, Mon and Tavoyan communities from Nigeria, Colombia, Northern Canada and Alaska, Australia and Burma calls from an end to fossil fuel subsidies, and an end to new exploration. The statement calls on 'governmental and international financial institutions to cease all fossil fuel subsidies and to invest immediately in clean, renewable and decentralised forms of energy, with a particular focus on meeting the needs of the two billion poorest people on Earth. We reaffirm our commitment to the defence of local people in their democratic struggle to regain their human dignity and protect the environments in which they live. We must all come together and demand clean energy – energy free of blood and environmental destruction – if we are all to survive.' [13]

A continued reliance on coal-fired power and fossil fuels flies in the face of the Kyoto Protocol, whereby countries defined as high greenhouse gas emitters are required to reduce their reliance on fossil fuels. Even Australia's so-called 'clean coal' exports are a contentious issue. While 'clean coal' contains a lower level of sulfur, the sulfur content has no bearing on levels of greenhouse gas emissions. There is an exponential increase in the demand for energy in East and South-east Asia, with current demand expected to increase by 41 per cent by 2010.[14] This could enable the creation of a renewable-energy infrastructure, yet the Australian Government simply sees it as a means of boosting coal exports.

Reusing and recycling are also important ways of increasing the efficiency and sustainability of the industry. There are copious amounts of high quality, processed minerals available above the ground for recovery. Metal re-use and recycling reduces the impacts of extraction, as well as ensuring energy savings, producing less waste and reducing air emissions. Goldmining, for example, creates a tremendous amount of waste and has long been associated with social dislocation and massive damage to natural ecosystems. However, goldmining is not essential, even to meet the current demand for gold. Of the 127,000 tonnes of gold ever dug out of the ground, over 35,500 tonnes lies in the vaults of central reserve banks. This represents more than 350 years of current, so-called 'essential' use.[15]

Whilst these steps may be necessary as initial moves towards sustainability, they do not offer a viable alternative without broader attention to the inequities and unsustainable nature of the global system. The answers are not simple. The needs of mining communities who depend on the industry for jobs must be addressed within any responsible agenda for change. Solidarity with indigenous cultures should not rest on an objectification of indigenous cultures as static or 'natural.' Change is a continual process found in all cultures. However, the direction of this change should not be imposed upon local communities without consent. Local communities have the right to forge their own development path on their own cultural terms.

What is needed is for the system itself to change. A clean environment should not just be the prerogative of those who can afford it. Sustainable communities are not created by externalising social and environmental costs. Imagine a closed and gated community that has addressed all its environmental and internal social needs but is reliant on low-paid nannies, housekeepers and gardeners, and consumes goods that have been exploitatively produced in other countries, whilst it exists on land from which families have been relocated. This is obviously an untenable situation on a local or a global scale, and directly raises the issue of distribution. The Report *Factor Four* that states 'we' can double 'our' wealth and halve 'our' resource use through conscientious resource efficiency by talking of 'us' and 'our' neatly sidesteps the major issues of wealth redistribution.

It is vital that the central question be asked: whose wealth is cut and at whose cost? There are many in this world that live off very few resources and to halve their intake would mean starvation. A leap to sustainability could perhaps be more usefully taken by altering the wealth and resource use of the world's richest. Perhaps rather than a doubling of wealth for those in the overdeveloped world, it should be cut to a tenth, or a hundredth, of its current level with resource use cut to a thousandth or ten-thousandth. This sounds like a challenge, and it is. While distribution is unequal – with those that benefit and those that pay – the system cannot be sustained. This directly raises the question of envisioning alternatives; how and where do they come from? How and who should create them?

Resistance Is Not Just a Mirror of Power

Contesting globalisation needs to be inclusive and to celebrate what neo-liberalism denies diversity of cultures, diversity of people and diversity of environments. There will not be one grand alternative, no easy one-size-fits-all band-aid to be used for every community and every situation. Instead, solutions and alternatives must spring from communities, and not merely the communities of the privileged global North. This means taking seriously the process of struggle.

Fighting transnational oil and mining companies must be understood on its own terms, not just as the underside of domination. Resistance is not just a mirror of power.[16] Resistance to exploitative mining and globalisation is not just about reacting to injustice, it is part of an envisioning process that provides alternative strategies and solutions. It is difficult when fighting a certain mine, or campaigning against a particular mining company, to suggest alternatives, but it is also crucial. As the cultural geographer, Steve Pile, argues, 'Resistance may take place as a reaction against unfairness and injustice, as a desire to survive intolerable conditions, but it may also involve a sense of remembering and dreaming of something better. If there is a beaten track ... then resistance will stray from this track, find new ways ... new futures.'[17]

Forms and patterns of globalisation itself have been and continue to be contested. Corporate globalisation is fluid and is not something to accept as a certainty. There is no predetermined, inevitable outcome.[18] Labour is just one force that plays an active role at the global scale and indeed in helping to create the global scale. The International Chemical Energy and Mining Union (ICEM), for example, brings together mining workers to fight for common concerns, and ICEM's campaign against Rio Tinto, outlined in this book, is an excellent example of this kind of activity.

Drawing on discourses of justice, democracy, human rights and environment, many other groups are trying to influence the agenda and instigate a bottom-up approach to globalisation. The approach is grounded in a vision of human communities, from the grassroots level, defining this as the source of legitimacy, not corporations or national or supranational institutions.[19] The emphasis is on communities of resistance challenging corporate globalisation from diverse standpoints. As Falk argues, a bottom-up globalisation, 'facilitates communication across civilisational, nationalist, ethnic, class, generational, cognitive, and gender divides, but there is also implicit respect and celebration of difference and an attitude of extreme scepticism towards exclusivist claims that deny space for expression and exploration to others, as well as toward variants of universalism that ignore the uneven circumstances and aspirations of peoples, classes and regions.'[20]

We need an open debate about the form and nature of the system. In the past, periods of economic change and reform have seen debates about the different alternatives.[21] As Jeremy Brecher and Tim Costello point out, in the responses to the Great Depression of the 1930s: 'various versions of Labor and political organisation and anti-monopoly policies, government regulation, socialism, communism, and communitarianism were hotly debated in schools, workplaces, unions, the press, and political organisations. Such an open discussion of alternative solutions should be a crucial part of today's global reconstruction.'[22]

The huge protests that have occurred against the institutions of neo-liberal globalisation such as the World Bank, the IMF and the WTO challenge supranational organisations and corporate rule not merely with the physical act of blockading streets, but with the multiplicity of voices, cultures, and approaches that flourish on the street, in bars, universities, schools and workplaces. A unionist at the Seattle protests explained:

'A year's worth of political discussion has been compressed into six days: the role of the different movements, the role of the folks from other countries, the question of violence and civil disobedience, etc... Trade unionists in the US don't exist in a vacuum, and we see ourselves more clearly when we see ourselves in relationship to others.'[23]

The breakdown of established experience in the planning and the implementation of these large protests creates a space of regeneration, and puts in place new decision-making practices, new opportunities for conversation, creativity and the formation of new communities and cross-cultural bridges. In this way, global protests provide a chance to take that first step in the process of generating solutions, namely the generation of discussion and ideas. As another Seattle protester explained:

'We are creating a festival of resistance... we are building movement. We are building bridges. By using art, it's a language that the police and the State don't understand. It's the language of the people. It's the language of creation. It's the opposite of war. It's the opposite of violence. It's the opposite of death. It's a language of people being creative and innovative together.' [24]

Yet it is not major events that generate solutions. Sustained local action is the key to envisioning change: this is where the problems themselves are felt, and where women and men who have the necessary intimate knowledge of specific situations are found. The struggle against neo-liberalism is a struggle that reflects the needs of a 'pluriverse'.[25] The refrain, 'More world, less bank,' seen and heard at the protests surrounding the first meetings of the IMF/World Bank for the new millennium, summed up this demand for multiplicity and difference: MORE world, MORE ways of working, thinking, acting and being, not less.

Strategies for change and the envisioning of new alternatives are springing from all corners of the globe. Responses to globalisation must be wary of focusing on myths of divisive communalism or nationalism, or of allowing the agenda to be set by liberal think-tanks in the global North.[26] As we fight against specific processes and injustices, we need to keep in our minds the dreams and visions for something better. Alternatives will spring from open discussions and recognition of strengths: they will not mirror structures that are put in place by the powerful. The alternatives to a reductionist, economic approach will spring from diversity and from culture.

Envisioning Alternatives

Advocates of 'free', globalised markets claim they are establishing 'a level playing field', and removing barriers to trade. Such a system is not about removing rules, but about changing them to favour corporations. The rhetoric of neo-liberal globalisation may revolve around freedom for capital, but it is important to realise the 'freedom' it brings is simply the freedom of the big and powerful to crush the small and marginal.

We need a redefinition of the focus of the global agenda from a corporate to a human-focused model. It is clear that we are in a process of major economic reconstruction. A liveable future depends on reversing the race to the bottom; turning around the rush towards the lowest working conditions, the poorest social and environmental standards. It relies upon activists and local communities taking power back from multinational corporations and corporate-oriented supranational organisations like the IMF, the World Bank and the WTO, returning it instead to accountable governments and to local communities.

Only by combining efforts can the world economy be brought under control. Within themselves, neither local, national or international institutions are capable of realising this diverse agenda. Such a program has to be implemented and conceived at multiple levels. As Korten has argued, 'It is time to make a fresh start toward re-thinking and recreating the global economy based on principles of decentralisation, diversity, and distribution – with full and open public debate.' [27]

One alternative, proposed by the Economic Working Group, a loose alliance of mostly US-based activists, was developed as a direct response to the General Agreement of Tariffs and Trade (GATT). This model, called the General Agreement on a New Economy (GANE), begins with three fundamental values: environmental sustainability, equity and meaningful work. Each set of values raises fundamental questions about the global economy. For instance, if environmental sustainability requires that goods are durable, reusable, repairable, and ultimately recyclable, then how will unneeded manufacturing jobs be replaced? If some communities have more resources than others, will only the rich become sustainable? For GANE, the economy begins at the local level with community needs linked to an environmentally and socially sustainable future, not just to individual needs that may be open to manipulation by marketeers.[28]

Within the community, work is linked with the needs of the community. Once a community has developed its own vision, it will realise what it needs as a community. This becomes the basis for defining what has real value locally and for identifying what work will be meaningful in the local context. Central to GANE's 'new economy' is the fact that productivity and wealth should be rooted in safe and rewarding work, in the sustainable use of resources and healthy communities. As Ruth Caplan explains, 'the General Agreement on a New Economy, GANE not GATT, is premised on the idea that people have the right to ask about the purpose of the economy and to imagine together how an economy could be structured to meet the needs of families and communities.'[29]

Such visions are important in stimulating debate, and in opening up new agendas. But it is the process of creating these agendas that is all-important – the process of realising radical hope – the essence of all social movements. At the Intercontinental Encounter for Humanity and Against Neo-liberalism hosted by the Zapatistas and held in Chiapas, Mexico in July-August 1996, thousands of people from more than 40 countries met in a small village in the Chiapas rainforest to envision a future without neo-liberalism and to plot a course for change.

This gathering conceptualised the movement for change as a web consisting of 'movements that are firmly local while being, at the same time and without contradiction, international in expressing the hopes of liberation across the world; of the people struggling to free themselves from the menace of global neo-liberalism.'[30] The web is not a centralised organisational structure leading to more committees and flow charts, but a supportive network of particular struggles and resistances. Building upon strong, local alliances and solidarities between groups, 'all of us who resist are the web.'[31] What is clear is that possibilities and prospective solutions do exist, and we need to intensify the challenge.

Conclusion

Free trade and liberalisation, most recently under the banner of globalisation, swept the world in the latter half of the 20th century. The movement of capital between countries is nothing new – the empires of Europe were founded on the 'unfettered' movement of resources, technology and even slaves from the global South to the global North. What we are seeing now, however, is a new form of colonisation whereby trade barriers are removed and markets prised open under the rhetoric of prosperity, peace and accountability. The minerals industry is one industry that has benefited immensely from such 'prosperity' and 'accountability'. Through the liberalisation of mining laws, the industry has the ability to skip over national and local concerns. Via the vast spatial separation between those people positively and negatively affected by developments, the international minerals industry has manipulated, promoted and benefited from this 'recolonisation' process.

What I have argued in this chapter is that ideologies of mining and globalisation need to be fundamentally changed. To do so, progressive movements must engage in local struggles to generate and articulate alternative visions for the future. There is a need for society to pull away from an obsession with free trade and an unfettered, super-conductive market to examine our most basic assumptions and structures. In the West, we need to look at patterns of consumption and at the very foundation of a lifestyle that is based on the exploitation of so many, and of so much.

It is time that we went back to the word 'freedom' and remembered its value. As Gandhi said, 'Freedom is never dear at any price. It is the breath of life.' Globalisation, as it stands today, is about the imposition of structures that will affirm and further ingrain established world hierarchies. To move beyond these, we must search for alternatives, speak of new possibilities and draw upon our diverse cultures to envisage a just and equitable future.

About the authors

Abigail Abrash has monitored human rights conditions in Indonesia, with a specific focus on indigenous rights and corporate responsibility issues in Papua, as Program Director and a consultant for the Robert F Kennedy Memorial Centre for Human Rights and as a Visiting Fellow at Harvard Law School's Human Rights Program. She is also a Board member of the Jayapura-based Institute for Human Rights Studies and Advocacy, and Project Underground, and serves on the Advisory Board of the Indonesia Human Rights Network.

Bob Burton is a Canberra based freelance journalist. He is editor of *Mining Monitor*, the investigative news-magazine of the Sydney based non-government organisation the Mineral Policy Institute (www.mpi.org.au) and a regular contributor to a number of media outlets including *PR Watch* (www.prwatch.org), *Inter-Press Service* and *Environment News Service*. With Nicky Hager, he co-authored *Secrets and Lies; the anatomy of an anti-environmental PR campaign*, Craig Potten Publishing, New Zealand 1999.

Peter Colley is National Research Director for the Mining & Energy Division of the Construction, Forestry, Mining and Energy Union – one of Australia's largest unions. He has worked at the national and international levels of labour unions since 1989. The thesis for his Master of Economics (Honours) degree was on trading and investment practices in the Australia–Japan coal trade. He is the author of *Reforming Energy – sustainable futures and global labour*, published by Pluto Press. UK in 1997.

Catherine Coumans has been Research Coordinator at MiningWatch Canada for the past two years, where her geographic focus, in addition to Canada, is on South-east Asia and the Pacific. Catherine researches and writes on issues related to water contamination, such as Submarine Tailings Disposal, as well as on Full Cost Accounting for the Canadian Mining Sector, Global Standards, Corporate Social Responsibility and Shareholder Activism. Catherine holds a Ph.D. (1993) in Anthropology and has done extensive anthropological research in the Philippines since 1984. In 1990 she became involved in the struggle of people of the Philippine island of Marinduque against mining by Canadian-based Placer Dome. Catherine has published several articles on mining and is working on a book on the history of struggle against mining in Marinduque.

Geoff Evans is the Director of the Mineral Policy Institute, Sydney. He is an environmental scientist and social ecologist, and has worked on mining and environmental justice issues with Aboriginal people in Central Australia, and in the Philippines and Papua New Guinea. He is an NGO representative on the Australian Government's Best Practice Environmental Management in Mining Steering Committee. He now lives in Newcastle, NSW, the centre of Australia's largest coalmining and fossil fuel power generation region.

Rick Fowler is Executive Officer of the Australian Construction, Forestry, Mining and Energy Union. His roles have included Strategic Campaigning trainer, and he played a key role in the Rio Tinto campaign and world network. He is a Board member of the Mineral Policy Institute, Sydney, a member of Advisory Committee to the University of NSW Institute of Environmental Studies, a member of Global Justice Coalition, and a member of APHEDA's Education and Campaign sub-committee. Rick Fowler holds an MA in Political Science, and a BA in Industrial Relations.

James Goodman is a lecturer in international political economy and cultural studies at the Faculty of Humanities and Social Sciences, University of Technology, Sydney. He is active in several campaign organisations, including being on the boards of Aid/Watch and the Mineral Policy Institute. He has co-edited several books on social movements, including *Protest and Globalisation: Prospects for Transnational Solidarity* (Pluto Press, 2001), *Stopping a Juggernaut: Public Interests versus the Multilateral Agreement on Investment* (2000) and *Dis/agreeing Ireland: Obstacles, Hopes* (1998).

Alison Harwood conducts Social Impact Assessments relating to sand and coalmining, and has worked with Aboriginal traditional owners of the southern Gulf of Carpentaria, Stradbroke Island, Queensland and the Upper Hunter Valley in New South Wales. Alison is currently employed by the NSW Department of Land and Water Conservation, assisting regional community-based committees to insert social and cultural aspirations and values within natural resource management plans, and to assess the social and cultural impacts of planning options.

Moses Havini is the International Political Representative and Human Rights Advocate of the Bougainville Interim Government in Australia.

During the war, Mr Havini played an active role and continues to represent his people on behalf of the Bougainville Peoples Congress.

Vikki John is an active member of the Bougainville Freedom Movement in Australia (www.eco-action.org/bv/bvupdate). In 1993, she met Moses Havini in the middle of the Australian desert whilst supporting Aboriginal land rights by protesting against the USA spy base at Nurrungar. She is a part-time student of Humanities at the University of Technology, Sydney.

Jacqui Katona is the former Executive Officer of the Gundjehmi Aboriginal Corporation. Gundjehmi Aboriginal Corporation is an organisation established, managed and controlled by the Mirrar people, the traditional owners of part of Kakadu National Park. The Gundjehmi Aboriginal Corporation provides for both its own members and those Aboriginal people affected by the existing Ranger uranium mine. It assists the Mirrar people to maintain their culture and protect their heritage, publishes and disseminates information and represent the interests of members in the development of regional agreements and other matters that will further self-determination. In 1999, Jacqui Katona was awarded the Goldman Environment Prize in the US.

Danny Kennedy was until recently the Director of Project Underground, a non-governmental organisation in the United States that supports the human rights of communities resisting mining and oil exploitation. He has also served on the Board of the Mineral Policy Institute in Australia, and is on the Board of the Pacific Environment and Resource Center in California. He now works for Greenpeace on climate change issues in California.

David Korten is the author of *When Corporations Rule the World* and *The Post Corporate World*, both published by Kumarian Press. He is also the founder and president of the People-Centered Development Forum, an international voluntary organisation whose activities centre on facilitating the sharing and interpretation of experience with an emerging people's development movement. Korten holds PhD and MBA degrees from the Stanford University Graduate School of Business, is a former faculty member of Harvard University's graduate Schools of Business and Public Health and a former advisor to the United States Agency for International Development.

Nina Lansbury is the Research Coordinator at the Mineral Policy Institute, Sydney. She is currently working on issues of mining in Socially Responsible Investment portfolios, coordinating an online, international database of mining companies and projects, and monitoring the role of mining companies in globalisation. Her background is in environmental science and Indonesian studies, and her previous work has involved environmental journalism, environmental education and socio-environmental research.

Jean McSorley coordinated the Rio Tinto campaign for the International Chemical, Mine, Energy and General Workers' Union from 1998 to 1999. She has over twenty years experience as a campaigner, most of which was spent on nuclear issues. She has been coordinator of the Nuclear & Energy Campaign in Asia for Greenpeace International and in 1999 was appointed to 'represent the interests of the general public' on the Nuclear Safety Committee of the Australian Radiation Protection and Nuclear Safety Agency.

Ruth Phillips completed her doctorate at the University of New South Wales, Sydney, in 2001 on non-Government Organisations and their experience with corporate engagement.

Gabrielle Russell currently manages the Futures Foundation which helps organisations explore the needs and opportunities of the future. Until July 2001 she was the Foreign Affairs Advisor for Australian Democrats Senator Vicki Bourne, and was instrumental in formulating the Corporate Code of Conduct Bill 2000. She has an MBA from the Macquarie Graduate School of Management and has written papers on governance, aid and corporate citizenship issues.

Rory Sullivan is the Convenor of the Amnesty International (Australia) Business Group and the Australian representative on Amnesty International's Working and Advisory Group on Economic Relations. He is currently completing a PhD at the University of London on the role of self-regulation in environmental and public policy. He is the author (with Hugh Wyndham) of *Effective Environmental Management: Principles and Case Studies* (Allen & Unwin, Sydney, 2001). He is also the author/co-author of over seventy papers and articles on various aspects of environmental management, environmental policy and human rights law.

Antonio Tujan Jr. is a well-known activist, scholar and lecturer in the Philippine progressive movement. In 1978, he was one of the pioneers of IBON Foundation, an independent research–education institution actively involved in Philippine social and economic issues. He since returned as its Executive Director from 1994–1999 and is currently its Executive Editor and Research Director. He is also a consultant to various Philippine NGOs and people's organisations and is the Chairperson of the Asia Pacific Research Network. Recent books published are *Globalizing Philippine Mining,* IBON Books, 1999 and *The Impact of the WTO Agreement on Agriculture*, IBON Books, 2000.

Sarah Wright is currently an instructor at the University of Washington where she researches intellectual property rights and corporate globalisation. She is a board member of PressurePoint, a Seattle-based NGO that works on redefining corporate power through sustained, non-violent direct action. She was previously the research coordinator for the Mineral Policy Institute and was co-coordinator for the corporate campaign against the Jabiluka mine in Australia. Sarah also worked in Cuba for two years helping coordinate the urban food production education project in Havana.

END NOTES

Introduction

[1] Junne Cosmos, Letter to the Mineral Policy Institute, October 1999.

[2] Center for International Environmental Law, Environmental Defense, Friends of the Earth, Greenpeace, Institute for Policy Studies, Natural Resource Defense Council, World Wildlife Fund, Physicians for Social Responsibility and Union of Concerned Scientists, Joint Position Letter to Dan Magraw, Acting Deputy Principal Assistant Administrator of US Environmental Protection Agency, prior to the Trieste G8 meeting, February 2001.

[3] 'Venezuela Finds Source of Wealth Is Also A Curse', *Section 1, New York Times*, August 2000, p. 3.

[4] 'Shell-Shocked Refugees', Project Underground, USA, 1999.

[5] W. Bello, 'Why reform of the EDB is the wrong agenda', Accounting for Development Conference, June, University of Sydney, 2000.

[6] World Wide Web Document: International Institute for the Environment and Development, 'What is MMSD?', www.iied.org, accessed 22 July 2001.

[7] Sir Robert Wilson, 'The Mining Industry: In Recuperation or Remission?' Securities Institute of Australia, Grand Hyatt Hotel, Melbourne, 7 December 1999.

[8] Sir Robert Wilson, 'How the world mining industry had to dig itself out of a hole', *The Observer*, London, 8 July 2001.

Chapter 1: Predatory Corporations

[1] M. Fox, *Sins of the Spirit, Blessings of the Flesh*, Harmony Books, 1992.

[2] K. M. Panikkar, *Asia and Western Dominance*, The Other Press, Kuala Lumpur, 1993, p. 46; and 'Dutch East India Company', Encyclopedia Britannica, (CD Edition) 1998.

[3] K. M. Panikkar, *Asia and Western Dominance*, The Other Press, Kuala Lumpur, 1993, p. 48.

[4] E. McNall Burns, *Western Civilizations: Their History and Their Culture*, Fifth Edition, W. W. Norton and Company, New York, 1958, p. 467; and 'The British East India Company', Encyclopedia Britannica, (CD Edition) 1998.

[5] 'The Opium Wars', Encyclopedia Britannica, (CD Edition) 1998.

[6] 'South Sea Company and Asiento de Negros', Encyclopedia Britannica, (CD Edition) 1998.

[7] M. Curtis, 'The Ambiguities of Power: British Foreign Policy Since 1945', *The Ecologist*, Vol. 26, No. 1, January/February 1996, pp. 5–12.

[8] G. Kennan, US State Department Policy Planning Study 23, 1948.

[9] UNDP Human Development Report 1998, Oxford University Press, New York, 1998, p. 2.

[10] *YES! A Journal of Positive Futures*, Bainbridge Island, Summer 1998 issue on 'Rx for the Earth' for a series of articles dealing with endocrine disrupters, corporate manipulation of related science, and the efforts of citizen groups.

Chapter 2: Political economy of mining

[1] P. Colley, *Reforming Energy: sustainable futures and global labour*, Pluto Press, London, 1997.

[2] Ministry of International Trade and Industry, White Papers, 1981–1982, cited in T. E. Kolenda 'Japan's Develop-for-import Policy', *Resources Policy*, December 1985, p. 257.

[3] H. Hotelling, H, 'The economics of exhaustible resources', *Journal of Political Economy*, 39, 1931 pp. 137–175.

[4] D. Meadows and D. Meadows (eds), *Limits to Growth A report for the Club of Rome's Project on the Predicament of Mankind*, Earth Island Ltd, London 1972.

[5] BP Amoco plc, 'Statistical review of world energy', London, June 2000.

[6] Joint Coal Board & Queensland Department of Mines and Energy, 1999 Australian Black Coal Statistics, Sydney, 2000.

[7] H. Aydin and J. Tilton, 'Mineral endowment, labour productivity and comparative advantage in mining', *Resource and Energy Economics*, 22, 2000 pp. 281–293.

[8] Tex Report, Iron Ore Manual 1999–2000, Tokyo, 1999.

[9] P. Colley, 'Investment practices in Australian coal: The practice and profit of quasi-integration in the Australia-Japan coal trade', *Energy Policy*, 25(12) 1997 pp1013–1025: P. Colley, 'Trading practices in the coal market: application of the theory of bilateral monopoly to the Australia-Japan coal Trade', *Resources Policy* 24(1), 1998 pp 59–75.

[10] 'Top 150 companies by market capitalisation', *The Sydney Morning Herald*, 4 December, 2000, p35.

[11] Note that BHP Ltd commenced a merger with Billiton plc of the UK in May 2001. The new entity was valued at A\$57 billion in market capitalisation in March 2001.

[12] International Monetary Fund, 'Statistical Appendix', IMF Staff Country Report 99/66 Papua New Guinea, Washington DC, 1999.

[13] Ok Tedi Mining Limited, 'Social and Sustainable Development Issues in relation to mine closure', Tabubil, PNG 2000.

[14]'Top 150 companies by market capitalisation', *The Sydney Morning Herald* 4 December, 2000, p35.

Chapter 3: Politicising mining and finance

[1] B. Hextall, 'Lack of funding on Diggers' minds', *Australian Financial Review*, 23 July 2001.

[2] B. Rich, 'Export Credit Agencies: the need for more rigorous, common policies, procedures and guidelines to further sustainable development', Environmental Defense Fund, Washington, 1998.

[3] B. Rich, B. 'Export Credit Agencies: the need for more rigorous, common policies, procedures and guidelines to further sustainable development', Environmental Defense Fund, Washington, p. 6.

[4] Friends Of The Earth International, 'Phasing Out Public Financing For Fossil Fuel And Mining Projects, Position Paper', Friends Of The Earth International, Washington DC, 2000.

[5] S. Chesters, 'Export Credit Agencies: new engines of globalisation', Aid/Watch, Sydney, 1999.

[6] B. Rich, 'Trading in dubious practices', *Financial Times*, February 24, 2000.

[7] Aid/Watch and Mineral Policy Institute (1999), 'Putting the ETHIC into EFIC: a discussion paper on accountability standards within the Export Finance and Insurance Corporation', Aid/Watch and Mineral Policy Institute, Sydney.

[8] Lihir Gold Ltd, 'Facts at a glance', October 1997; P. Chatterton, 'RTZ dumps on Lihir', *Mining Monitor*, 1(1), February 1996.

[9] B. Rich, 'Export Credit Agencies: the need for more rigorous, common policies, procedures and guidelines to further sustainable development', Environmental Defense Fund, Washington, 1998, p. 13.

[10] M. van Voorst, *Debt creating aspects of export credits*, Eurodad, Brussels, 1998.

[11] S. Freid, and T. Soentoro, 'Export Credit Agency Finance in Indonesia', Export Credit Agency Workshop, April, Jakarta, 2000, p. 2–3.

[12] J. Nettleton, 'Snouts in the trough; ECAs, corporate welfare and policy incoherence', The Corner House Briefing 14, Dorset, UK, 1999, p. 15.

[13] Friends Of The Earth International (2000), 'Phasing Out Public Financing For Fossil Fuel And Mining Projects, Position Paper', Friends Of The Earth International, Washington DC.

[14] G. Lawless, 'Address by Managing Director of Export Finance and Insurance Corporation', PNG Mining and Petroleum Conference, 31 Aug– 1 Sept, Sydney. 1992.

[15] J. Nettleton, 'Snouts in the trough; ECAs, corporate welfare and policy incoherence', The Corner House Briefing 14, Dorset, UK, 1999, p. 15.

[16] G. Bridge, 'Harnessing the bonanza: economic liberalisation and capacity building in the mineral sector', *Natural Resources Forum*, 23, 1999, pp. 43–55.

[17] G. Bridge, 'Harnessing the bonanza: economic liberalisation and capacity building in the mineral sector', *Natural Resources Forum*, 23, 1999, pp. 43–55.

[18] J. Otto, 'Global changes in mining laws, agreements and tax systems', Resources Policy, 24, 1998 2, p. 85.

[19] Berne Declaration, Bioforum, Centre for International Law, Environment Defense Fund, Eurodad, Friends of the Earth, Narmada Bachao Andolan, Pacific Environment and Resources Centre, and Urgewald (1999), 'A Race to the Bottom: Creating Risk, Generating Debt and Guaranteeing Environmental Destruction', Berne Declaration, Switzerland.

[20] Berne Declaration, Bioforum, Centre for International Law, Environment Defense Fund, Eurodad, Friends of the Earth, Narmada Bachao Andolan, Pacific Environment and Resources Centre, and Urgewald (1999), 'A Race to the Bottom: Creating Risk, Generating Debt and Guaranteeing Environmental Destruction', Berne Declaration, Switzerland.

[21] D. Knight, 'Environment-Finance: NGOs seek global environmental standards', *World News Interpress Service*, 24 April 1998.

[22] Aid/Watch and the Mineral Policy Institute, 'Putting the ETHIC into EFIC: a discussion paper on accountability standards within the Export Finance and Insurance Corporation', Aid/Watch and Mineral Policy Institute, Sydney, 1999, p 37–9.

[23] J. Nettleton, 'Written comments in response to the Export Credit Guarantee Department questionnaire', The Corner House, Dorset, UK, 1999, p. 1.

[24] Western Mining Activist Network, 'Follow the Money: An Activist Toolkit for Direct Corporate Campaigning', Environmental Mining Council of British Columbia, Vancouver, 2000.

[25] World Wide Wed document: Social Investment Forum, 'Report on Socially Responsible Investing Trends in the United States', 1999, and World Wide document, 'Site Social Investment Forum', www.socialinvest.org. accessed, November 4, 2000.

[26] People and Planet, 2000. 'Meeting the Responsibilities of Ownership: A Proposal for Ethical and Environmental Investment Policy for the Universities Superannuation Scheme', Oxford, 2000

[27] S. Viederman, 'Can Financial Institutions Contribute to Sustainability?' *Sustainable Banking*. Greenleaf Publishing, USA, 2001.

[28] B. Fine, 'Developmental State is Dead? Long Live Social Capital?' *Development and Change,* = 30, 1996, p 1–19; R. O'Brien, A. Goetz, J.A.

Schlote, and M. Williams, '*Contesting Global Governance*', Cambridge University Press, Cambridge, 2000.

[29] J. Nettleton, 'Written comments in response to the Export Credit Guarantee Department questionnaire', The Corner House, Dorset, UK, 1999, p. 10.

[30] 'Editorial comment: discreditable exports', *Financial Times*, 14 July, 2000.

[31] Sir Robert Wilson, 'The Mining Industry: In Recuperation or Remission?', Securities Institute of Australia, Grand Hyatt Hotel, Melbourne, 7 December, 1999.

[32] Friends Of The Earth International, 'Phasing Out Public Financing For Fossil Fuel And Mining Projects', Position Paper, Friends Of The Earth International, Washington DC, 2001.

[33] AMP Henderson Global Investors, 'Socially Responsible Investment Draft Position Paper: Mining and Minerals – Overview', Sydney, AMP Henderson Global Investors, March 2001

[34] A. Rankin, and H. Vélez , 'Mining in the Crossroads of Sustainability', Friends of the Earth Colombia – Censat Agua Viva, 12 March 2001.

[35] G. Evans, 'Inside the Eye: Miners' $7M Compliment', *Mining Monitor,* September 2000, p11.

Chapter 4: Repressive mining in West Papua

[1] A. Abrash, 'The Victims of Indonesia's Pursuit of Progress,' *The New York Times*, March 2001.

[2] P. Waldman 'Hand in Glove: How Suharto's Circle and a Mining Firm Did So Well Together,' *The Wall Street Journal*, 29 September 1998, p. A1.

[3] T. Beanal and K. Asmareyao, 'Complaint from Timika,' Letter to the provincial governor, published in *Tifa Irian*, February 1995.

[4] World Wide Web document: LEMASA (Amungme's traditional Council) Resolution, Timika, Indonesia, www.org/international/shareholders/LEMASAesol.htm accessed, June 2000

[5] Private correspondence, on file with the authors, 5 December 1999.

[6] R. W. Phelps,'Moving a Mountain a Day-Grasberg Grows Six-Fold' *Engineering & Mining Journal*, McGraw Hill Publishing Company, New York, June 2000.

[7] R. W. Phelps, 'Moving a Mountain a Day-Grasberg Grows Six-Fold' *Engineering & Mining Journal,* McGraw Hill Publishing Company, New York June 2000.

[8] G. Mealey, 'Grasberg: Mining the Richest and Most Remote Deposit of Copper and Gold in the World, in the mountains of Irian Jaya, Indonesia, Freeport McMoRan Copper & Gold', New Orleans, 1996, p.273.

[9] World Wide Web document: Montgomery Watson Environmental Process Audit 1999 fcx.com/news/fcxaudit.pdf accessed June 2000; Dames & Moore, PTFI Environmental Audit Report, March 1996.

[10] World Wide Web document: Minewatch report on Dames & Moore audit, 'A fossil of the sixties,' 2 September 1996, www.moles.org/projectunderground, accessed June 2000.

[11] PT Freeport Indonesia 1999 External Environmental Audit (Excluding Social, Cultural and Economic Impacts); PT FreeportIndonesia Operations; Irian Jaya, Indonesia; December 1999; Montgomery Watson Indonesia, Jakarta, Indonesia and Steamboat Springs, Colorado USA.

[12] 'PNG mine closure urged', *BBC World News*, Tuesday, 7 March 2000, 22:05 GMT.

[13] World Wide Web document: Letter to Freeport-McMoRan Copper & Gold, Inc.; US Overseas Private Investment Corporation; Washington, D.C.; 10 October 1995 available online at www.cs.utexas.edu/users/boyer/fp.html accessed June 2000.

[14] 'US envoy frustrated over Freeport',*Indonesian Observer*, 14 March 2000.

[15] S. Paul 'Ok Tedi owners seek new ways to ease mine harm', Melbourne, 25 November 2000.

[16] R. Howitt and J. Connell (ed.), *Mining and Indigenous Peoples in Australasia*, Sydney University Press, 1991.

[17] 'Mission to Indonesia and East Timor on the issue of violence against women', Report of the Special Rapporteur on violence against women, its causes and consequences, U.N. Economic and Social Council, E/CN.4/1999/68/ Add.3, 21 January 1999.

[18] 'The Amungme and Kamoro Demand Justice for the Destruction caused by Freeport Indonesia in Irian Jaya,' translated letter by Tom Beanal, in his capacity as Director of the Lorentz Foundation, a nongovernmental organisation founded by the Kamoro and Amungme people; circa 1993 (on file with authors).

[19] 'Arti Tanah Bagi Suku Amungme', *Kompas*, 25 September 1995 English translation; and cited in M. Easton, 'Land Tenure Issues Surrounding the PT Freeport Indonesia Concession in Irian Jaya', unpublished manuscript (on file with authors).

[20] National Human Rights Commission of Indonesia, 'Results of Monitoring and Investigating of Five Incidents at Timika and One Incident at Hoea, Irian Jaya During October 1994–June 1995,' September 1995; and Violations of Human Rights in the Timika Area of Irian Jaya, Indonesia, Catholic Church of Jayapura; August 1995.

[21] 'Violations of Human Rights in the Timika Area of Irian Jaya, Indonesia', Catholic Church of Jayapura; August 1995; p. 6.

[22] 'Amungme People's Response to National Commission on Human Rights Findings' announced on 22 September 1997, on file with authors

[23] 'The Victims Residing in the Area of the PT Freeport Mining Concession in the Villages of Banti, Arwanop, Tsinga, Hoeya, Waa, and Timika,' statement from Amungme community members, sent to Komnas HAM, Freeport management and the Robert F. Kennedy Center for Human Rights, February 7, 2000.

[24] Public Statement, Forum for the Reconciliation of Irian Jaya Society (FORERI), Jayapura, 24 July 1998.

[25] P. Madani and J. Solomon 'Indonesia Orders Freeport To Reduce Mining Output', *The Wall Street Journal*, 24 May 2000.

[26] M. Shari and S. Prasso 'Freeport McMoRan: A Pit of Trouble', *Business Week*, 31 July 2000.

[27] 'Amungme, Kamoro and Freeport Indonesia Announce Agreement'. *New Orleans Business Wire,* 18 August 2000.

[28] T. Dodd, 'Risky Business – Freeport dances to a new tune', *Australian Financial Review*, 16 December 2000.

Chapter 5: Indigenous sovereignty and Century Zinc

[1] R. Howitt, J. Connell and P. Hirsch, 'Resources, Nations, and Indigenous Peoples' in R. Howitt, J. Connell and P. Hirsch (Eds.) *Resources, Nations, and Indigenous Peoples: Case Studies from Australasia, Melanesia and South East Asia,* Oxford University Press, Melbourne, 1996, p.6.

[2] A. Escobar, 'Imagining a post-development era? Critical thought, development and social movements', *Social Text* 31/32, 1992, pp.20–56; R. Howitt, 'Developmentalism, Impact Assessment and Aborigines: re-thinking regional narratives at Weipa', NARU discussion paper No.24, Darwin: North Australia Research Unit, 1995, p.1.

[3] M. Christie, 'Aboriginal science for the ecologically sustainable future', *Ngoonjook*, November 1990, pp. 56–68.

[4] D.S. Trigger, *Whitefella Comin': Aboriginal Responses to Colonialism in Northern Australia*, Cambridge University Press, Cambridge 1992, p. 17; D. B. Rose, *Nourishing Terrains*, Australian Heritage Commission, Canberra, 1996; D. B. Rose, 'Indigenous Ecology and an Ethic of Hope', paper prepared for the Conference 'Environmental Justice: Global Ethics for the 21st Century', Melbourne, 1–3 October 1997; D. B. Rose, 'Exploring an Aboriginal Land Ethic', *Meanjin*, 47(3), 1988, pp. 378–386.

[5] S. Schneirer, *Aboriginal Cultural Values and Native Vegetation*, Southern Cross Univeristy, Lismore; the NSW Native Vegetation Advisory Committee, 2000.

[6] D.B. Rose, *Nourishing Terrains*, Australian Heritage Commission, Canberra, 1996, p.34.

[7] Trigger, *Whitefella Comin': Aboriginal Responses to Colonialism in Northern Australia'*, Cambridge University Press, Cambridge 1992

[8] D. B. Rose, 'Indigenous Ecology and an Ethic of Hope', paper prepared for the Conference 'Environmental Justice: Global Ethics for the 21st Century', Melbourne, 1–3 October 1997, pp.3–4.

[9] G. Crough, *Aboriginal People in the Economy of Northern Australia*, Northern Territory University Press, Darwin 1983, p.25; M. Massey, 'Huge Zinc Discovery 'Back of Burketown'', *Australian Financial Review*, 3 September, 1991, p.52.

[10] R. Howitt, '*Terra nullius* no more? Changing Australian geographies through negotiation', Paper presented to the Inaugural International Conference in Critical Geography, August 10–13, 1997, Vancouver, British Columbia, p.5.

[11] Trigger, *Whitefella Comin': Aboriginal Responses to Colonialism in Northern Australia*, Cambridge University Press, Cambridge 1992, p. 20.

[12] Trigger, *Whitefella Comin':Aboriginal Responses to Colonialism in Northern Australia*, Cambridge University Press, Cambridge 1992 p. 40.

[13] Trigger, *Whitefella Comin':Aboriginal Responses to Colonialism in Northern Australia*, Cambridge University Press, Cambridge 1992; G. Crough and D. Cronin, 'Aboriginal People and the Century Project: The 'Plains of Promise' Revisited?', Brisbane: Report prepared for the Carpentaria Land Council, commissioned by CZL through Kinhill Cameron MacNamara Pty Ltd, 1995, p.10.

[14] ADVYZ, 1995, 'Carpentaria Land Council Organisational Review', paper prepared by ADVYZ Community And Corporate Planners, July 1995, p. 3.

[15] Mining Warden's Court, 1995, Report and Recommendation of Warden Pursuant to Section 7.26 and 7.27 of the Mineral Resources Act 1989 – Application for Mining Lease number 90045 and 90058, Mount Isa: 3 July 1995.

[16] S. Cowell, 'Aboriginal Interests and the Century Zinc Proposal: Resource Planning, Development and Impact Assessment in the Gulf of Carpentaria', Honours thesis, Griffith University 1996, p. 77.

[17] D. B. Rose, 'Indigenous Ecology and an Ethic of Hope', paper prepared for the Conference 'Environmental Justice: Global Ethics for the 21st Century', Melbourne, 1–3 October 1997, p.3.

[18] D. S.Trigger, 'Reflections on Century Mine: preliminary thoughts on the politics of indigenous response', in D.E. Smith and J. Finlayson (eds), *Fighting Over Country: Anthropological Perspectives*, Canberra: Centre for Aboriginal Economic Policy Research, Australian National University, 1997.

[19] P. Memmott and P. Kelleher, 'Social impact study of the proposed Century Project on the Aboriginal people of Normanton and surrounds', A study carried out for the Bynoe Community Advancement Co-operative Society Ltd, Normanton, commissioned by Century Zin Limited through Kinhill Cameron McNamara Pty Ltd, Brisbane, 1995 p. 64.

[20] CZL [Century Zinc Ltd.], 'The Century Project – Response to IAS Submissions: Supplementary Report', Draft Impact Assessment Study Report

March 1995, Brisbane; S.Cowell, 'Aboriginal Interests and the Century Zinc Proposal: Resource Planning, Development and Impact Assessment in the Gulf of Carpentaria', Honours thesis, Griffith University, 1996, p. 54.

[21] DFSAIA [Department of Family Services, Aboriginal and Islander Affairs], Minutes, Meeting between CLC and Doomadgee Communities, Brisbane, 12 March1991; and DFSAIA Minutes, Meeting between Robert Blowes, Lawyer and Representative of Mornington Shire Council, Carpentaria Land Council and Kaidilt Corporation at Mornington Island, Brisbane, 16 August, 1991

[22] CZL [Century Zinc Ltd.], 'The Century Project – Response to IAS Submissions: Supplementary Report', Draft Impact Assessment Study Report March 1995, Brisbane.

[23] DFSAIA [Department of Family Services, Aboriginal and Islander Affairs], 'Minutes, Meeting Between CRA Mining Company and Doomadgee Community at Doomadgee', Brisbane, 15 August 1991.

[24] FOE [Friends of the Earth], 'From the frontlines – an interview with Wadjularbinna', in FOE (Fitzroy) newsletter, 8–9 December 1996, p.8.

[25] Trigger, 'Reflections on Century Mine: preliminary thoughts on the politics of indigenous response', in D.E. Smith and J. Finlayson (eds), *Fighting Over Country: Anthropological Perspectives*, Canberra: Centre for Aboriginal Economic Policy Research, Australian National University, 1997.

[26] CLC [Carpentaria Land Council], 'Briefing Paper, World Council of Churches Delegate for CLC', May 1996.

[27] J. Buckell, 'Dispossessed Aborigines claim land in national park', in *The Weekend Australian*: 12 October 1994, p12.

[28] B. Williams, 'Aborigines Vow to Stay in Park', *Courier Mail*, 26 October 1994 p.6; CLC [Carpentaria Land Council], File Note – 'Lawn Hill National Park Claim under the Aboriginal Land Act 1991 (Qld)', 29 January 1997

[29] T. Piper, fieldwork interview, 24 October, 1996

[30] Howitt, 'Social Impact Assessment as Applied Peoples' Geography', *Australian Geographical Studies*, 31(2), 1993 p 131

[31] Howitt, 'Social Impact Assessment as Applied Peoples' Geography', *Australian Geographical Studies*, 31(2), 1993 p 131

[32] Howitt, 'Social Impact Assessment as Applied Peoples' Geography', *Australian Geographical Studies*, 31(2), 1993 p 130

Chapter 6: Mining, Water, Survival and the Diavik diamond mine

[1] Adapted from the slogan of the US–based Okanagan Highlands Alliance, 'Pure Water is More Precious than Gold'.

[2] International Union for the Conservation of Nature and World Wildlife Fund for Nature, 'Metals from the Forests: Mining and Forest Degradation', *Arborvitae*, January 1999.

[3] Environmental Mining Council of British Columbia, and British Columbia Wild. 'Acid Mine Drainage: Mining & Water Pollution Issues in BC', 1996.

[4] World Wide Web document: CIA, 'Global Trend 2015: A dialogue about the future with non-governmental experts', available from Africa 2000 website, www.africa2000.com/index/trends2015.html, accessed June 2000.

[5] Council of Canadians.' Fact Sheet #2: Privatisation', Council of Canadians. 1998

[6] Mineral Policy Center, 'Golden Dreams, Poisoned Streams: How Reckless Mining Pollutes America's Waters, and How We Can Stop It', Mineral Policy Center, Washington DC, 1997, p 76.

[7] Mineral Policy Center, 'Golden Dreams, Poisoned Streams: How Reckless Mining Pollutes America's Waters, and How We Can Stop It', Mineral Policy Center, Washington DC, 1997, p 4.

[8] Mineral Policy Center, 'Golden Dreams, Poisoned Streams: How Reckless Mining Pollutes America's Waters, and How We Can Stop It', Mineral Policy Center, Washington DC, 1997. p 5

[9] *Philippine Daily Inquirer*, 3 September, 2000, p.7.

[10] C. Coumans, 'Placer Dome Inc. in the Philippines: An Illustration of the Need for Binding International Regulations on Mining', *Canadian Mining Industry Focus Report,* Social Investment Organisation, Toronto, Canada. 1997.

[11] World Wide Web Document: Water Watch, *Information Pamphlet,* Water Watch. Available from waterwatch@canadians.org, accessed December 2000.

[12] Canadian Fisheries Act, Section 35.

[13] Canadian Fisheries Act, Section 36.

[14] Northwatch, Unpublished fact sheet provided by one of the non-governmental organisations involved in the review of Metal Mining Liquid Effluent Regulations.

[15] B. Lloyd, The Dome Mine, Placer Dome (Draft), 2000.

[16] 'Tails of Woes', *New Scientist*, 11 November, 2000, p 46–48.

[17] Louise Hardy, Member of Parliament for the Yukon, quoted in *The Whitehorse Star*, 15 November, 1999.

[18] T. Pearse, 'Diavik Diamonds Project: An Environmental Assessment', Dogrib Diavik Working Group on Dogrib Treaty 11 Council, June 1999; Government of Canada, *News Release*, 18 June, 1999.

[19] Government of Canada, 'Comprehensive Study Report Diavik Diamonds Project', Government of Canada, June 1999, p.xi.

[20] MiningWatch Canada, 'Diavik Diamonds Comprehensive Study Report: Comments from MiningWatch Canada', MiningWatch Canada. July 1999; Canadian Arctic Resources Committee, 'Response to Comprehensive Study Report on the Diavik Diamonds Project', Canadian Arctic Resources Committee, July 1999.

[22] Canadian Federal Environment Minister David Anderson, Press Release, Ottawa, 3 November, 1999.

[23] Canadian Federal Indian Affairs and Northern Development Minister Robert Nault, Press Release, Ottawa, 3 November, 1999.

[24] John Zoe, 'Dogrib First Nation', *Globe and Mail*, November 2, 1999.

[25] Louise Hardy, Member of Parliament for the Yukon, quoted in *The Whitehorse Star*, November 15, 1999.

[27] Kevin O'Reilly, quoted in MiningWatch Canada and the Canadian Consortium for International Social Development, 'On the Ground Research: A Workshop to Identify the Research Needs of Communities Affected by Large-Scale Mining – Workshop Report', MiningWatch Canada and the Canadian Consortium for International Social Development, Canada, 2000.

[28] Little Salmon Carmacks First Nation, Press Release, 9 August , 2000.

[29] Ross River Kaska Dene First Nation, Press Release, 14 August, 2000.

[30] *Globe and Mail*, 1 November, 1999.

[31] *Globe and Mail,* 26 October, 1999

[32] Canadian Federal Court Judgement, 'Alberta Wilderness et al. v. Cardinal Rivers Coal Ltd. ('Cheviott').

[34] T. Pearse, 'Diavik Diamonds Project: An Environmental Assessment', Dogrib Diavik Working Group on Dogrib Treaty 11 Council. June 1999, p 66.

[35] Pearse, 'Diavik Diamonds Project: An Environmental Assessment', Dogrib Diavik Working Group on Dogrib Treaty 11 Council. June 1999, p 66.

[36] Pearse, 'Diavik Diamonds Project: An Environmental Assessment'. Dogrib Diavik Working Group on Dogrib Treaty 11 Council. June 1999:ii and p.66–82.

[37] Pearse, 'Diavik Diamonds Project: An Environmental Assessment'. Dogrib Diavik Working Group on Dogrib Treaty 11 Council. June 1999, iv

[38] Government of Canada, 'Comprehensive Study Report Diavik Diamonds Project', Government of Canada, June 1999, p.145–146

[39] Government of Canada, 'Comprehensive Study Report Diavik Diamonds Project', Government of Canada, June 1999, p.151

[40] T. Pearse, 'Diavik Diamonds Project: An Environmental Assessment'. Dogrib Diavik Working Group on Dogrib Treaty 11 Council, June 1999, p.v.

[42] Department of Fisheries and Oceans, 'Authorization for Works or Undertaking Affecting Fish Habitat', File No. SC98001.

[43] World Wide Web document: Department of Fisheries and Oceans. 'Decision Framework for the Determination and Authorization of Harmful Alternation, Disruption or Destruction of Fish Habitat', available at www.dfo-mpo.gc.ca/habitat/HADD/english/hadd_e_2.htm, accessed July 2001.

[43] *Northern News Services*, 19 June, 2000.

[44] North Slave Metis Alliance, 'Can't Live Without Work: North Slave Metis Alliance Environmental, Social, Economic and Cultural Concerns. A Companion to the Comprehensive Study Report on the Diavik Diamonds Report*',* North Slave Metis Alliance, July 1999. p.i.

[45] Author's personal notes taken at Gaining Ground: Women, Mining and the Environment conference, September 2000. See also Cleghorn, C., Edelson, N. and Moodie, S., 'Gaining Ground: Women, Mining and the Environment', Yukon Status of Women Council, April 2001.

[46] T. Pearse, 'Diavik Diamonds Project: An Environmental Assessment', Dogrib Diavik Working Group on Dogrib Treaty 11 Council. June 1999

[47] Government of Canada, 'Comprehensive Study Report Diavik Diamonds Project', Government of Canada, June 1999, p.211

[48] *Northern News Services*, 2 February, 2000

[49] John Zoe, *Globe and Mail*, 2 November, 1999.

[50] John Zoe, *Globe and Mail*, 2 November, 1999.

[51] North Slave Metis Alliance, 'Can't Live Without Work: North Slave Metis Alliance Environmental, Social, Economic and Cultural Concerns. A Companion to the Comprehensive Study Report on the Diavik Diamonds Report', North Slave Metis Alliance, July 1999.

[52] North Slave Metis Alliance, 'Can't Live Without Work: North Slave Metis Alliance Environmental, Social, Economic and Cultural Concerns. A Companion to the Comprehensive Study Report on the Diavik Diamonds Report', North Slave Metis Alliance, July 1999, p.ii–iv.

[53] North Slave Metis Alliance, 'Can't Live Without Work: North Slave Metis Alliance Environmental, Social, Economic and Cultural Concerns. A Companion to the Comprehensive Study Report on the Diavik Diamonds Report', North Slave Metis Alliance, July 1999, p.ii–v.

[54] Mackenzie Valley Environmental Impact Review Board, 'Views on the Diavik Diamonds Project Comprehensive Study Report*',* Mackenzie Valley Environmental Impact Review Board, 7 October, 1999, p.16.

[55] MiningWatch Canada, 'Diavik Diamonds Comprehensive Study Report: Comments from MiningWatch Canada', MiningWatch Canada. July 1999.

[56] Mackenzie Valley Environmental Impact Review Board. 'Views on the Diavik Diamonds Project Comprehensive Study Report, Mackenzie Valley Environmental Impact Review Board, October 7, 1999.p.16.

[57] Correspondence between Rio Tinto and the Office of the Canadian High Commission in London was obtained by Canadian Arctic Resources Committee through an access to information request.

[58] World Wide Web document: Rio Tinto, *Community Policy,* Rio Tinto website www.riotinto.com/community/policies/access.asp, accessed December 2000.

Chapter 7: When corporations want to cuddle

[1] Sir Robert Wilson, 'The Mining Industry: In Recuperation or Remission?', *Securities Institute of Australia*, Grand Hyatt Hotel, Melbourne, 7 December 1999.

[2] See Bob Burton 'Peter Sandman plots to make you a winner: Advice on making nice', *PR Watch*, Volume 6 Number 1, First Quarter 1999, www.prwatch.org, pages 1–6.

[3] Bob Burton, 'Some clients of Peter Sandman', *PR Watch*, Volume 6 Number 1, First Quarter 1999, www.prwatch.org, page 4.

[4] Bob Burton, 'Packaging the beast: a public relations lesson in type-casting', *PR Watch*, Volume 6 Number 1, First Quarter 1999, www.prwatch.org, page12.

[5] Bob Burton, 'Community advisory panels: corporate cat herding' *PR Watch*, Volume 6 Number 1, First Quarter 1999, www.prwatch.org, pages 9–10.

[6] Mining Watch Canada, Mineral Policy Center USA, Mineral Policy Institute Australia, 'Chairperson Quits Over River Pollution at Placer Dome's Porgera Mine in Papua New Guinea', *Media Release*, 14 June 2001.

[7] CRA, 'Results of CRA's 1996 Community Issues and Priorities Survey', CRA, December 1996.

[8] Bob Burton, 'WWF signs $1.2m partnership with Rio Tinto', *Mining Monitor*, Volume 5 Number 1, March 2000, pages 9–10.

[9] See Nicky Hager and Bob Burton, 'Building bridges and splitting greens', *PR Watch*, Volume 7 Number 1, First Quarter 2000, www.prwatch.org. See also Nicky Hager and Bob Burton, 'Secrets and Lies: the anatomy of an anti-environmental PR campaign, Craig Potton Publishing, 1999.

[10] See Nicky Hager and Bob Burton, 'Building bridges and splitting greens', *PR Watch*, Volume 7 Number 1, First Quarter 2000, www.prwatch.org. See also Nicky Hager and Bob Burton, 'Secrets and Lies: the anatomy of an anti-environmental PR campaign', Craig Potton Publishing, 1999.

[11] WWF Australia, 'WWF Australia: guidelines for corporate relations', undated memo.

[12] Bob Burton, 'WWF signs $1.2m partnership with Rio Tinto', *Mining Monitor*, Volume 5 Number 1, March 2000, page 9.

[13] World Wide Fund for Nature Australia, 'WWF & Rio Tinto partner for frogs', *Media Release*, December 1999.

[14] Dr Ray Nias, fax to author, 16 March 2000.

[15] Guy Espiner, 'WWF has links with oil company', *Sunday Star Times*, 8 October 2000, page 1.

[16] Australian Legal Resources International, *Annual Report 1998*, Sydney, page 10.

[17] Rio Tinto, 'Business with Communities Program: Partnering', Rio Tinto, undated, page 9.

[18] Bob Burton, 'Rio Tinto's deal with NGO to write Indonesian laws', *Mining Monitor*, Volume 5 Number 1, March 2000, www.mpi.org.au, pages 7–8.

[19] Bob Burton, 'Small donation for a big payoff?', *The Jakarta Post*, 25 July 2000, page 4.

[20] Australian Legal Resources International, 'Australian support to legal and judicial reform', June 2000, www.alri.org.au

[21] World Wide Web Document: PT Kelian Equatorial Mining (2000), *Social and Environmental Report'*, PT Kelian Equatorial Mining website, www.keliangold.com/news/03052000-7.html accessed May 3, 2000.

[22] Tim Dodd (2000), 'Rio Tinto Faces Sex Claims in Borneo', *Australian Financial Review,* June 30, pp1, 42.

[23] Rio Tinto, 'The way we work: our statement of business practice', www.riotinto.com, January 1998, page 3.

[24] Rio Tinto, '1999 Social and Environment report', www.riotinto.com, page 27.

[25] Kenny Bruno and Joshua Karliner, 'Tangled up in Blue: Corporate Partnerships at the United Nations', Transnational Resource and Action Center, September 2000, www.corpwatch.org.

[26] Bob Burton, 'UNEP seconds Rio Tinto adviser for mining review', *Mining Monitor*, Volume 5 Number 2, July 2000, www.mpi.org.au, page 1.

Chapter 8: Mining, self-determination and Bougainville

[1] Douglas Oliver, 'Bougainville: A Personal History', Melbourne, 1973.

[2] J. Mayo, 'The Protectorate of British New Guinea 1884–1888: An Oddity of Empire', 2nd Waigani Seminar: The History of Melanesia, University of PNG Australian National University, 1969, p17; Hank, N. (1972), *Papua New Guinea – Black Unity or Black Chaos*? Penguin Books, 1972 Vic Australia, p 11.

[3] J.A. Moses, 'The German Empire in Melanesia 1884 – 1914', 2nd Waigani Seminar: The History of Melanesia, University of PNG and Australian National University, 1969, p 59.

[4] Douglas Oliver, 'Bougainville: A Personal History', Melbourne, 1973, p 83

[5] 'Convention on Declaration between Germany and Great Britain for the Settlement of the Samoan and other Questions', London, 14th November 1899.

[6]'Everyone's United Nations, A Handbook on the United Nations, its Structure and Activities', 9th Edition, New York, 1975, p 20.

[7] T. Miriung, 'The North Nasioi View of the Bougainville Crisis', Keynote Address, The Bougainville Crisis: The Search for Peace and Rehabilitation,

Dept. of Political and Social Changes, Australian National University, 22nd June 1995, p 3.

[8] J. Ryan, 'The Hotland: Focus on New Guinea', p 291.

[9] J. Ryan, 'The Hotland: Focus on New Guinea'.

[10] J. Ryan, 'The Hotland: Focus on New Guinea', p137

[11] M. Havini, L. Hannett, L, and others, September 1, 1970.

[12] L. Hannett, L., 'Bougainville Island's move for Separate Independence'; Havini, M. (1995), 'A Manifesto for the Independence Struggle of The People of Bougainville', 1973, a Paper written towards a Masters Degree, University of Sydney, 1995.

[13] M. Havini, A 'Manifesto 'For the Independence Struggle for the People of Bougainville', a Paper written towards a Masters Degree, University of Sydney, 1995.

[14] J. Ryan, 'The Hotland: Focus on New Guinea'.

[15] 'Mining Ordinance of Papua New Guinea', 1928.

[16] R. Moody, 'Plunder!' PARTiZANS/CAFCA, London, 1991, p68

[17] R. Bedford, and A. Mamak, *Compensation for Development: The Bougainville Case*, Christchurch, 1977, p 104.

[18] D. Denoon, *Getting under the skin – The Bougainville Copper Agreement and the Creation of the Panguna Mine*, Melbourne University Press, 2000, p 66.

[19] D. Denoon, *Getting under the skin – The Bougainville Copper Agreement and the Creation of the Panguna Mine*, Melbourne University Press, 2000, p 66.

[20] R. Moody, *Plunder!*, PARTiZANS/CAFCA, London, 1991 p70

[21] K.M. Phillips, 'Personal Notes 1964 – 1966', in P. Quodling, 'Bougainville, The Mine and the People', The Centre for Independent Studies, St Leonards 1991 p 107.

[22] K.M. Phillips, 'Personal Notes 1964 – 1966', in P. Quodling, *Bougainville, The Mine and the People*, The Centre for Independent Studies, 1991, p 107.

[23] R. Bedford, and A. Mamak, *Compensation for Development: The Bougainville Case*, Christchurch, 1977.

[24] R. Bedford, and A. Mamak, *Compensation for Development: The Bougainville Case*, Christchurch, 1977, p 13.

[25] D. Denoon, 'Getting under the skin – The Bougainville Copper Agreement and the Creation of the Panguna Mine', Melbourne University Press, 2000, p 66; Bougainville Copper Limited *Annual Reports*

[26] R. Bedford, and A. Mamak, *Compensation for Development: The Bougainville Case*, Christchurch, 1977.

[27] Applied Geology Associates Limited, 'Environmental Socio-Economic Public Review – The Bougainville Copper Mine Panguna', Applied Geology Associates Limited, 1988 pp 3–13.

[28] R. Moody, *Plunder!* PARTiZANS/CAFCA, London, 1991, p70

[29] R. Moody, *Plunder!* PARTiZANS/CAFCA, London, 1991, p71

[30] *The Daily Mirror*, 6 August 1969

[31] P. Quodling, *Bougainville: The Mine and the People*, Centre for Independent Studies Ltd, St Leonards, 1991, p29

[32] P. Quodling, *'Bougainville: The Mine and the People*, Centre for Independent Studies Ltd, St Leonards, 1991, p29

[33] P. Quodling, *'Bougainville: The Mine and the People*, Centre for Independent Studies Ltd, St Leonards, 1991, p29

[34] R. Moody, *Plunder*!, PARTiZANS/CAFCA, London, 1991, p69

[35] M. Tossol and B. Bartlett B, *Danger: Artists at Work*, D. W. Thorpe, Melbourne, 1991, p141

[36] D. Oliver, *Bougainville: A Personal History*, Melbourne, 1973, p137

[37] D. Oliver, *Bougainville: A Personal History*, Melbourne, 1973, p137

[38] R. Moody, *Plunder!* PARTiZANS/CAFCA, London, 1991, p66

[39] R. Moody, *Plunder!* PARTiZANS/CAFCA, London, 1991, p66

[40] R. West, *River of Tears The Rise of Rio Tinto Zinc Corporation, Ltd.,* Earth Island Institute, 1972 p121

[41] R.J. May and M. Spriggs, (Eds), *The Bougainville Crisis*, Crawford House Press, Bathurst, 1990, p41

[42] R. Moody, *Plunder!* PARTiZANS/CAFCA, London, 1991, p67

[43] R. Moody, *Plunder!* PARTiZANS/CAFCA, London, 1991, p68

[44] P. Quodling, *Bougainville: The Mine and the People*, Centre for Independent Studies Ltd, St Leonards, 1991, p31

[45] R. Moody, *Plunder!* PARTiZANS/CAFCA, London, 1991, p72

[46] P. Quodling, *Bougainville: The Mine and the People*, Centre for Independent Studies Ltd, St Leonards, 1991, p60

[47] C. Mark, 'The Return of Mercenary Corporations', Proceedings of the 1999 Conference of the Australian Political Studies Association, Sydney, 1999.

[48] M. and R.Havini, *Bougainville: The long struggle for freedom*, New Age Publishers Pty Ltd, Sydney, 1997, p1.

Chapter 9: Corporate imperialism in the Philippines

[1] A. Tujan Jr. and R. B Guzman, *Globalizing Philippine Mining*, IBON Books, Manila, 1998.

[2] J. Haygood, The Mining Act of 1995: National Patrimony Megasale, IBON Special Release, April 1996.

[3] 'Mining Revisited: Can An Understanding of Perspectives Help?', Environmental Science for Social Change and Bishops-Businessmen's Conference, 1999.

[4] Roberto Padilla, national president of Marcopper labour union, MELU-NAMAWU, undated speech.

[5] J. Haygood, 'The Mining Act of 1995: National Patrimony Megasale', IBON Special Release, April 1996.

[6] Bagong Alyansang Makabayan press release, 6 March 1998.

[7] C. Catalino Jr., 'National Situation: the Mining Industry', International Solidarity Conference, Utrecht, The Netherlands, 30 November 1999.

[8] 'International Conference Against Mining Transnational Corporations', Manila 14–16 November 1998 ; Indigenus Pilipinas press release, 19 April 2000.

[9] World Metal Statistics, Mines and Geosciences Bureau, Philippines.

[10] Bagong Alyansang Makabayan press release, 6 March 1998.

[11] J. Carling, Media Release from Cordillera People's Alliance, Philippines, May 2000.

Chapter 10: Mineworkers on the offensive

[1] International Confederation of Free Trade Unions, *1998 Trade Union Survey*, International Confederation of Free Trade Unions, 1998.

[2] International Confederation of Free Trade Unions, *1998 Trade Union Survey*, International Confederation of Free Trade Unions, 1998.

[3] World Wide Web Document: for details see website of the Korean Confederation of Trade Unions http://www.nodong.org/english/index.htm or http://kctu.org , accessed March 2001.

[4] World Wide Web Document: for details see website of the Mining and Energy Division of the Construction, Forestry, Mining and Energy Union, Australia http://www.cfmeu.asn.au/mining-energy, accessed March 2001.

[5] International Federation of Chemical, Energy, Mine and General Workers' Unions, 'Rio Tinto – Tainted Titan: The Stakeholders' Report 1997', International Federation of Chemical, Energy, Mine and General Workers' Unions, Belgium, 1997.

[6] Australian Industrial Relation Commission, Weipa Decision, M8600, January 23, 1996.

[7] Atkinson, J., 'Undermined: The Impact of Australian Mining in Developing Countries', Community Aid Abroad, Melbourne, 1998.

[8] World Wide Web Document: United Nations General Assembly, 'Universal Declaration of Human Rights: Article 23.4', United Nations website http://www.un.org/Overview/rights.html, accessed March 2001.

[9] International Federation of Chemical, Energy, Mine and General Workers' Unions, 'Rio Tinto – Tainted Titan: The Stakeholders' Report 1997', International Federation of Chemical, Energy, Mine and General Workers' Unions, Belgium, 1997.

Chapter 11: Engagement or confrontation?

[1] World Wide Web Document: Control Risks Group, *About Us,* Control Risks Group website, http://www.crg.com/about/aboutus.html, accessed September, 2000.

[2] M. McIntosh, D. Leipziger, K. Jones, and G. Coleman, G. 'Corporate Citizenship, Successful Strategies for Responsible Companies', *Financial Times* Pitman Publishing, London, 1998, p 4.

[3] Rio Tinto, *The Way We Work*, Westersham Press, England, 1998.

[4] Personal communication with Dr Tim Duncan, Director, External Affairs, Australia, Rio Tinto, 28 April 2000.

[5] International Confederation of Free Trade Unions, 'Response to Rio Tinto's Statement of Business Practice "The Way We Work"', Letter to Chairman of Rio Tinto, Mr Wilson from the General Secretary, International Confederation of Free Trade Unions, 1999, p 2.

[6] D. Bryer, and Magrath 'New Dimensions of Global Advocacy', *Nonprofit and Voluntary Sector Quarterly*, Vol 28, No. 4, Supplement, 1998, p 172.

[7] D. Bryer, and Magrath, 'New Dimensions of Global Advocacy', *Nonprofit and Voluntary Sector Quarterly*, Vol 28, No. 4, Supplement, 1998, p 176.

[8] C. Marsden, and J. Andriof, 'Towards an Understanding of Corporate Citizenship and How to Influence It', *Citizenship Studies*, Vol 2, No 2: 1998, pp 329 – 352; M. McIntosh, D. Leipziger, K. Jones, and G. Coleman, 'Corporate Citizenship, Successful Strategies for Responsible Companies', *Financial Times* Pitman Publishing, London, 1998; N. Tichy, A. McGill, and L. St Clair, (eds) *Corporate Global Citizenship, Doing Business in the Public Eye,* The New Lexington Press, San Francisco, 1997.

[9] R. Falk, *'Predatory Globalization: A Critique'*, Polity Press, Cambridge; 1999, W. Hutton, and Q. Giddens, *On the Edge, Living with Global Capitalism*, Jonathon Cape, London, 2000; D. Korten, *The Post-Corporate World, Life after Capitalism*, Pluto Press, Australia, 2000.

[10] N. Tichy, A. McGill, and L. St Clair, (eds), *Corporate Global Citizenship, Doing Business in the Public Eye,* The New Lexington Press, San Francisco, 1997; M. McIntosh, D. Leipziger, K. Jones and G. Coleman, G. *Corporate Citizenship, Successful Strategies for Responsible Companies*, Financial Times Pitman Publishing, London., Elkington 1998.

[11] D. Birch, J. Batten, *Corporate Citizenship in Australia; A Survey of Corporate Australia*, Corporate Citizenship Research Unit, Deakin University, Melbourne, 2001.

[12] V. Shiva, 'The World on the Edge', in Hutton, W. & Giddens, A. (eds) *On the Edge, Living with Global Capitalism*, Jonathon Cape, London, 2000, p 118.

[13] R. Lipschutz, 'Reconstructing World Politics: The Emergence of Global Civil Society', *Millennium*, Winter 1992, Vol. 21 No 3, p. 395.

[14] J. Atkinson, 'Undermined; The Impact of Australian Mining Companies in Developing Countries', Community Aid Abroad, Melbourne, 1998, p. 10.

[15] R. Phillips, 'From Confrontation to Sponsorship? Multinational Corporations, Corporate Citizenship and Social Movement NGOs', Chapter 12 in J. Goodman, (ed) *Protesting Globalisation: Prospects for Transnational Solidarity*, Pluto Press, Sydney, 2001.

[16] D. Korten, *The Post-Corporate World, Life after Capitalism*, Pluto Press, Australia, 200o, p. 261.

[17] Personal communication with Dr Tim Duncan, Director, External Affairs, Australia, Rio Tinto, 28 April 2000.

[18] Susan Blackburn, *Practical Visionaries A Study of Community Aid Abroad*, Melbourne University Press, Melbourne, 1993.

[19] Personal communication with Jeff Atkinson, Mining Campaign Coordinator, Community Aid Abroad, 27 July 1999.

[20] Personal communication with Dr Tim Duncan, Director, External Affairs, Australia, Rio Tinto 28 April 2000.

[21] Personal communication with Jeff Atkinson, Mining Campaign Coordinator, Community Aid Abroad 27 July 1999.

[22] Campaign correspondence by the Indonesian Mining Advocacy Network (JATAM), 9 September 1999.

[23] Campaign correspondence by the Indonesian Mining Advocacy Network (JATAM), 9 September 1999.

[24] Campaign material by the Indonesian Mining Advocacy Network (JATAM), 9 September 1999.

[25] Direct correspondence with the Indonesian Mining Advocacy Network (JATAM), 9 September 1999.

[26] D. Murphy, 'Business and NGOs in the Global Partnership Process', Partners for Development Summit, United Nations Conference on Trade and Development, Lyon, France, November 9–12, 1998, p9.

[27] Personal communication with Michael Boud, Corporate Affairs, Aurora Gold 27 September 1999.

[28] D. Bryer, and Magrath 'New Dimensions of Global Advocacy', *Nonprofit and Voluntary Sector Quarterly*, Vol 28, No. 4, Supplement, 1998, pp 169–177.

[29] N. Tichy, A. McGill, and L. St Clair, (eds) *Corporate Global Citizenship, Doing Business in the Public Eye,* The New Lexington Press, San Francisco, 1997; M. McIntosh, D. Leipziger, K. Jones and G. Coleman, *Corporate Citizenship, Successful Strategies for Responsible Companies*, Financial Times Pitman Publishing, London, 1998.

[30] D. Murphy, 'Business and NGOs in the Global Partnership Process', Partners for Development Summit, United Nations Conference on Trade and Development, Lyon, France, November 9–12, 1998; H. Fabig, and R. Boele, 'The Changing Nature of NGO Activity in a Globalising World, Pushing the

Corporate Responsibility Agenda', *IDS Bulletin* Vol 30 No 3, 1999, pp 58–67.

Chapter 12: Mining uranium and indigenous Australians: The fight for Jabiluka

[1] World Wide Web Document: For further information visit the Mirrar peoples' website at www.mirrar.net.
[2] Mirrar Submission to the World Heritage Committee Mission to Kakadu (October 1998), 'Mirrar Living Tradition In Danger – World Heritage In Danger'
[3] D. J. Mulvaney 'The Landscape of the Aboriginal Imagination and its Heritage Significance', Unpublished Paper, September, 1998.
[4] D. J. Mulvaney 'The Landscape of the Aboriginal Imagination and its Heritage Significance', Unpublished Paper, September, 1998.
[5] *Minutes*, Gundjehmi Aboriginal Corporation, September 15, 1998.
[6] Australian Government (1991), 'World Heritage Renomination document', p 88.
[7] *Report 1*, 'Ranger Uranium Environmental Inquiry ('the Fox Inquiry')', 28 October 1976; *Report 2*, 'Ranger Uranium Environmental Inquiry ('the Fox Inquiry')', 17 May 1977.
[8] *Report 1*, 'Ranger Uranium Environmental Inquiry ('the Fox Inquiry')', 28 October 1976; *Report 2*, 'Ranger Uranium Environmental Inquiry ('the Fox Inquiry')', 17 May 1977.
[9] *Report 1*, 'Ranger Uranium Environmental Inquiry ('the Fox Inquiry')', 28 October 1976; Report 2, 'Ranger Uranium Environmental Inquiry ('the Fox Inquiry')', 17 May 1977.
[10] Katona, J. (1999), *Address by Gundjehmi Aboriginal Corporation to Public Health Association of Australia Conference*, September, Darwin.
[11] Katona, J. (1999), *Address by Gundjehmi Aboriginal Corporation to Public Health Association of Australia Conference*, September, Darwin.

Chapter 13: An international regulatory framework?

[1] C. Harris, 'Trade Liberalisation and Mining: The Corporate Agenda', *The Ecologist Asia*, Vol. 6, No. 2, 1998 p. 5.
[2] J. Gordon, 'The Ok Tedi lawsuit in retrospect' in Banks, G. and Ballard, C. 'The Ok Tedi Settlement: issues, outcomes and implications', *Pacific Policy Paper 27*, Research School of Pacific and Asian Studies, ANU, Canberra, 1997, p 157; T. Kaye, 'BHP had Ok Tedi bill drafted', *Sydney Morning Herald*, 16 August 1995, p41.
[3] World Wide Web document: S. Zadek, and M. Forstater, 'Strengthening Civil Regulation: Building Competency Based Alliances'. Unpublished

report commissioned by the Ford Foundation, New Economics Foundation, London, 1998, http://www.zadek.net/papers.html, accessed January 2001.

⁴ World Wide Web document: S. Zadek and M. Forstater, Earthrights, 2001 'Burma Project – Doe Vs. Unocal' 1998 http://www.earthrights.org/unocal/index.html, accessed January 2001.

⁵ World Wide Web document: OECD (Organisation for Economic Co-operation and Development), 'The OECD Guidelines for Multinational Enterprises June 2000' http://www.oecd.org/daf/investment/guidelines/mnetext.htm, last updated 29 May 2001, accessed January 2001.

⁶ World Wide Web document: Business and Industry Advisory Council, 'Statement on the Revised OECD Guidelines for Multinational Enterprises', 2000 (BIAC, Paris, France) http://www.oecd.org/daf/investment/guidelines/ last updated 29/05/01, accessed January 2001.

⁷ European Union Resolution (1998), 'Code of Conduct for European Enterprises Operating in Developing Countries', Ref. A4-0508/1998, Minutes of 15/01/1999 – Provisional Edition.

⁸ S. Joseph, 'Taming the Leviathians: Multinational Enterprises and Human Rights', *Netherlands International Law Review*, Vol. XLVI, Issue 2, 1998 pp. 175 –177.

⁹ H. Ward, 'Foreign Direct Liability: A New Weapon in the Performance Armoury?' *AccountAbility Quarterly*, Vol. 14, No. 3, 2000 pp. 22 – 24.

¹⁰ S. Joseph, 'Taming the Leviathians: Multinational Enterprises and Human Rights', *Netherlands International Law Review*, Vol. XLVI, Issue 2, 1998 pp. 175 –177.

¹¹ J. Greer, 'US Petroleum Giant to Stand Trial over Burma Atrocities', *The Ecologist*, Vol. 28, No. 1, 1998 pp. 34–37.

¹² World Wide Web document: S. Zadek and M. Forstater, Earthrights, 2001 'Burma Project – Doe Vs. Unocal' 1998 http://www.earthrights.org/unocal/index.html, accessed January 2001; J. Greer, 'US Petroleum Giant to Stand Trial over Burma Atrocities', *The Ecologist*, Vol.28, No. 1, 1998 pp. 34–37.

¹³ World Wide Web document: United States District Court, 1997 United States District Court for the Central District Court of California, 1997, John Doe I, et al., Plaintiffs, vs. Unocal Corp., et al., Defendants. Case No. CV 96–6959 Rap III C28, http://www.earthrights.org/unocal/index.html, last updated 19 April, 2001, accessed January 2001.

¹⁴ World Wide Web document: S. Zadek and M. Forstater, Earthrights, 2001 'Burma Project – Doe Vs. Unocal' 1998, http://www.earthrights.org/unocal/index.html, accessed January 2001; J. Greer, 'US Petroleum Giant to Stand Trial over Burma Atrocities', *The Ecologist*, Vol. 28, No. 1, 1998 pp. 34–37.

[15] World Wide Web document: House of Lords, Judgements – Schalk Willem Burger Lubbe (Suing as administrator of the estate of Rachel Jacob Lubbe) and 4 others and Cape Plc. and Related appeals, House of Lords, London, 20 July 2000, http://www.parliament.the-stationery-office.co.uk/pa/ld199900/ldjudgmt/jd000720/lubbe-1.htm, accessed January 2001.

[16] H. Ward, 'Foreign Direct Liability: A New Weapon in the Performance Armoury?' *AccountAbility Quarterly*, Vol. 14, No. 3, 2000 pp. 22 – 24.

[17] C. McKinney, 'Corporate Code of Conduct Act', 106th Congress, 2nd Session H.R. 4596 I.H, US House of Representatives, Library of Congress, 2000.

[18] World Wide Web document: V. Bourne, 'Corporate Code of Conduct Bill, 2000', The Parliament of Australia (The Senate), Ref. 0016320-355/7.9.200 – (163/00) http://www.aph.gov.au, last updated 18th April 2001, accessed January 2001.

[19] World Wide Web document: International Council of Metals and the Environment, Sustainable Development Charter, www.icme.com/icme/SDcharter.htm, accessed September 2000.

[20] World Wide Web document: Minerals Council of Australia, 'Australian Minerals Industry Code For Environmental Management', February 2000 <http://www.minerals.org.au (accessed January 2001).

[21] World Wide Web document: IIED (International Institute for Environment and Development), *What is MMSD?* 1999, http://www.iied.org/mmsd, last updated 30th May 2001, accessed January 2001.

[22] N. Gunningham, and J. Rees, 'Industry Self-Regulation: An Institutional Perspective', *Law & Policy*, Vol. 19, No. 4, 1997, pp. 363–414.

[23] D. Spar, 'The Spotlight and the Bottom Line: How Transnationals Export Human Rights', *Foreign Affairs*, Vol. 77, No. 2, 1998 pp. 7–12.

[24] N. Gunningham, and J. Rees, 'Industry Self-Regulation: An Institutional Perspective', *Law & Policy*, Vol. 19, No. 4, 1997 pp. 363–414.

[25] World Wide Web document: Organisation for Economic Co-operation and Development [OECD], 'Voluntary Approaches for Environmental Protection in the European Union', (OECD, Paris, France), 1999 http://www.oecd.org, last update 11th June 2001, accessed January 2001.

[26] World Wide Web document: Minerals Council of Australia, 'Australian Minerals Industry Code For Environmental Management', February 2000, http://www.minerals.org.au, accessed January 2001.

[27] World Wide Web document: Organisation for Economic Co-operation and Development [OECD], *Voluntary Approaches for Environmental Protection in the European Union* (OECD, Paris, France), 1999 http://www.oecd.org, last update 11th June 2001, accessed January 2001.

[28] R. Sullivan, 'The Rules of Engagement: Dealing with the Corporate Sector'. Presented at Protesting Globalisation: Prospects for Transnational Solidarity, University of Technology, Sydney, 10–11 December 1999.

[29] R. Sullivan, 'The Rules of Engagement: Dealing with the Corporate Sector'. Presented at Protesting Globalisation: Prospects for Transnational Solidarity, University of Technology, Sydney, 10–11 December 1999.

[30] R. Sullivan, 'The Rules of Engagement: Dealing with the Corporate Sector'. Presented at Protesting Globalisation: Prospects for Transnational Solidarity, University of Technology, Sydney, 10–11 December 1999.

[31] N. Gunningham, and J. Rees, 'Industry Self-Regulation: An Institutional Perspective', *Law & Policy*, Vol. 19, No. 4, 199 pp. 363–414.

[32] K. Bart and M. Baetz, 'The Relationship Between Mission Statements and Firm Performance: An Exploratory Study', *Journal of Management Studies*, Vol. 33, No. 6, 1998, pp. 823–853.

[33] N. Gunningham, and J. Rees, 'Industry Self-Regulation: An Institutional Perspective', *Law & Policy*, Vol. 19, No. 4, 1997 pp. 363–414.

[34] R. Wilson, 'The Mining Industry: In Recuperation or Remission?'. Presentation to The Securities Institute of Australia, Grand Hyatt Hotel, Melbourne, 7 December 1999.

[35] World Wide Web document: S. Zadek and M. Forstater, Earthrights, 2001 'Burma Project – Doe Vs. Unocal' 1998 http://www.earthrights.org/unocal/index.html, accessed January 2001; J. Greer, 'US Petroleum Giant to Stand Trial over Burma Atrocities', *The Ecologist*, Vol. 28, No. 1, 1998 pp. 34–37.

[36] World Wide Web document: Organisation for Economic Co-operation and Development [OECD], 'Voluntary Approaches for Environmental Protection in the European Union' (OECD, Paris, France), 1999 http://www.oecd.org, last update 11th June 2001, accessed January 2001.

Chapter 14: Strategies for change: What next?

[1] World Wide Web document: World Trade Organisation (WTO) 'The WTO in brief', 1999, http://www.wto.org, accessed June 2000.

[2] United Nations Development Program, *Human Development Report,* Oxford University Press, New York, 1996.

[3] A. Herod, G. Tuathail and S. Roberts, *An unruly world? Globalisation, governance and geography*, Routledge London, 1998.

[4] A. Herod, G. Tuathail and S. Roberts, *An unruly world? Globalisation, governance and geography*, Routledge London, 1998.

[5] Moody, R , *The Gulliver File*, Minewatch, London, 1992.

[6] Moody, R , *The Gulliver File*, Minewatch, London, 1992.

[7] N. Jhaveri, N, 'Human Dimensions of Environmental Change', Unpublished lecture notes, 1999.

[8] T. O'Riordan and J. Cameron, (Eds.) *Interpreting the Precautionary Principle* Earthscan Publications Ltd, London, 1994.

[9] E. von Weizsacher, A.B. Lovins and L.H.Lovins, *Factor Four: Doubling Wealth – Halving Resource Use,* Allen and Unwin, Australia, 1997.

[10] E. von Weizsacher, A.B. Lovins and L.H.Lovins, *Factor Four: Doubling Wealth – Halving Resource Use,* Allen and Unwin, Australia, 1997.

[11] N. Lansbury, 'How to Mine, or Whether to Mine?' *Chain Reaction*, Issue 81 Friends of the Earth, Australia, Summer, 1999/2000, p32–34.

[12] Oilwatch/NGO 'Declaration on Climate Change, Fossil Fuels and Public'. Kyoto, December 2, 1997.

[13] World Wide Web document: Earth Day Indigenous Solidarity Statement, 'Clean Energy Now!' 2000, http://www.moles.org/ProjectUnderground/drillbits/5_07/diary.html, accessed January 2001.

[14] N. Lansbury, 'How to Mine, or Whether to Mine?' *Chain Reaction*, Issue 81 Friends of the Earth, Australia, Summer, 1999/2000, pp32–34.

[15] N. Lansbury, 'How to Mine, or Whether to Mine?' *Chain Reaction*, Issue 81 Friends of the Earth, Australia, Summer, 1999/2000 pp32–34.

[16] S. Pile, *Geographies of Resistance*, Routledge, London, 1997.

[17] S. Pile, *Geographies of Resistance*, Routledge, London, 1997, p.30.

[18] P.F. Kelly, 'The Geographies and Politics of Globalization', *Progress in Human Geography*, 1999, p.386

[19] R. Falk, *On Humane Governance: Toward a New Global Politics.* Cambridge: Polity Press, 1995.

[20] R. Falk, *On Humane Governance: Toward a New Global Politics.* Cambridge: Polity Press, 1995, p.242

[21] J. Brecher, and T. Costello, *Global Village or Global Pillage: Economic Reconstruction from the Bottom-Up*, South End Press, Boston, 1994.

[22] J. Brecher, and T. Costello, *Global Village or Global Pillage: Economic Reconstruction from the Bottom-Up*, South End Press, Boston, 1994, p.17.

[23] J. Crosby, *The kids are allright: The WTO protests from a Union Activists perspective.* London: Freedom Press International. 6 December 1999.

[24] W. Carlton, W 'Statement on art and dance in the streets' from video of the WTO demonstrations. Seattle: Independent Media Center. Recorded December 2 1999.

[25] G. Esteva and M. Prakesh. 1998, *Grassroots Postmodernism: Remaking the soil of cultures,* Zed Books, London, 1998.

[26] S. Roberts, 'Geo-Governance in Trade and Finance and Political Geographies of Dissent', in Herod, A., O Tuathail, G. and Roberts, S. (eds.) *An unruly world: globalization, governance and geography*, Routledge, London.1998

[27] D. Korten, *When corporations rule the world*, Kumarian Press, West Hartford, 1995.

[28] R. Caplan and D. Lewit, *Positive alternatives to corporate globalization*, Massachussetts: Alliance for Democracy, 1999.

[29] R. Caplan 'Social Protections that De-Commodify the Earth, Labor, Money,' in T. Schroyer (Ed.) *A World That Works: Building Blocks for a Just and Sustainable Society*, Apex Press, June 1997.

[30] G. Esteva and M. Prakesh, 1998, *Grassroots Postmodernism: Remaking the soil of cultures*, Zed Books, London, 1998.

[31] G. Esteva and M. Prakesh, 1998, *Grassroots Postmodernism: Remaking the soil of cultures*, Zed Books, London, 1998.

INDEX

271